ALAN ROGERS'
GOOD CAMPS GUIDE

Rented Accommodation
on Quality Sites in
FRANCE

Compiled by: Deneway Guides & Travel Ltd
Cover design: Design Section, Frome
Cover photography: Near Macon, Saume et Loire, by
Michael Busselle
Clive Edwards, Lois Edwards & Sue Smart
have asserted their rights to be identified as the
authors of this work.

First published in this format 1998

© **Haynes Publishing & Deneway Guides & Travel Ltd 1998**

Published by: Haynes Publishing, Sparkford, Nr Yeovil, Somerset BA22 7JJ
in association with
Deneway Guides & Travel Ltd, West Bexington, Dorchester, Dorset DT2 9DG

British Library Cataloguing-in-Publication Data:
A catalogue record for this book is available from the British Library.

ISBN: 0 901586 61 7

Printed in Great Britain by J H Haynes & Co Ltd

Contents

Foreword 4

Alan Rogers' Carte d'Or 4

Bienvenue en France 5

The Départements and Regions of France 6

How to use the Guide 8

Travel Information 10

Car Ferry Services 13

SELECTED AND INSPECTED CAMPSITES

AQUITAINE 14   MIDI-PYRÉNÉES 88

AUVERGNE 37   NORMANDY 97

BRITTANY 43   PARIS/ILE DE FRANCE 101

BURGUNDY 57   PICARDY 103

CÔTE D'AZUR 63   POITOU-CHARENTES 106

FRANCHE-COMTÉ 65   PROVENCE 111

LANGUEDOC-ROUSSILLON . 67   RHÔNE VALLEY 119

LIMOUSIN 81   SAVOY/DAUPHINY ALPS . . . 127

LOIRE VALLEY 83   WESTERN LOIRE 130

Carte d'Or Application Form 137

The Essential Travel Pack 138

'The Bluffer's Guide to Wine' by Mike Cazelet 143

'Exploring French Canals' by Dennis Needham 153

Campsite map 158

Index by Département 159

Index by Region 160

Foreword

The Alan Rogers team have produced campsite guides for Britain, France and Europe for more than thirty years, which have been nominated as the "best campsite guides" on several occasions. What has distinguished our guides from the many others on the market is the fact that we monitor all our featured sites for high quality, good maintenance and efficient management by means of a regular personal inspection system, which affords us the opportunity to describe sites exactly as we find them and to ensure continuing high standards.

We have now put our considerable experience to wider effect by producing the first English language guide to accommodation for rent on campsites in France. The aim is to provide objective information to satisfy the many enquiries we receive from potential clients who would like to enjoy the freedom of staying on a campsite in Europe's most popular camping destination without the hassle of towing a caravan or tent around with them.

All the campsites featured in this new guide have already been inspected and selected by us for our 1998 Good Camps Guide for France, so they are all known to us personally. However, we have only had the opportunity to carry out an internal inspection of a sample of the wide range of accommodation offered in this selection of over 100 campsites throughout France.

We have also tried to give you a flavour and feel for the 'real' France by providing information on the tourist regions and featuring articles about the wine regions and France's amazing system of waterways. We hope that this will inspire you to go out and about, to savour the past and to perhaps taste and buy.

The Alan Rogers' Carte d'Or

A particular feature of this new guide is that most of the sites have agreed to offer a special discount for readers who purchase our unique 'Carte d'Or'. These discounts on the rental of accommodation range from 5% in the high season to 15% or more in the low seasons. Similarly we have also been able to negotiate very favourable terms for our readers for ferry travel, personal and breakdown insurance, tourist guides and maps through special arrangements with the Caravan & Camping Service. Their 'Essential Travel Pack' is available only to holders of the Alan Rogers' Carte d'Or and is described in detail on pages 138 and 139. The application form for the Carte d'Or is on page 137. The cost is just £10 and the value of the discounts available with the card will normally exceed the cost both of the Carte d'Or and the cover price of this guide! Of course you can still use the guide and stay on any of the featured campsites without buying the Carte d'Or, but in that case you won't benefit from the special Alan Rogers' campsite discounts.

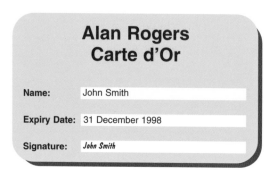

Alan Rogers Carte d'Or

Name: John Smith

Expiry Date: 31 December 1998

Signature: *John Smith*

BIENVENUE EN FRANCE
Welcome to France

France is the third largest country in Europe (after Russia and the Ukraine) and one of the most beautiful and varied. It has a rich and diverse geography – mountains, beaches, orchards, vineyards and forests are complemented by big cities, an excellent road and rail network, enormous hypermarkets and major industrial infrastructure.

However, to the British eye the most striking feature of the French countryside is the space. There are huge tracts of woodland and undeveloped land without a house in sight. Towns and villages have changed little, their old houses and streets intact, as much a part of the natural landscape as the rivers, hills and fields giving a sense of timelessness, providing an amazing feel for the history and culture without having to seek out major sights. Another feature is the outdoor life of the streets, the pavement cafés, restaurants and markets where people sit, talk and watch the world go by. The people themselves are witty, humorous and sensual, with a great sense of style. There is much to see, from the Gothic cathedrals of the north to the Romanesque churches of the centre and west, the châteaux of the Loire, the Roman monuments of the south, the ruined castles of the English and the Cathars and the prehistoric cave paintings of the Dordogne; hopefully identified in our regional introductions.

As you travel south the climate becomes more and more Mediterranean, with short winters and long, hot, dry summers. In the west it is tempered by the nearness of the Atlantic though a great deal warmer than Britain. The central and upland areas have a more extreme continental climate with colder, snowy winters and hot summers. The Pyrénées and especially the Alps are snowbound from the end of October to May. It is important to note that from mid-July to nearly the end of August the entire country (except for those employed in tourism) is on holiday. The French love their country and have so much choice that many stay in France for their own holidays, which does mean that during this period the main resort areas can get very crowded. Outside this time it can be very quiet.

The problem of overcrowding in the main season has been exacerbated by the tendency in recent years for many of the small traditional French hotels to have disappeared to be replaced by large, impersonal chains of hotels aimed primarily at the business or overnight sector. These are usually quite unsuitable for a holiday, especially one with children. Campsites, by contrast, offer the ideal environment for families, and the French themselves have long taken the view that one doesn't necessarily need to own a caravan, motorhome or even a tent to enjoy the essentially holiday ambience of a good quality campsite – hence the thinking behind the provision of an ever increasing range of 'static accommodation' on French campsites.

In this guide we are featuring this type of accommodation – small to large mobile homes, wooden chalets or 'bungalows', as the French call them, of various styles, all available to rent. This static accommodation is fully furnished and usually with a patio or veranda to take advantage of good weather. In some cases sites also provide 'Trigano' tents which have a solid wooden floor and are equipped for sleeping and cooking, but have no running water. In this situation the site's sanitary and washing-up facilities must be used (where this is the case reference has been made to these facilities in our site report).

French campsites are, on the whole, amazing places providing lots of facilities and activities. Nearly all have a bar with that unique French ambience and provide food, either simply as a takeaway facility (frites, etc) or have restaurants (rustic or stylish) featuring local specialities. All will be open for the high season when the French are on holiday. Outside that time the provision can vary and we have tried to provide that information in the our site report. The French are also very keen on 'animation' – entertainment for both adults and children. They usually engage young 'animateurs', often young Dutch or even English students who are learning the language. All sorts of events are organised, for example tennis or petanque tournaments, water polo, activities such as horse riding, trekking, excursions to visit local attractions and entertainment on stage – singing, dancing, etc. Where the campsite has informed us, we have tried to indicate when and what range of entertainment is on offer. All have a fully geared up 'reception' in the high season, again often utilising tourism students. It is very rare to find no one speaking some English in the high season; outside that period you may have to practise your French! So you can be entertained, exercised, acquire a suntan or a hangover, should you wish to do so; BUT you can, if you wish, also find a simple site which will offer you no more than peace and quietness ('tranquil' as the French say). Just study the site reports carefully to meet your own requirements and choose your accommodation.

The Départements of France

France is divided administratively into 95 'départements' (including Corsica) which are approximately the equivalent of our counties but with rather more autonomy. The départements are numbered in alphabetical order and these numbers form the first two digits of all post codes within each département. For example, the Dordogne is département 24, so every large town in the Dordogne has a post code commencing 24. We have adopted a similar system for numbering our French campsites; thus all our sites in the département of Dordogne start with the numbers 24.

The Regions of France

France is also divided into larger areas known as Regions, each of which consists of several départements. For example, the Region known as Normandy comprises five départements (14 Calvados, 27 Eure, 50 Manche, 61 Orne and 76 Seine-Maritime). Although this may seem a little confusing, it is actually quite straightforward and more definite than the English equivalent (for example, East Anglia comprises Norfolk, Suffolk and Essex, but also arguably Cambridgeshire). The Regions, listed alphabetically with the départements (each with its official number) within each, are:

ALSACE	67 Bas-Rhin, 68 Haut-Rhin
AQUITAINE	24 Dordogne, 33 Gironde, 40 Landes, 47 Lot-et-Garonne, 64 Pyrénées-Atlantiques
AUVERGNE	03 Allier, 15 Cantal, 43 Haute-Loire, 63 Puy-de-Dôme
BRITTANY	22 Côtes d'Armor, 29 Finistère, 35 Ille-et-Vilaine, 56 Morbihan
BURGUNDY	21 Côte d'Or, 58 Nièvre, 71 Saône-et-Loire, 89 Yonne
CHAMPAGNE-ARDENNE	08 Ardennes, 10 Aube, 51 Marne, 52 Haute-Marne
CÔTE D'AZUR	06 Alpes-Maritimes
FRANCHE-COMTÉ	25 Doubs, 39 Jura, 70 Haute-Saône, 90 Tré. de Belfort
LANGUEDOC-ROUSSILLON	11 Aude, 30 Gard, 34 Hérault, 48 Lozère, 66 Pyrénées-Orientales
LIMOUSIN	19 Corrèze, 23 Creuse, 87 Haute-Vienne
LOIRE VALLEY	18 Cher, 28 Eure-et-Loir, 36 Indre, 37 Indre-et-Loire, 41 Loir-et-Cher, 45 Loiret
LORRAINE VOSGES	54 Meurthe-et-Moselle, 55 Meuse, 57 Moselle, 88 Vosges
MIDI-PYRÉNÉES	12 Aveyron, 31 Haute-Garonne, 32 Gers, 46 Lot, 65 Hautes-Pyrénées, 81 Tarn, 82 Tarn-et-Garonne, 90 Ariège
NORD/PAS-DE-CALAIS	59 Nord, 62 Pas-de-Calais
NORMANDY	14 Calvados, 27 Eure, 50 Manche, 61 Orne, 76 Seine-Maritime
PARIS/ILE DE FRANCE	75 Paris, 77 Seine-et-Marne, 78 Yvelines, 91 Essonne, 92 Hauts-de-Seine, 93 Seine-St-Denis, 94 Val de Marne, 95 Val d'Oise
PICARDY	02 Aisne, 60 Oise, 80 Somme
POITOU-CHARENTES	16 Charente, 17 Charente-Maritime, 79 Deux Sèvres, 86 Vienne
PROVENCE	04 Alpes-de-Haute-Provence, 05 Hautes-Alpes, 13 Bouches-du-Rhône, 83 Var, 84 Vaucluse
RHÔNE VALLEY	01 Ain, 07 Ardèche, 26 Drôme, 42 Loire, 69 Rhône
SAVOY/DAUPHINY ALPS	38 Isère, 73 Savoie, 74 Haute-Savoie
WESTERN LOIRE	53 Mayenne, 49 Maine-et-Loire, 72 Sarthe, 85 Vendée

How to Use the Guide

Finding a Campsite

This guide is organised geographically using the official French regional structure – these regions are listed alphabetically in the guide and a sketch map on page 6 shows their geographical location within France. Each of these regions contains a number of `départements' (see page 7), each of which has an official number. We have used these numbers to prefix our site numbers (the four figure number which preceeds the site name). The map on page 158 shows the approximate location of each of the featured campsites using these numbers. We include two indexes at the back of the guide. Index 1 is by region (as the campsites appear in the guide) and Index 2 lists the campsites using the département in which each one is situated (i.e. numerically by département and campsite number).

The Campsite Descriptions

Each individual campsite is provided with a full page entry – the first part of each page is used to feature our Site Assessor's objective description of the site; the second part of the page is for the campsite's own description of the type(s) of accommodation available to rent at the site and a summary of their tariff, whilst the final part of the page is used for photographs of the site, etc. Readers should note that we have not normally carried out an internal inspection of the accommodation described by the campsite. When a site is described as `small' we mean one with less than about 120 pitches, whereas `medium' is between 120-300 pitches and `large' is 300 plus. These figures include all types of pitch, including those for touring caravans, etc.

In most cases mobile homes, chalets and bungalow style accommodation will, of course, have their own sanitary facilities `en-suite'. However, tents for rent will not have such facilities, and in these cases readers should expect to share the campsite's sanitary facilities with clients occupying the touring pitches. In this event we have included a short description of the sanitary block(s).

We would stress that the quoted tariffs published in this guide are essentially a summary of the charges as at the date of publication (March '98) and are provided for guidance only. They do not usually include items such as the local French holiday tax (usually from Ffr 1.00 – 2.50 per night for adults, less for children under 7 years) or any 'extras' you may require such as the hire of sheets and linen.

Campsite booking conditions, forms, brochures and discounts

Before committing yourself to making a firm booking with the site we recommend that you avail yourself of our free brochure distribution service (page 135) which will provide you with a campsite brochure, full tariff, booking conditions and booking form. If you want to take advantage of the very cost-effective discount arrangements we have made with the campsites and travel services, you will also need to complete the Carte d'Or application form, also on page 137, and send this to us along with your remittance for £10.

Booking a campsite and paying a deposit

To make a booking at any of the featured campsites, you then simply complete the campsite's own booking form and send this off direct to the campsite along with the required deposit (as stipulated in the campsite's own booking conditions/form) and, to qualify for the Alan Rogers' Discount, details of your Carte d'Or card number. Please note that we do not undertake a booking service.

Campsite deposits, payable in French Francs, are best made by Eurocheque, which are readily obtainable from your local bank, or you can ask your bank to effect a bank transfer.
On arrival at the site you may also be asked to pay a `damage deposit' and/or a fee for cleaning. The damage deposit is refundable on departure, subject to your leaving the accommodation in a condition acceptable to the site. Usually the cost of a reasonable amount of gas and electricity is included in the tariff but if you use more than one cylinder of gas you may be asked to pay for any subsequent one needed.
You will find various references in our descriptions and in the sites' own tariffs to 'high' and 'low' seasons. So far as the sites are concerned, there is often a significant variation as to the precise dates that each individual site uses to describe its own particular high season. So, as a general rule, we have taken the

months of July and August as the standard 'high' season, the rest of the year being 'low' season. In some instances you will see that a site will accept bookings in its accommodation to rent at a period of the year when the site's facilities for 'tourers' are still closed. On a somewhat cautionary note, therefore, we would emphasise that this may mean the site may be very quiet, with few of the facilities such as the restaurant, swimming pool, etc. likely to be open. Similarly, even when a site is open for tourers, you will often find in the early or late season that not all the facilities are fully open. Where we know this to be the case we have quoted the dates when the various different facilities are advertised as being open, but if you are in any doubt it would be wise to check at the time of booking.

Ferry bookings, discounts, travel insurance, maps, etc.

To take advantage of the ferry savings, travel and breakdown insurance cover, and other benefits available with our Carte d'Or you should complete the travel booking form on page 139 and send it direct to the Caravan & Camping Service at the address shown on the form – do not forget to include your Carte d'Or number!

Of course there is no obligation for you to purchase the Alan Rogers' Carte d'Or, but the campsite and travel discounts are only available to readers who do have such a card, so in most circumstances you will be able to make a significant saving by having the Carte d'Or.

Rules and regulations

Of course, most campsites in France, as elsewhere, have their own rules and regulations which are too complex and varied to include in this Guide. However, it is worth noting one or two rules in particular which are becoming rather more commonplace. For example, many French campsites now ban the wearing of 'boxer' or 'bermuda' style shorts in swimming pools on hygiene grounds. Our advice would be to ensure that everyone takes a proper swimming costume. Similarly it is worth noting that many campsite swimming pools (where the general public are not admitted) are designated as 'private' and are not required under French law to be supervised.

Safety

We would emphasise the need for readers to exercise discretion on behalf of themselves and their children in respect of their participation in sports or leisure activities. Our site assessors have neither the time, nor are they qualified to evaluate the safety aspects of the very wide variety of sports and leisure pursuits available on or nearby campsites in France; nor are the safety regulations necessarily the same or as strict as in the UK. All we can do is to mention what sports and leisure facilities are available without comment. The continental approach to safety is somewhat different to the prevailing attitude in Britain in so far as consumers are expected to exercise their own precautions (and to take responsibility for their children's actions) to a greater extent than is the case nowadays in the UK.

The other titles in the ALAN ROGERS' series for independent campers and caravanners are:

• **Good Camps Guide – Britain & Ireland**

• **Good Camps Guide – France**

• **Good Camps Guide – Europe**

• **Camping & Caravanning All Year Round**

Travel Information

The following is a resumé of some of the more important considerations in connection with travel to France; those seeking more detailed advice and guidance on specific subjects should contact:

French Government Tourist Office, 178 Piccadilly, London W1V 0AL Tel: 0891 244123

Passports

Visitors to France must hold a valid full 10 year passport. The old 1 year British Visitors Passport has been abolished.

Health

There are no obligatory inoculations and, as Britain enjoys reciprocal agreement with France for health care, it is possible to obtain treatment in France by producing Form E111, obtainable in advance in the UK through post offices. As only about 80% of the cost of treatment is covered in this way, personal travel insurance, including medical expenses cover, is a wise precaution.

Insurance

Third party motor insurance is obligatory and a Green Card is strongly recommended; you should contact your motor insurance company or broker for details. Comprehensive personal travel and breakdown insurance, including cancellation cover is a sensible precaution. Several organisations can arrange cover to suit virtually every need, including the Caravan & Camping Service who offer our readers special terms – see advertisement on pages 138 and 139.

Finance

There is no limit to the amount of Sterling which you may take into France and you can change Sterling notes at banks or bureaux de change once there. Most holidaymakers prefer to take French currency or Travellers Cheques with them, and most banks in the UK provide a foreign currency service, although smaller branches may need a few days notice of your requirements. Eurocheques, backed up by a Eurocheque Card, are accepted at many establishments and can be used to obtain cash at most banks in France. French banking hours differ from the UK – they normally open Monday – Friday, 09.00-12.00 and 14.00-18.00, but close either on Saturday or on Monday. They also normally close at mid-day on the day prior to a public holiday.
Bank holidays in France are different from the UK and full details can be obtained from the French Government Tourist Office in London – the most important are:

New Year's Day, Easter,	Labour Day (early May),	
Liberation Day (early May),	Ascension Day,	Whit Monday,
Bastille Day (14 July),	Assumption Day (mid Aug)	All Saints Day (early Nov),
Remembrance Day (11 Nov),	Christmas Day	

Credit Cards: The major (i.e. Access, Visa, American Express and Diners Club) credit and charge cards are acceptable at many establishments (including a good few campsites) throughout France. However, we have heard of instances where credit cards issued in Britain have been refused by French retailers; this is because French credit cards have a microprocessor built in, whereas British cards have a magnetic strip. If you do encounter any difficulty (and in many visits every year we have never personally encountered such a problem), Visa International says there is no reason for the French to refuse British cards, and recommends the following statement:

"Les cartes brittaniques ne sont pas des cartes a puce, mais a piste magnetique.
Ma carte est valable et je vous serais reconnaissant d'en demander la confirmation
aupres de votre banque ou de votre centre de traitement"

Shopping

French shopping hours vary considerably, although shops are often open later than in the UK and many close for lunch, often for up to two hours. Supermarkets and hypermarkets are normally open until 8-10 pm (20.00 – 22.00 hrs).

Customs

Formalities for EC residents travelling between the UK and France are now minimal. It is, however, important to distinguish between 'duty free' goods (where the limits are more or less unchanged) and 'duty paid in the EC' goods which are no longer subject to strict limits.

Motoring Information

Both the AA and the RAC can provide full details of continental motoring regulations, including those applying in France, but the following points should be borne in mind in particular:

Vehicle: You should display a GB plate or sticker on the rear of your vehicle and you should carry a spare set of light bulbs and a red warning triangle for use in the event of an accident or breakdown. Similarly you should ensure that your headlights dip to the RIGHT (conversion kits are available from motor accessory shops). Riders and passengers of motorcycles exceeding 50 cc. must wear crash helmets and special speed limits apply to machines up to 80 cc.

Documentation: It is advisable to carry your vehicle registration document and/or, if the vehicle is not registered in your name, a letter of authority signed by the registered owner to the effect that you have permission to take the vehicle abroad. A valid full (not provisional) UK driving licence is required and car drivers must be over 18 years of age. An International Driving Licence (obtainable from the AA or RAC) is not required for France, but may well be necessary if you intend to make excursions into neighbouring countries, such as Spain. You must have valid third-party insurance cover as a minimum requirement. An International Green Card (obtained from your insurers, but now included with many standard motor insurance policies) is strongly recommended and comprehensive breakdown insurance is also a wise precaution.

Drinking and Driving: Historically the French were pretty relaxed about this, irrespective of the fact that they had laws not unlike ours. However, French drink and drive laws, and their implementation, have been considerably tightened up (the alcohol limit is now LOWER than in Britain) and they are now implementing the law with some enthusiasm. The upshot is that if you have a couple of glasses of wine at lunch-time you are probably no longer (legally) fit to drive for the rest of the afternoon at least. Similarly speed limits are also being enforced more rigorously with hefty (we mean huge) on-the-spot fines for offenders.

Roads: France has a comprehensive road system, ranging from motorways (Autoroutes), Routes National (N roads), Routes Départemental (D roads) down to purely local C class roads. The Autoroute system is extensive but expensive! The use of Autoroutes nearly always involves the payment of substantial tolls and it is a matter of personal choice as to whether you prefer to use the normally much faster Autoroute, and pay the tolls, use the equivalent N road, or even avoid main roads altogether. Autoroutes are expensive, but they are fast and some savings in terms of the cost of overnight stops can sometimes offset the cost of tolls on a long journey. Most toll booths accept payment by credit card. Up-to-date information on the prevailing toll charges is available from the French Government Tourist Office (tel: 0891 244123).

Maps and Guides: We have relied on Michelin maps for France for over 30 years, but in recent years the need for lots of maps has been obviated by the introduction of the Michelin Motoring Atlas covering all France on 1:200,000 scale pages. Excellent value, easy to use and almost indispensable unless you intend to stick to main roads only. Arguably the spiral-bound version is the best. A map of France and a local map will be included if you use our Carte d'Or to book your ferry, insurance, etc. through the Caravan & Camping Service (see pages 138/139).

For users of personal computers, we also recommend Microsoft's Autoroute Express programme which we have found very useful for assistance in navigating around France, and the latest versions of this includes the Alan Rogers' Campsite Database, with our sites shown on the map and highlighted with our logo. Your interest and enjoyment of travelling in or through France can be much enhanced by use of a 'travel guide', Of course there are lots to choose from; our own favourites are the books by Richard Binns (e.g. 'French Leave', 'French Leave Encore' and his latest book, 'French Leave Finesse'). We find his book `Allez France' particularly useful. Directly related to the individual pages of the Michelin Atlas, it also includes an excellent 'Bon Rapport Qualité-Prix' section on good value restaurants.

Post

Post Offices and many Tabacs (tobacconists) sell stamps; charges are roughly similar to those in the UK.

Telephone

Since October '96 all telephone numbers in France have been changed. The access code from the UK remains 00 33, followed by the new 10 figure local 'phone number MINUS the initial '0' – in other words from the UK you will dial 0033 followed by the last NINE digits of the subscriber's telephone number. For a full explanation a free full-colour leaflet is available from the London office of France Telecom.

To telephone the UK from France you need to dial 00 (instead of 19) followed by the UK country code of 44, then the exchange code MINUS the first 0, followed by the subscriber's number. For example: to telephone 01308 123456 from France you dial: 00 44 1308 123456.

Most French 'phone boxes now take 'phone cards not coins; 'phone cards (Telecartes) can be bought at post offices, tabacs and at most campsites.

Taking your dog to France

At present, all cats and dogs coming into the UK must go into quarantine for six months at one of the UK's 81 quarantine kennels. Approximately 10,000 cats and dogs go through UK quarantine each year. At the time of writing (March '98) the Government are carrying out a further review of this system.

As dog owners ourselves, we look forward to the time when we can take our pets to France. We have included whether our selected campsites accept dogs in their accommodation (which, of course, may be of interest to other readers who are not fond of dogs). The RSPCA and QUAFF (Quarantine Abolition Fighting Fund) are campaigning to enable animals from EU and rabies-free countries to enter the UK without quarantine if they have been vaccinated, blood-tested and microchipped.

For further information, the contact telephone numbers for these organisations are:
RSPCA – 01403 264181
QUAFF – 01243 264173

The other titles in the ALAN ROGERS' series for independent campers and caravanners are:

- **Good Camps Guide – Britain & Ireland**

- **Good Camps Guide – France**

- **Good Camps Guide – Europe**

- **Camping & Caravanning All Year Round**

Car Ferry Services

The number of different services from the UK to France provides a wide choice of sailings to meet most needs. The actual choice is a matter of personal preference, influenced by factors such as where you live, your actual destination in France, cost and whether you see the channel crossing as a potentially enjoyable part of your holiday or, (if you are prone to sea-sickness) as something to be endured!

For the latest information on ferry services to and from France contact the Caravan & Camping Service (tel: 0171-792 1944, fax: 0171-792 1956). The following table is a provisional summary of services expected to operate in 1998.

ROUTE	OPERATOR	SEASON	FREQUENCY	TIME
Dover-Calais	P&O Stena Lynx	all year all year	up to 25 daily up to 7 daily	90 mins 45 mins
Dover-Calais	SeaFrance	all year	up to 15 daily	90 mins
Dover-Calais	Hoverspeed	not January	up to 27 daily	35 mins
Folkestone-Boulogne	Hoverspeed	not January	up to 6 daily	55 mins
Newhaven-Dieppe	P&O Stena Lynx	all year all year	up to 4 daily up to 4 daily	4 hours 120 mins
Portsmouth-St. Malo	Brittany Ferries	all year	up to 2 daily	9/11 hours*
Portsmouth-Caen	Brittany Ferries	all year	up to 4 daily	6/7 hours*
Portsmouth-Le Havre	P&O European Ferries	all year	up to 4 daily	5¾ hours
Portsmouth-Cherbourg	P&O European Ferries	all year	up to 4 daily	5/9 hours*
Southampton-Cherbourg	Stena Line	all year	up to 3 daily	6/8 hours*
Poole-Cherbourg	Truckline	all year	up to 4 daily	4/7 hours*
Poole-St. Malo	Brittany Ferries	mid May-Sept.	up to 4 weekly	8/9 hours*
Plymouth-Roscoff	Brittany Ferries	all year	up to 3 daily	6/8 hours*
Weymouth-St Malo	Condor Ferries	1 May-15 Oct	daily	4½ hours
Cork-Roscoff/St Malo	Brittany Ferries	May-Sept.	weekly	13 hours
Rosslare-Cherbourg	Irish Ferries	all year	varies	18 hours
Cork-Le Havre	Irish Ferries	from 25 March	varies	18+ hours

the longer time is for night sailings

Aquitaine

Major city: Bordeaux

Départements: 24 Dordogne; 33 Gironde; 40 Landes; 47 Lot et Garonne; 64 Pyrénées Atlantiques

The history of Aquitaine goes back many thousands of years when man lived in the caves of the Périgord and left cave paintings at sites such as Les Eyzies and Lascaux. The ancient dukedom of Aquitaine was ruled by the English for 300 years following the marriage of Eleanor of Aquitaine to Henry Plantagenet, who became King of England in 1154. The fortified villages and castles of the area bear evidence of the resulting conflict between the French and English for control of Aquitaine, and today add charm and character to the countryside. It is a diverse region of mountains and vineyards, vast beaches and fertile river valleys, rolling grasslands and dense forests. Within its boundaries are the beautiful valleys of the Dordogne and Vézère, with the forest of the Landes and the beaches of the Atlantic stretching from the Gironde estuary to the Basque country, and the rocky Pyrénées mountains on the Spanish border. Some of the world's most famous vineyards are around Bordeaux, the capital of the region. The vineyards of Bordeaux are especially well known for their Médoc, Sauternes and St Emilion wines. Most châteaux open their doors to allow visits to their cellars and wine tastings.

Cuisine of the region
Foie Gras – specially prepared livers of geese and ducks, seasoned and stuffed with regional truffles
Confits – (preserved goose and duck) are a key ingredient in a number of dishes
Fish and seafood – like carp stuffed with foie gras, mullet in red wine and besugo (sea bream)
Chorizos – spicy sausages
Jambon de Bayonne – raw ham, cured in salt and sliced paper thin
Lamproie – eel-like fish with leeks, onions and red Bordeaux wine
Gâteau Basque – shallow custard pastry, often with fruit fillings
Cèpes – fine, delicate mushrooms; sometimes dried
Chou farci – stuffed cabbage, sometimes aux marrons (with chestnuts)
Huile de noix (walnut oil) – many magnificent walnut trees in the Dordogne area

Wine
There are three distinctive areas:
Médoc – famous for its fine red wines
Graves and Sauternes – found to the left of the Garonne
Saint-Emilion and its surroundings – known for Entre-Deux-Mers and Côtes de Blaye

Places of interest
Agen – rich agricultural area, famous for its prunes
Bayonne – old streets and fortifications; Basque Museum
Monflanquin – well preserved fortified village
Pau – famous motor racing circuit on (closed) public highway
St Jean-de-Luz – seaside resort and fishing village
St Jean-Pied-de-Port – ancient city with citadel; bright Basque houses in steep streets
Sarlat – heart of the Périgord region, old town with medieval dwellings

2400 Camping La Tuilière, St Rémy-sur-Lidoire

Traditional French site with small pool and acres of space.

St Rémy is in the western Dordogne, not far from Ste Foy la Grande, and well positioned to visit the wine areas of St Emilion, Pomerol and Bergerac. This small, but spacious, site is laid out on a gently sloping hillside. The reception building houses a small shop (July/August) and a bar/restaurant with takeaway (weekends only outside July/August). Outside is a terrace overlooking a little swimming pool and children's pool. A good playground is close, as is a tennis court. A walk down the hill leads to a small lake used for fishing or inflatable boats. Activities include bicycle hire, minigolf, table tennis and pool. There are hypermarkets in Ste Foy, and fresh bread in the mornings from the bar. Whilst not the most well appointed site in the region, there is enough here to keep families occupied, and plenty of peace and quiet.

Directions: Take the D708 from Montpon-Ménestérol to Ste Foy la Grande. St Rémy is 8 km. south of Montpon and the site is on a junction just past the village.

Open: 15 April – 15 September

Address: St Rémy-sur-Lidoire, 24700 Montpon-Ménestérol. Tel: (0)5.53.82.47.29. Fax: as phone.

RENTED ACCOMMODATION	MOBILE HOMES Types A (17ft), B (22ft)	MOBILE HOMES Type C (28ft)
Number of persons	2/4 persons	6 persons
Bedrooms	One or two bedrooms: 1 x double bed, 1 x bunk beds	Two bedrooms: 1 x double bed, 1 x twin beds
Living/Dining area	Gas fire, table and seating	Gas fire, table and seating, double convertible bed
Kitchen area	Hot-plates, refrigerator, sink, utensils, crockery and cutlery	Hot-plates, refrigerator, sink, utensils, crockery and cutlery
Bathroom/shower	Shower, washbasin, WC	Shower, washbasin, WC
Additional facilities	Garden table and chairs	Garden table and chairs
Bedding	Pillows and blankets provided	Pillows and blankets provided
Pets	Pets accepted	Pets accepted
Charges per week (98): From Ffr: (low season) to Ffr: (high season)	17 ft Ffr 1,600 - 2,000, 22 ft 1,840 - 2,300	Ffr 2,000 - 2,500
Amount/% of deposit	30% (plus Ffr 150 fee in high season)	30% (plus Ffr 150 fee in high season)

Aquitaine

2403 Camping Les Périères, Sarlat

Good quality small site with large pitches and swimming pool very close to town.

This little site is in a pleasant setting amid attractive trees on the edge of the town of Sarlat. It is arranged mainly on terraces on a semi-circle of a fairly steep hillside with shade in many parts. On the more level ground there is a small swimming pool, a paddling pool and two tennis courts. A recent addition is an indoor spa pool which is open all season. The main buildings house a small shop, pleasant bar and just beyond these, a terrace restaurant with takeaway (15 June – 15 Sept). Interestingly, the owners have made space for a library, where visitors can read, study or play board games and Dutch billiards. Sports include table tennis (indoors or outdoors), a football ground and a fitness track with exercise halts. The site has a spacious air and is quite free from overcrowding. It is one of the most thoughtfully improved sites we have visited.

Directions: Site is east of town on the D47 in the direction of 'Sous-Préfecture', towards Croix d'Alon.
Open: Easter – 30 September.
Address: Route Sainte-Nathalène, 24203 Sarlat Cedex. Tel: (0)5.53.59.05.84. Fax: (0)5.53.28.57.51.

RENTED ACCOMMODATION	BUNGALOWS (small stone 'villas' – 50 sq.m or 60 sq.m) These bungalows are over 10 years old but, as they are constructed from stone, remain in good condition)
Number of persons	Up to 5 persons
Bedrooms	Two bedrooms: 1 x double bed, 1 x twin beds
Living/Dining area	Table and 6 chairs, 2 armchairs, sideboard; extra bed
Kitchen area	Gas cooker with oven, sink, refrigerator, dishwasher in 60 sq.m, crockery, cutlery and utensils
Bathroom/shower	Washbasin, shower or bath, WC
Additional facilities	Patio with furniture, barbecue
Bedding	Blankets, bedspreads and pillows provided; sheets and extra bedding to hire
Pets	Pets accepted
Charges per week (98): From Ffr: *(low season)* to Ffr: *(high season)*	50 sq.m. Ffr 1,911 - 4,001, 60 sq.m. 2,101 - 4,401, 2 weeks 3,184 - 6,668 or 3,502 - 7,335; rates for extra days or weeks available; gas on meter Low season rates include Carte d'Or discount
Amount/% of deposit	50%

2404 Castel Camping Le Moulin du Roch, Sarlat

Family run site based around old water mill midway between Sarlat and Les Eyzies.

Set amongst traditional stone buildings, Le Moulin du Roch is ideally situated to visit the medieval Dordogne and prehistoric Vézère valleys. On the medium sized site are a swimming pool and children's paddling pool, both open all season. There is a small shop and the site has enlarged the bar (with satellite TV, games and billiards) and terrace. The cosy restaurant serves local dishes (from early May) and there is an excellent takeaway. The site becomes full for most of July/August. Activities include table tennis, tennis, boules, lake fishing, there are forest trails for walking and a children's playground. Daily entertainment, a children's club and sporting activities (tennis, aqua gym, arts and craft, etc) are organised in high season. There are frequent canoe trips and horse riding excursions in mid and high season. The toilet blocks are of very good quality with free hot water and contain well equipped washing areas and British style WCs. English is spoken. A number of pitches is taken by tour operators.

Directions: Site is 10 km. from Sarlat on the D47 road to Les Eyzies.
Open: 25 April – 13 September.
Address: Route des Eyzies D47, 24200 Sarlat en Perigord. Tel: (0)5.53.59.20.27. Fax: (0)5.53.29.44.65.

RENTED ACCOMMODATION	MOBILE HOMES *Type 6*	MOBILE HOMES *Type 4*	BUNGALOW TENTS *(BTM)*
Number of persons	6 persons	4 persons	4 persons
Bedrooms	Two bedrooms: 1 x double bed, 1 x twin beds	Two bedrooms: 1 x double bed, 1 x bunk beds	Two bedrooms: 1 x double bed, 1 x twin beds
Living/Dining area	Electric heating, table and seating; double sofa bed	Electric heating, table and seating	Table and 4 chairs
Kitchen area	3 ring gas hob, fridge/freezer, sink, utensils, crockery and cutlery	3 ring gas hob, fridge/freezer, sink, utensils, crockery and cutlery	2 ring gas hob, fridge/freezer, utensils, crockery and cutlery
Bathroom/shower	Shower, washbasin, WC	Shower, washbasin, WC	None
Additional facilities	Picnic table, 2 sunbeds, sunshade and clothes dryer	Picnic table, 2 sunbeds, sunshade and clothes dryer	Sunshade, 2 sunbeds and clothes dryer
Bedding	Pillows and blankets provided	Pillows and blankets provided	Pillows and blankets provided
Pets	Pets not accepted	Pets not accepted	Pets not accepted
Charges per week (98): From Ffr: *(low season)* to Ffr: *(high season)*	Ffr 1,268 - 3,585; nightly rates available in low season	Ffr 1,080 - 3,140; nightly rates available in low season	Ffr 820 - 2,323; nightly rates available in low season
Amount/% of deposit	20% plus Ffr 120 fee	20% plus Ffr 120 fee	20% plus Ffr 120 fee

Aquitaine

2405 Castel Camping Les Hauts de Ratebout, Belvès, nr Sarlat

Good family site with pool, on a hill away from habitations southwest of Sarlat.

Not a particularly large site, this one is in a fine, hill top situation with different aspects. On site is an outdoor, unheated swimming pool, a small children's pool and a new 100 sq.m. heated indoor pool. Amenities, including the pools, are available all season. There is a self-service shop with a takeaway service, including pizzas. A pleasant restaurant and bar area opens to the pool-side terrace, which has a small stage for live entertainment. A general room has a library, pool table, football table and TV. Sports facilities include volleyball, table tennis, bicycle hire and two tennis courts, plus an adventure playground. Many activities are organised in season, including canoe trips, nightly videos and sports for children. No dogs are accepted on site, or discos – it is a site more suitable for families with children under 16 years.

Directions: From Belvès, just off the D710 road 60 km. south of Périgueux, proceed 2 km. on D710 then left on D54 at camp sign and follow through to site.

Open: 25 April – 12 September.

Address: Ste Foy de Belvès, 24170 Belvès. Tel: (0)5.53.29.02.10. Fax: (0)5.53.29.08.28. E-mail: ratebout@msn.com.

RENTED ACCOMMODATION	MOBILE HOMES
Number of persons	4-6 persons
Bedrooms	Two bedrooms: 1 x double bed, 1 x twin beds
Living/Dining area	Electric heating, table and seating, colour TV to rent; double sofa bed
Kitchen area	3 hot-plates, microwave and grill, refrigerator, sink, utensils, crockery and cutlery
Bathroom/shower	Shower, washbasin, WC
Additional facilities	Garden table and chairs, sunbeds and sunshade, barbecue
Bedding	Pillows and blankets provided
Pets	Pets not accepted
Charges per week (98): From Ffr: *(low season)* to Ffr: *(high season)*	4 persons: Ffr 2,114 - 3,020; extra person 168 - 240
Amount/% of deposit	Deposit: 25%, plus Ffr 90 fee

Photo: L. Roulland – Imp. Lambert – 24150 Lalinde

2409 Camping Soleil Plage, Vitrac, nr Sarlat

Spacious, medium sized site with enviable location beside the Dordogne.

The site is in one of the most attractive sections of the Dordogne Valley, right on the riverside. Divided into two sections, one is adjacent to the reception, bar, shop and restaurant complex, which is housed in a renovated Perigourdine farmhouse. It is also close to a small sandy river bank from which canoes and kayaks can be hired. Near the reception area is a swimming pool (all season), paddling pool, tennis court and minigolf. The friendly bar provides an excellent takeaway and the attractive refurbished restaurant serves excellent Perigourdine menus. The larger section of the site is about 250 m. from the reception area, and offers river bathing from a sizeable pebble bank. Open air table tennis, volleyball and a children's playground occupy part of a large central recreation space. Fishing and bicycle hire are available. The site is used by tour operators. A 'Sites et Paysages' member.

Directions: Site is 8 km south of Sarlat. Take D704 and it is signed from Montfort castle. Coming from the west on D703, turn first right 1 or 2 km. after the bridge at Vitrac-Port, and follow the signs.
Open: 1 April – 11 November.
Address: Vitrac, 24200 Sarlat. Tel: (0)5.53.28.33.33. Fax: (0)5.53.29.36.87.

RENTED ACCOMMODATION	CHALETS (Rêve)	CHALETS (Palace)
Number of persons	4/5 persons	5/6 persons
Bedrooms	Two bedrooms: 1 x double bed, 1 x twin beds (2 or 3)	Two bedrooms: 1 x double bed, 1 x twin beds (2 or 3)
Living/Dining area	Table and seating, colour TV	Table and seating, colour TV; convertible sofa bed
Kitchen area	Electric hot-plates and oven, refrigerator, sink, utensils, crockery and cutlery	Electric hot-plates and oven, refrigerator, sink, utensils, crockery and cutlery
Bathroom/shower	Shower, washbasin, WC	Shower, washbasin, WC
Additional facilities	Covered terrace with garden furniture	Covered terrace with garden furniture
Bedding	Blankets and pillows provided; sheets for hire	Blankets and pillows provided; sheets for hire
Pets	Pets accepted	Pets accepted
Charges per week (98): From Ffr: (low season) to Ffr: (high season)	Ffr 2,000 - 2,700	Ffr 3,400 - 4,100
Amount/% of deposit	20% plus Ffr 150 fee	Deposit: 20% plus Ffr 150 fee

Aquitaine

2410 Camping-Caravaning Le Moulinal, Biron

Lakeside site with wide range of activities for all ages.

Le Moulinal provides a good base for exploring the southern Dordogne and also has extensive wooded grounds to explore. The 5-acre lake with sandy beach is suitable for swimming, boating and fishing. The medium sized site has a shop, excellent restaurant and bar which also serves snacks. A rustic children's play area on grass overlooks the lake. The large swimming pool has a jacuzzi and children's pool. Ambitious, well organised animation is run as a series of programmes and excursions with a very wide range of activities (some free, some charged). There is a full programme of evening entertainment in high season. The site is popular with tour operators. Sanitary facilities have mostly British style toilets, washbasins (some in cabins) and hot showers.

Directions: From D104 Villeréal – Monpazier road, 9 km from Villeréal, take D53 south to Biron (3 km). Continue on D53 to Lacapelle Biron (4½ km – the D53 becomes the DI50 on crossing the regional boundary before Lacapelle Biron). Site is signed from west from Lacapelle Biron on the D255; or, from D911 Fumel – Villeneuve road take D162 and after 6½ km, turn right at sign for Lacapelle Biron.
Open: 11 April – 12 September, with all services.
Address: 24540 Biron. Tel: (0)5.53.40.84.60. Fax: (0)5.53.40.81.49.

RENTED ACCOMMODATION	MOBILE HOMES *Types A and B*	BUNGALOWS *Edena*	BUNGALOW TENTS *'Trigano' Bengali*
Number of persons	Type A: 4 persons, type B: 6 persons	6 persons	4-5 persons
Bedrooms	Two bedrooms: 1 x double bed, 1 x twin beds	Two bedrooms: 2 x 2 single beds	Two bedrooms: 1 x double bed, 1 x single beds
Living/Dining area	Heating, table and seating; type B double sofa bed	Gas heating, table and seating, double sofa bed	Table, seating
Kitchen area	2 hot-plates, refrigerator, sink, utensils, crockery and cutlery	Kitchen area: 2 hot-plates, refrigerator, sink, utensils, crockery and cutlery	2 gas hot-plates, refrigerator, utensils, crockery and cutlery (no sink)
Bathroom/shower	Shower, washbasin, WC (type B separate WC)	Shower, washbasin, WC	None
Additional facilities	Awning with garden table and chairs	Awning with garden table and chairs	Table and chairs with awning
Bedding	Pillows and blankets provided; sheets for hire	Pillows and blankets provided; sheets for hire	Pillows and blankets provided; sheets for hire
Pets	Pets accepted	Pets accepted	Pets accepted
Charges per week (98): From Ffr: *(low season)* to Ffr: *(high season)*	4 persons: type A Ffr 850 - 3,150, type B 1,050 - 3,820; extra person 10 -39, child 2-7 yrs free - 33	4 persons: Ffr 950 - 3,650; extra person 10 -39, 3 child 2-7 yrs free - 3	4 persons: Ffr 750 - 3,150; extra person 10 -39, child 2-7 yrs free - 33
Amount/% of deposit	25%, plus Ffr 220 fee	25%, plus Ffr 220 fee	25%, plus Ffr 220 fee

© Pascal Rousse

le Moulinal
CAMPING·VILLAGE
DORDOGNE·PÉRIGORD

2411 Camping-Caravaning Aqua Viva, Carsac, nr Sarlat

Clean site with good pool complex in heart of the Perigord Noir.

This medium sized site is divided into two sections. One side is very quiet and spacious with pitches and chalets terraced in woodland. The other half has pitches on flat grass and the excellent main swimming pool, children's pool, small lake (for fishing), table tennis, a floodlit basketball and boules area, minigolf, children's tennis court and under 7's play park. Canoe lessons and guided trips on the Dordogne are organised, as are many other sporting activities. Between the two sections is the reception area, with a small reasonably priced restaurant, a bar and terrace where evening entertainment is arranged in season, a small shop and takeaway. The site is well situated for visits to Rocamadour and Padirac. It is also close to Sarlat for markets and hypermarkets. The site is very popular with families, especially those with pre-teen and younger teenage children.

Directions: Site is 6 km. from Sarlat on the D704 road from Sarlat to Souillac.
Open: Easter – 31 October.
Address: Carsac, 24200 Sarlat. Tel: (0)5.53.59.21.09. Fax: (0)5.53.29.36.37.

RENTED ACCOMMODATION	CHALETS *Evasion*	CHALETS *Relax, Rêve and Fugue*	CHALETS *Espace and Aqua Viva*
Number of persons	2/3 persons	4/5 persons	6 persons
Bedrooms	One bedroom with double bed	Two bedrooms: 1 x double bed, 1 x twin beds	Two bedrooms: 1 x double bed, 1 x twin beds, Espace with upper mezzanine with extra twin beds.
Living/Dining area	Electric heating, table and seating, some with telephone, convertible sofa bed	Electric heating, table and seating, most with telephone, some TV, double sofa bed	Central heating, table and seating, Aqua Viva with phone and TV, double sofa bed
Kitchen area	2 ring gas hob, refrigerator, coffee machine, sink, utensils, crockery and cutlery	4 ring gas hob, refrigerator, coffee machine, sink, utensils, crockery and cutlery	4 ring gas hob, refrigerator, coffee maker, sink, utensils, crockery and cutlery
Bathroom/shower	Shower, washbasin, WC	Shower, washbasin, WC (separate WC in Relax)	Shower, washbasin, WC; (separate WC in Aqua Viva)
Additional facilities	Covered terrace with furniture	Covered terrace with table, 6 chairs and sunshade	Covered terrace (only small in Espace) with garden furniture
Bedding	Blankets and pillows provided; sheets for hire	Blankets/duvets and pillows provided; sheets for hire	Blankets/duvets and pillows provided; sheets for hire
Pets	Pets accepted in some chalets (not all)	Pets accepted in some chalets (not all)	Pets accepted in some chalets (not all)
Charges per week (98): From Ffr: *(low season)* to Ffr: *(high season)*	Ffr 1,100 - 2,950	Ffr 1,500 - 3,600	Ffr 1,800 - 4,000
Amount/% of deposit	Ffr 300 (plus 150 fee in July/August)	Ffr 300 (plus 150 fee in July/August)	Ffr 300 (plus 150 fee in July/August)

Aquitaine

2416 Camping-Caravaning Le Grand Dague, Atur, Périgueux

Good quality, small site with pool on the outskirts of Périgueux.

Having negotiated the narrow access road, Le Grand Dague is found to be a very spacious, clean and pretty site. Created around an old Dordogne style farmhouse, the main building houses reception, a small shop which provides essentials (from 1 May) and the very attractive restaurant and bar with its shady terrace. A takeaway service and an appetising restaurant menu make the most of this provision (1 May – early Sept). On the lawns in front of the house are the swimming pool and children's pool which have paved surrounds for sunbathing. Sports amenities on the site include football, volleyball, badminton, petanque, minigolf and table tennis courts. Le Grand Dague is approximately 6 km. from Périgueux and also close to hypermarkets and tennis. There are no tour operators. A 'Sites et Paysages' member.

Directions: Site is signed from the N89 south of Périgueux.
Open: Easter – 30 September.
Address: Atur, 24750 Périgueux. Tel: (0)5.53.04.21.01. Fax: (0)5.53.04.22.01.

RENTED ACCOMMODATION	MOBILE HOMES Type A	MOBILE HOMES Type B	CHALETS
Number of persons	4 persons	6 persons	4/6 persons
Bedrooms	Two bedrooms: 1 x double bed, 1 x twin beds	Two bedrooms: 1 x double beds, 1 x bunk beds	Two bedrooms: 1 x double beds, 1 x bunk beds
Living/Dining area	Fireplace, table and seating	Fireplace, table and seating	Table and seating, double sofa bed
Kitchen area	3 hot-plates, refrigerator, sink, crockery, cutlery and utensils	3 hot-plates, refrigerator, sink, crockery, cutlery and utensils	4 hot-plates, refrigerator, sink, crockery, cutlery and utensils
Bathroom/shower	Washbasin, shower, WC	Washbasin, shower, WC	Washbasin, shower, WC
Additional facilities	Garden table and 4 chairs, sunshade	Garden table and 6 chairs, sunshade	Garden table and 6 chairs, sunshade
Bedding	No bedding provided	No bedding provided	Pillows and blankets provided
Pets	Pets accepted	Pets accepted	Pets accepted
Charges per week (98): From Ffr: *(low season)* to Ffr: *(high season)*	Ffr 1,185 - 2,635	Ffr 1,325 - 3,160	Ffr 1,650 - 3,450
Amount/% of deposit	30% plus Ffr 100 fee	30% plus Ffr 100 fee	30% plus Ffr 100 fee

2420 Camping de la Plage, Saint-Aulaye

Pretty, small riverside site run by the municipality.

Beside the River Dronne, which runs around three of its sides, this prettily situated municipal site shares a river beach with the village community, with a bar and snacks and a children's playground. Activities available nearby include tennis, minigolf, canoe/kayak and mountain bike hire. River or lake fishing is possible and guided walks are arranged from the town. Saint-Aulaye is located quite close to Bordeaux and Bergerac vineyards. The site is only open for a short season.

Directions: Take the D5 from Riberac to La Roche-Chalais. Saint-Aulaye is 19 km. along the road and the site is just after the village.

Open: 27 June – 29 August

Address: Contact the Mairie at 24410 Saint-Alaye. Tel: (0)5.53.90.62.20. Fax: (0)5.53.90.59.89.

RENTED ACCOMMODATION	MOBILE HOMES	CHALETS Type A	CHALETS Type B
Number of persons	4/5 persons	4 persons	6 persons
Bedrooms	Two bedrooms: 1 x double bed, 1 x twin beds	Two bedrooms: 1 x double beds, 1 x bunk beds	Three bedrooms: 1 x double beds, 2 x bunk beds
Living/Dining area	Table and seating	Table and seating	Table and seating
Kitchen area	Hot-plate, sink, refrigerator, sink, crockery, cutlery and utensils	Hot-plate, sink, refrigerator, sink, crockery, cutlery and utensils	Hot-plate, sink, refrigerator, sink, crockery, cutlery and utensils
Bathroom/shower	Washbasin, shower, WC	Washbasin, shower, WC	Washbasin, shower, WC
Additional facilities	Terrace with garden seating	Terrace with garden seating	Terrace with garden seating
Bedding	Duvets and pillows provided	Duvets and pillows provided	Duvets and pillows provided
Pets	One small dog accepted	One small dog accepted	One small dog accepted
Charges per week (98): From Ffr: *(low season)* to Ffr: *(high season)*	Ffr 900 - 1,900	Ffr 850 - 1,750	Ffr 950 - 2,000

Aquitaine

3301 Camping de la Dune, Pyla-sur-Mer, nr Arcachon

Large, busy site with pool and other amenities separated from sea by famous giant dune.

La Dune, a good example of a busy French family site, is informal, friendly and lively with a comprehensive range of amenities. From its situation at the foot of the enormous dune you can reach the beach either by climbing over the dune or driving round, or you can use the medium-size swimming pool at the far side of the site. The site is shaded by pine trees and some of the roads are quite narrow with parts quite sandy. There are several small shops and a pleasant little bar and restaurant which can get busy at times (opens June, all other facilities are all season), with a takeaway. A purpose built barbecue is provided. Sports and tournaments are organised mid-June to end August and there is a children's playground with mini-club. Riding. English is spoken in season.

Directions: Take the new D259 road signed from the N250 to Biscarrosse and Dune du Pilat, just before La Teste (avoiding Pyla-sur-Mer). At the end of the new road turn right at roundabout onto D218 coast road. La Dune is second site on right.
Open: 1 May – 30 September.
Address: Route de Biscarrosse, Pyla sur Mer, 33260 La Teste. Tel: (0)5.56.22.72.17. Fax: as phone.

RENTED ACCOMMODATION	MOBILE HOMES *ABI Lock 17*	MOBILE HOMES *Lock 28-22*	CHALETS *Campéco and Campitel*
Number of persons	4 persons	4-6 persons	4 or 6 persons
Bedrooms	Two bedrooms: 1 x double bed, 1 x bunk beds	Two bedrooms: 1 x double bed, 1 x single beds	Campéco: Two bedrooms: 1 x double bed, 1 x single beds Campitel: Two bedrooms: 1 x double bed, 1 x double bed and 2 bunk beds
Living/Dining area	Table and seating;	Table and seating; convertible double bed	Table and seating, plus two twin beds
Kitchen area	Gas hot-plates, refrigerator, sink, utensils, crockery and cutlery	Gas hot-plates, refrigerator, sink, utensils, crockery and cutlery	Gas hot-plates, refrigerator, sink, utensils, crockery and cutlery
Bathroom/shower	Shower, washbasin, WC	Shower, washbasin, WC	Shower, washbasin, WC
Additional facilities	Garden table and chairs, sunshade	Garden table and chairs, sunshade	Garden table and chairs; Campitel with covered terrace
Bedding	Pillows provided; sheets and blankets to hire	Pillows provided; sheets and blankets to hire	Pillows provided; sheets and blankets to hire
Pets	Pets accepted	Pets accepted	Pets accepted
Charges per week (98): From Ffr: *(low season)* to Ffr: *(high season)*	Ffr 1,500 - 2,900	Ffr 2,000 - 3,400	Campéco: Ffr 1,500 - 2,900, Campitel: 2,000 - 3,400
Amount/% of deposit	25% plus Ffr 120 fee	25% plus Ffr 120 fee	25% plus Ffr 120 fee

3304 Camping-Caravaning Airotel Les Viviers, Claouey, nr Arcachon

Very large site on Cap Ferret peninsula, with frontage to the Bassin d'Arcachon.

Les Viviers is an attractive wooded site covering a large area with a pleasant, holiday atmosphere. On the shores of the Bassin d'Arcachon, the site is divided by sea water channels and lakes which have been developed to form a positive feature – sluice gates allow the water level to be maintained in this very tidal area so that bathing from a sandy beach, fishing and use of non-powered boats is possible all day within the site. Canoes, pedaloes and boats are provided free of charge and there are swimming instructors and lifeguards. A commercial area near the entrance provides a shop (15 May – 15 Sept), bar with TV, takeaway and other high season facilities including a cinema, restaurant, crêperie and disco. On an 'island' formed by the waterways are a bar and grill, also minigolf. A children's play area is on another island. Sports are organised in July/August. Bicycle hire. Barbecues are not permitted. Atlantic beaches are only ten minutes drive.

Directions: From Bordeaux take the D106 to Lège-Cap Ferret (40 km) and on through Claouey; site entrance is 1 km. further on.
Address: Claouey, 33950 Lège-Cap Ferret. Tel: (0)5.56.60.70.04. Fax: (0)5.56.60.76.14.
Open: 1 May – 27 September.

RENTED ACCOMMODATION	MOBILE HOMES Type C	CHALET
Number of persons	4/6 persons	4 persons
Bedrooms	Two bedrooms: 1 x double bed, 1 x twin beds	One bedroom with double bed
Living/Dining area	Gas fire, table and seating; convertible double bed	Table and seating, plus two twin beds
Kitchen area	4 gas hot-plates, oven, refrigerator, sink, utensils, crockery and cutlery	2 gas hot-plates, refrigerator, sink, utensils, crockery and cutlery
Bathroom/shower	Shower or bath, washbasin, WC	Shower, washbasin, WC
Additional facilities	Terrace with garden table and chairs	Terrace with garden table and chairs
Bedding	Pillows and blankets provided	Pillows and blankets provided
Pets	Pets accepted	Pets accepted
Charges per week (98):l From Ffr: *(low season)* to Ffr: *(highseason)*	Ffr 1,590 - 3,590	Ffr 1,390 - 3,190
Amount/% of deposit	Deposit and fee required	Deposit and fee required

Aquitaine

3306 Camping Palace, Soulac-sur-Mer, nr Royan

Large, traditional site close to beach, south of Royan across the estuary.

This large, flat site is regularly laid out on sandy ground amongst a variety of trees which provide good shade. A wide, sandy beach is 400 m. from the site gates and bathing, said not to be dangerous in normal conditions, is controlled by lifeguards. However, the site has its own small swimming pool, also with lifeguards, which is attractively set in a raised, part grass, part tiled area with its own shower facilities, etc. Arranged around a lush green roundabout with a fountain at the centre of the site are several shops (mostly 1 June – 10 Sept), restaurant (15 June – 10 Sept) and a bar with dancing and concerts. On the site are a supervised children's playground with paddling pool, bicycle hire and a programme of sports, entertainment and excursions in July/August. There are tennis courts adjacent to the site.

Directions: Site is 1 km. south of Soulac and well signed. The shortest and simplest way is via the ferry which runs from Royan across the Gironde estuary to the Pointe de Grave, but this is quite expensive. Alternatively make the trip via Bordeaux.
Open: 1 April – 30 September.
Address: BP 33, Bvd. Marsan de Montbrun, 33780 Soulac-sur-Mer. Tel: (0)5.56.09.80.22. Fax: (0)5.56.09.84.23.

RENTED ACCOMMODATION	MOBILE HOMES	CHALETS Type A	CHALETS Type B
Number of persons	4-6 persons	4 persons	5 persons
Bedrooms	Two bedrooms: 1 x double bed, 1 x two single beds	Two bedrooms: 1 x double bed, 1 x two single beds	Two bedrooms: 1 x double bed, 1 x three single beds
Living/Dining area	Sofa bed (2 persons), table, seating and chairs	Table seating and chairs	Table, seating and chairs
Kitchen area	4 ring gas hob (no oven or grill), refrigerator, sink, utensils, crockery and cutlery	4 electric hot-plates, refrigerator, sink, utensils, crockery and cutlery	4 electric hot-plates, refrigerator, sink, utensils, crockery and cutlery
Bathroom/shower	Shower, washbasin; separate WC	Shower, washbasin, WC	Shower, washbasin, WC
Additional facilities	Open terrace with table and chairs	Covered terrace with table and chairs	Covered terrace with table and chairs
Bedding	Duvet, duvet cover, sheets and pillows provided	Duvet, duvet cover, sheets and pillows provided	Duvet, duvet cover, sheets and pillows provided
Pets	Pets accepted	Pets accepted	Pets accepted
Charges per week (98): From Ffr: (low season) to Ffr: (high season)	Ffr 1,750 - 3,300	Ffr 1,260 - 2,800	Ffr 1,400 - 2,900
Amount/% of deposit	25% plus fee Ffr 120	25% plus fee Ffr 120	25% plus fee Ffr 120

4003 Les Pins du Soleil, Saint-Paul-lès-Dax, nr Dax

Family orientated, medium-sized site with swimming pool close to spa town of Dax.

Tthis site will appeal to families, particularly those with younger children who prefer to be some way back from the coast within easy reach of shops, cultural activities, etc., and well placed for touring the area. Dax is a busy spa town with many attractions – Les Pins du Soleil is actually at St Paul lès Dax, some 3 km. from Dax itself. The attractive, medium-sized swimming pool (open 5 June – 23 Sept) has a surrounding sunbathing area. There is a children's playground with an organised 'mini-club' in high season, volleyball and table tennis. Amenities include a takeaway (from June), small supermarket and a bar on the site, but there is no restaurant (many in Dax). Excursions can be arranged by bus to St Sebastian, Lourdes, etc., and there is a bus service to the thermal baths. English is spoken. The site is used by tour operators.

Directions: From the west on N124, avoid bypass and follow signs for Dax and St Paul. Almost immediately, turn right onto the D495 and follow signs. The site is a little further on the left. It is also well signed from the town centre, north of the river.
Open: 4 April – 31 October.
Address: 40990 Saint-Paul-lès-Dax. Tel: (0)5.58.91.37.91. Fax: (0)5.58.91.00.24.

RENTED ACCOMMODATION	MOBILE HOMES
Number of persons	2-6 persons
Bedrooms	Two bedrooms: 1 x double bed, 1 x twin beds
Living/Dining area	Table and seating, double sofa bed
Kitchen area	4 gas hot-plates, fridge/freezer, sink, crockery, cutlery and utensils
Bathroom/shower	Washbasin, shower, WC
Additional facilities	Garden furniture
Bedding	Sheets, blankets and pillows provided
Pets	Pets accepted
Charges per week (98): From Ffr: *(low season)* to Ffr: *(highseason)*	Ffr 1,470 - 2,891
Amount/% of deposit	Ffr 1,000 per week and 70 fee

Aquitaine

4004 Camping La Paillotte, Azur, nr Soustons

Very attractive, good lakeside site with an individual atmosphere.

La Paillotte is a large site with a character of its own. The buildings are all Tahitian in style, circular and constructed from local woods with the typical straw roof; some are now being replaced but still in character. It lies right by the edge of the Soustons lake, 1½km. from Azur village, with its own sandy beach. This is particularly suitable for young children because the lake is shallow and slopes extremely gradually. For boating the site has a small private harbour and sailing (with lessons) and rowing boats are for hire. The Atlantic beaches are 10 km. Alternatively there are two swimming pools with a water toboggan. There is a shop and a good restaurant with a very pleasant terrace overlooking the lake and bar (all season). Takeaway (high season). Sports, games and activities are organised. Amenities include a TV room, table tennis, an amusement room with juke box, library and bicycle hire. Member 'Sites et Paysages'.

Directions: From the north on N10, turn west on D150 at Magescq. From south go via Soustons.
Open: 21 May – 13 September.
Address: Azur, 40140 Soustons. Tel: (0)5.58.48.12.12. Fax: (0)5.58.48.10.73.
Internet: http://www.francecom.com/aft/camping/la.paillotte.

RENTED ACCOMMODATION	MOBILE HOMES *Type A*	BUNGALOWS *Types B and C*	CHALETS *Faré model*
Number of persons	4 persons	Type B: 4/5 persons, type C: 5/6 persons	6/8 persons
Bedrooms	Two bedrooms: 1 x double bed, 1 x twin beds	Two bedrooms: 1 x double bed, 1 x twin beds	Ground floor: one bedroom with twin beds; first floor: two bedrooms 1 x double bed, 1 x twin beds
Living/Dining area	Table and seating	Table and seating; convertible double bed	Living/dining area: table, seating; sofa bed (2 persons)
Kitchen area	4 hot-plates, refrigerator, sink, utensils, crockery and cutlery	4 hot-plates, refrigerator, sink, utensils, crockery and cutlery	Electric hot-plates, refrigerator, microwave, sink, utensils, crockery and cutlery
Bathroom/shower	Shower, washbasin, WC	Shower, washbasin, WC (type C separate WC)	Shower, washbasin; separate WC
Additional facilities			Two terraces
Bedding	Pillows and blankets provided	Pillows and blankets provided	Pillows and blankets provided
Pets	Pets not accepted	Pets not accepted	Pets not accepted
Charges per week (98): From Ffr: *(low season)* to Ffr: *(high season)*	Ffr 2,600 - 3,300; daily rates available outside 6 July - 23 August	Type B Ffr 2,700 - 3,400, type C 3,100 - 3,780; daily rates available outside 6 July - 23 August	Ffr 4,000 - 4,800; daily rates available outside 6 July - 23 August
Amount/% of deposit	25% plus Ffr 200 fee	25% plus Ffr 200 fee	25% plus Ffr 200 fee

LA PAILLOTTE

4010 Camping du Domaine de la Rive, Biscarrosse

Landes site with excellent beach on the Lac de Sanguinet.

This large site, set in pine woods, has generally good shade and is normally very quiet (except near the bar/disco area before 11 pm). The bar serves snacks and takeaway meals and the unpretentious restaurant provides cheap family meals (pizzas, burgers, etc), all from 15 June. The hour-glass shaped pool and other new pools are perfectly adequate (open from 25 April), but many visitors prefer to use the excellent lake beach. The lake shelves very gently, providing safe swimming for all ages and in another section, an ideal place to learn how to fall off a sail-board! Small craft and dinghies can be launched from the site's own slipway. Facilities for the energetic include a children's playground, two good tennis courts, table tennis and a boules court. There is a shop from 15 May.

Directions: Take the D652 from Sanguinet to Biscarrosse, and the site is signed on the right.
Open: 1 April – 30 October.
Address: 40600 Biscarrosse. Tel: (0)5.58.78.12.33. Fax: (0)5.58.78.12.92.
Internet: http://www.francecom.com/aft/camping/la.rive/

RENTED ACCOMMODATION	MOBILE HOMES *Type B*	MOBILE HOMES *Type D*	CHALETS
Number of persons	2/4 persons	4/6 persons	4/6 persons
Bedrooms	Two bedrooms: 1 x double bed, 1 x bunk bed	Two bedrooms: 1 x double bed, 1 x two single beds	Two bedrooms: 1 x double bed, 1 x double bed plus 2 x bunk beds
Living/Dining area	Table and seating	Table and seating; sofa bed (2 persons)	
Kitchen area	Gas hot-plates, refrigerator, sink, crockery, cutlery and utensils	Gas hot-plates, refrigerator, sink, crockery, cutlery and utensils	Gas hot-plates, refrigerator, sink, crockery, cutlery and utensils
Bathroom/shower	Washbasin, shower, WC	Washbasin, shower, WC	Washbasin, shower; separate WC
Additional facilities	Garden furniture	Garden furniture	Garden furniture
Bedding	Blankets and pillows provided; sheets for hire	Blankets and pillows provided; sheets for hire	Blankets and pillows provided; sheets for hire
Pets	Pets not accepted	Pets not accepted	Pets not accepted
Charges per week (98): From Ffr: *(low season)* to Ffr: *(high season)*	Ffr 1,650 - 2,990	Ffr 1,540 - 3,520	Ffr 1,640 - 3,990
Amount/% of deposit	Ffr 1,000 per week Available 30 May - 26 September	Ffr 1,000 per week	Ffr 1,000 per week

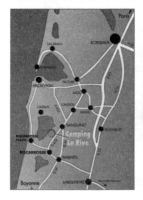 

Aquitaine

4013 Camping de la Côte, Messanges, nr Vieux-Boucau

Peaceful family site near the beaches of the Landes.

This small, family oriented site is surrounded by farmland and pine woods, with the beaches and dunes within walking distance. It should provide for a peaceful, relaxed stay. The purpose-built reception provides bread and drinks in high season and tomatoes, eggs and lettuce are available from the farm in season. Amenities include a barbecue, games room, children's play area, petanque, football, volleyball and table tennis. There are two modern sanitary blocks, built in the traditional Landes style, of very good quality and well maintained. Facilities are unisex, semi-open with controllable hot showers, washbasins (some private cabins), British style toilets, provision for disabled people including ramps, and a washing machine. There is a supermarket nearby, plus the amenities of the modern resort of Vieux-Boucau.

Directions: Site is signed off the D652, 1.5 km. north of Vieux-Boucau.
Open: 1 April – 30 September.
Address: Route de Vieux-Boucau, 40660 Messanges. Tel: (0)5.58.48.94.94. Fax: (0)5.58.48.94.44.

RENTED ACCOMMODATION	MOBILE HOMES *Type A*	MOBILE HOMES *Type B*
Number of persons	4 persons	4/5 persons
Bedrooms	Two bedrooms: 1 x double bed, 1 x twin beds	Two bedrooms: 1 x double bed, 1 x twin beds
Living/Dining area	Gas fire, table and chairs	Gas fire, table and chairs
Kitchen area	4 ring gas hob, refrigerator, coffee machine, sink, utensils, crockery and cutlery	4 ring gas hob, refrigerator, coffee machine, sink, utensils, crockery and cutlery
Bathroom/shower	None	Shower, washbasin, WC
Additional facilities	Shady terrace	Shady terrace
Bedding	Blankets and pillows provided	Blankets and pillows provided
Pets	Pets accepted	Pets accepted
Charges per week (98): From Ffr: *(low season)* to Ffr: *(high season)*	Ffr 800 - 2,000	Ffr 950 - 2,600
Amount/% of deposit	Contact site	Contact site

4014 Camping Caravaning Lou P'tit Poun, St Martin de Seignanx

Friendly, family run site in a quiet setting with swimming pool.

The manicured grounds that surround Lou P'tit Poun give a well kept appearance, a theme that is carried out throughout this very pleasing, medium sized site. It is only after arriving at the car park and security barrier that you feel confident it is not a private estate. Beyond this point the site unfolds to reveal an abundance of thoughtfully positioned shrubs and trees. Behind a central sloping flower bed lies the swimming pool which fronts the open plan reception area, café/snack bar and shop. Activities include a children's play area, games room, TV, half tennis court, table tennis and bicycle hire. The jovial owners not only make their guests welcome, but extend their enthusiasm to organising weekly entertainment for young and old during the high season. Despite its tranquil surroundings, this site is within 6 km. of Bayonne and a ten minute drive from the sandy beaches of the Basque coast.

Directions: Leave the A63 at exit 6 and join N117 in the direction of Pau. Continue for 5.5 km. Site clearly signed on right (at Leclerc supermarket).
Open: 1 May – 30 September.
Address: 40390 St Martin de Seignanx. Tel: (0)5.59.56.55.79. Fax: (0)5.59.56.53.71.

RENTED ACCOMMODATION	MOBILE HOMES	CHALETS
Number of persons	5/6 persons	5/6 persons
Bedrooms	Two bedrooms: 1 x double bed, 1 x two single beds	Two bedrooms: 1 x double bed, 1 x two single beds
Living/Dining area	Table and bench seating, sofa bed (2 persons)	Table and bench seating; sofa bed (2 persons)
Kitchen area	Gas hot-plates, sink, utensils, crockery and cutlery	Gas hot-plates, sink, utensils, crockery and cutlery
Bathroom/shower	Shower, washbasin, WC	Shower, washbasin, WC
Additional facilities	Open terrace	Covered terrace
Bedding	Pillows and blankets provided; sheets for hire	Pillows and blankets provided (sheets for hire)
Charges per week (98): From Ffr: *(low season)* to Ffr: *(high season)*	Ffr 1,500 - 3,250	Ffr 1,700 - 3,400
Amount/% of deposit	Ffr 1,000, plus 200 fee	Ffr 1,000, plus 200 fee

Aquitaine

4701 Moulin du Périé, Sauveterre-la-Lémance, Fumel

Immaculate, pretty little site tucked away in rolling wooded countryside.

The attractive main buildings at this site are converted from an old mill and its outhouses. Flanking the courtyard, as well as the restaurant (open air, but covered), are the bar/reception area where people can meet. A small shop sells essentials, with a small supermarket in the village and hypermarkets in Fumel. Snacks and takeaway are available. There is a clean but rather small swimming pool, with a children's pool much the same size. A small lake is used for inflatable boats and swimming and by this is a large games field for football, volleyball, etc. There is also a 'boulodrome', table tennis, bicycle hire, a trampoline and a children's playground. Activities are organised on and off the site in season, including a weekly French meal and barbecues round the lake. A 'Sites et Paysages' member.

Directions: Sauveterre-la-Lémance is by the Fumel – Périgueux (D710) road, midway between the Dordogne and Lot rivers. From the D710, cross the railway, straight through the village and turn left (northeast) at the far end onto a minor road and past the Château. Site is 3 km. up this road.

Open: 4 April – 30 September

Address: Sauveterre-la-Lémance, 47500 Fumel. Tel: (0)5.53.40.67.26. Fax: (0)5.53.40.62.46.

RENTED ACCOMMODATION	MOBILE HOMES *Model A*	MOBILE HOMES *Models B and C*	CHALETS
Number of persons	7 persons	6/7 persons	6/7 persons
Bedrooms	Two bedrooms: 1 x double bed, 1 x single beds (2 or 3)	Two bedrooms: 1 x double bed, 1 x single beds (2 or 3)	Two bedrooms: 1 x double bed, 1 x single beds (2 or 3)
Living/Dining area	Electric or gas heating, table and seating; sofa bed (2 persons)	Electric or gas heating, table and seating; sofa bed (2 persons)	Electric or gas heating, table and seating; sofa bed (2 persons)
Kitchen area	2 or 3 hot-plates, refrigerator, sink, utensils, crockery and cutlery	2 or 3 hot-plates, refrigerator, sink, utensils, crockery and cutlery	2 or 3 hot-plates, refrigerator, sink, utensils, crockery and cutlery
Bathroom/shower	Shower, washbasin, WC	Shower, washbasin, separate WC	Shower, washbasin, WC
Additional facilities	Garden furniture	Garden furniture	Terrace with garden furniture
Bedding	Pillows and blankets provided	Pillows and blankets provided	Pillows and blankets provided
Pets	Pets accepted in some units (not all)	Pets accepted in some units (not all)	Pets accepted in some units (not all)
Charges per week (98): From Ffr: *(low season)* to Ffr: *(high season)*	5 persons: Ffr 1,550 - 3,100; extra person per day 20.50 - 34,00, child (under 7 yrs) 9.25 - 18.50	5 persons: model B Ffr 1,625 - 3,250, C 1,700 - 3,400; extra person per day 20.50 - 34,00, child (under 7 yrs) 9.25 - 18.50	5 persons: 2,000 - 3,900; extra person per day 20.50 - 34,00, child (under 7 yrs) 9.25 - 18.50
Amount/% of deposit	Ffr 1,000 plus 200 fee (UK cheques accepted)	Ffr 1,000 plus 200 fee (UK cheques accepted)	Ffr 1,000 plus 200 fee (UK cheques accepted)

MOULIN DU PÉRIÉ

★★★★
CAMPING - CARAVANING

4703 Castel Camping Château de Fonrives, Rives, Villeréal

Neat, orderly site with swimming pool, in southwest of the Dordogne.

This is one of those very pleasant Dordogne sites of medium size, set in pretty part-farmed, part-wooded countryside. The park is a mixture of hazelnut orchards, woodland with lake, château (mostly 16th century) and camping areas. Barns adjacent to the château have been tastefully converted – the restaurant particularly – to provide for the reception, the bar, B&B rooms, shop and games areas. The swimming pool is on the south side of this. The lake has a small beach and can be used for swimming, fishing or boating. A small field is set aside by the pool for volleyball and football. There is a children's play area and paddling pool, a reading room, minigolf and bicycle hire. Amenities include a shop, restaurant, bar and snacks (all mid June - 31 August). Plenty of activities are organised in season, including excursions and walks. The original sanitary block is clean and adequate with free hot water, showers, washbasins in private cabins and British style WCs. Two additional blocks have private bathrooms (weekly hire), facilities for children and babies and laundry rooms.

Directions: Site is about 2 km. northwest of Villeréal, on the Bergerac road (D14/D207).

Open: 9 May – 19 September.

Address: 47210 Rives. Tel: (0)5.53.36.63.38. Fax: (0)5.53.36.09.98.

RENTED ACCOMMODATION	MOBILE HOMES	CHALETS *Fun and Rêve*	BUNGALOW TENTS `Trigano' Bengali*
Number of persons	4/6 persons	Fun: 2-4 persons, Rêve: 2-6 persons	2-4 persons
Bedrooms	Two bedrooms: 1 x double bed, 1 x single beds	Two bedrooms: 1 x double bed, 1 x two single beds	Two bedrooms: 1 x double bed, 1 x two single beds
Living/Dining area	Gas heating, table and seating, double sofa bed	Gas heating, table and seating, Rêve: double sofa bed	Table, seating
Kitchen area	4 gas hot-plates, refrigerator, sink, utensils, crockery and cutlery	3 electric hot-plates, refrigerator, sink, utensils, crockery and cutlery	2 gas hot-plates, fridge-freezer, utensils, crockery and cutlery (no sink)
Bathroom/shower	Shower, washbasin, WC	Shower, washbasin, WC	None
Additional facilities	Garden table and chairs, sunshade	Terrace with table and chairs, sunshade	Awning with table and chairs
Bedding	Pillows and blankets provided	Pillows and blankets provided	Pillows and blankets provided
Pets	Pets not accepted	Pets accepted	Pets accepted
Charges per week (98): From Ffr: *(low season)* to Ffr: *(high season)*	Ffr 1,200 - 3,250; nightly rates available outside 27 June - 29 August	Fun: Ffr 950 - 2,950, Rêve: 1,600 - 3,650; nightly rates available outside 27 June - 29 August	Ffr 790 - 2,250; nightly rates available outside 27 June - 29 August
Amount/% of deposit	25%, plus Ffr 120 fee	25%, plus Ffr 120 fee	25%, plus Ffr 120 fee

Aquitaine

6407 Castel Camping Le Ruisseau, Bidart, nr Biarritz

Pleasant, busy site with swimming pool, just back from sea.

This site, just behind the coast, is about 2 km. from Bidart and 21/2 km. from a sandy beach but it does have two swimming pools on the site, one large complex with slides and an indoor heated pool. There is also a little lake, where boating is possible, in the area at the bottom of the site which has a pleasant open aspect and includes a large play area. The terrain is wooded so the great majority of pitches have some shade. There is a shop, a large, self-service restaurant with takeaway and a separate bar with terraces. Activities include 2 tennis courts (free outside July/Aug), volleyball, table tennis, riding from the site, TV and games rooms, minigolf, fitness room, sauna and solarium. In the main season there are organised sports and evening entertainment. Bicycle and surf board hire is available. The site is popular with tour operators.

Directions: Site is east of Bidart on a minor road towards Arbonne. From autoroute take Biarritz exit, turn towards St Jean-de-Luz on N10, take first left at traffic lights and follow camp signs. When travelling south on N10 the turning is the first after passing the autoroute entry point.
Open: 15 May - 15 September, with all amenities.
Address: 64210 Bidart. Tel: (0)5.59.41.94.50. Fax: (0)5.59.41.95.73.

RENTED ACCOMMODATION	MOBILE HOMES
Number of persons	6 persons
Bedrooms	Two bedrooms: 1 x double bed, 1 x two single beds
Living/Dining area	Table and seating; sofa bed (2 persons)
Kitchen area	Hot-plates, refrigerator, sink, utensils, crockery and cutlery
Bathroom/shower	Shower, washbasin, WC
Additional facilities	Garden table and chairs
Bedding	Blankets and pillows provided
Pets	Pets not accepted
Charges per week (98): From Ffr: (low season) to Ffr: (high season)	Ffr 1,400 - 3,300
Amount/% of deposit	Contact site for details

LES CASTELS
Camping & Caravaning

LES CASTELS

The 'Castels' group comprises 49 campsites which have been created in the grounds of chateaux and mature country estates. They are individually owned and this contributes to their individuality, although they all conform to the high standards which are the main criteria for membership of this well known chain. This is evidenced by the fact that most of the Castels sites have been selected for the Alan Rogers' Good Camps Guide for France.

The majority of owners have opened their estates and residences and have created a variety of sport and leisure facilities, swimming pools, bars, restaurants and entertainment programmes for adults and children, making them among the finest holiday sites in France.

6409 Camping La Chêneraie, Bayonne

Good class, quite large site with swimming pool in pleasant situation 8 km. from sea.

A good quality site in a mature, pleasant setting, La Chêneraie is only 8 km. from the coast at Anglet where there is a long beach and big car park. It also has a medium sized free swimming pool on site (open June - August) which makes it a comfortable base for a holiday in this attractive region. Bayonne and Biarritz are near at hand. There are distant mountain views from the site which consists of generally well shaded meadows. A wooded area, not used for camping, is available for strolls. The sanitary blocks provide baby baths, facilities for disabled people and a washing machine and dryer. Facilities include a shop, general kiosk and restaurant with an all day snacks and takeaway (shop, restaurant and pool 1 June – 15 Sept). Activities include tennis (free outside July/August), table tennis, a children's playground and a small pool for fishing, boating with inflatables, etc. English is spoken.

Directions: Site is 4 km. northeast of Bayonne just off the main N117 road to Pau. From new autoroute A63 take exit 6 marked 'Bayonne St Esprit'.
Open: 1 April – 15 October (Trigano tents June - September only).
Address: 64100 Bayonne. Tel: (0)5.59.55.01.31. Fax: (0)5.59.55.11.17.

RENTED ACCOMMODATION	MOBILE HOMES	CHALETS	BUNGALOW TENTS *Trigano' Bengali*
Number of persons	4-6 persons	6 persons	4 persons
Bedrooms	Two bedrooms: 1 x double bed, 1 x two single beds	Three bedrooms: 2 x double beds, 1 x bunk beds	Two bedrooms: 1 x double bed, 1 x two single beds
Living/Dining area	Sofa bed (2 persons), table, seating and stools	Table, seating	Table, seating
Kitchen area	3 gas hot-plates, fridge-freezer, sink, utensils, crockery and cutlery	4 gas hot-plates, fridge-freezer, sink, utensils, crockery and cutlery	2 gas hot-plates, fridge-freezer, utensils, crockery and cutlery (no sink)
Bathroom/shower	Shower, washbasin, WC	Shower, washbasin; separate WC	None
Additional facilities	Terrace with garden furniture and sunshade	Covered terrace with garden furniture	Terrace with awning
Bedding	Pillows and blankets provided	Pillows and blankets provided	Pillows and blankets provided
Pets	Pets not accepted	Pets not accepted	Pets not accepted
Charges per week (98): From Ffr: *(low season)* to Ffr: *(high season)*	Ffr 1,100 - 3,000; nightly rates available for April, May, June, and September	Ffr 1,600 - 3,500; nightly rates available for April, May, June, and September	Ffr 950 - 2,500; nightly rates available for June and Sept
Amount/% of deposit	25%, plus Ffr 150 fee	25%, plus Ffr 150 fee	25%, plus Ffr 150 fee (available June - Sept only)

Aquitaine

6411 Camping du Col d'Ibardin, Urrugne

Family owned site with swimming pool at foot of Basque Pyrénées.

This medium sized site is well run with an emphasis on personal attention which ensures that all are made welcome. It is attractively set in the middle of an oak wood, with a modern reception area set in a forecourt decorated by brightly coloured shrubs. A small shop sells basic foodstuffs and bread orders are taken (1 June – 15 Sept), but a large supermarket and shopping centre is within 5 km. In July/August there is a catering service and takeaway, also a bar and occasional evening entertainment which includes Flamenco dancing. Other amenities include a swimming pool and paddling pool, tennis courts, bicycle hire, boules, table tennis, video games and a children's playground and club with adult supervision. From this site you can enjoy the mountain scenery, be on the beach at Socoa within minutes or cross the border into Spain approximately 14 km. down the road. The site is used by tour operators.

Directions: Leave A63 autoroute at St Jean-de-Luz sud, exit 2 and join the RN10 in the direction of Urrugne. Turn left at roundabout (signed Col d'Ibardin) onto the D4 and site is on right after 5 km.
Open: 1 May – 30 September.
Address: 64122 Urrugne. Tel: (0)5.59.54.31.21. Fax: (0)5.59.54.62.28.

RENTED ACCOMMODATION	MOBILE HOMES
Number of persons	4-5 persons (8.5 x 3 m)
Bedrooms	Two bedrooms: 1 x double bed, 1 x twin beds
Living/Dining area	Table and seating, heating, colour TV if required, sofa bed
Kitchen area	4 hot-plates, refrigerator, sink, utensils, crockery and cutlery
Bathroom/shower	Shower, washbasin, WC
Additional facilities	Garden table and chairs, barbecue
Bedding	Pillows and blankets provided
Pets	Pets not accepted
Charges per week (98): From Ffr: *(low season)* to Ffr: *(high season)*	2 persons Ffr 1,200 - 2,800; extra adult 100 - 200
Amount/% of deposit	Details from site

Auvergne

Major city: Clermont-Ferrand
Départements: 03 Allier; 15 Cantal; 43 Haute-Loire; 63 Puy-de-Dôme

The Auvergne, set in the heart of the Massif Central, is a dramatic region of awe-inspiring non-active volcanoes, lakes, rivers and forests. It is a wonderful destination for nature lovers and for those who enjoy active outdoor pursuits. The `Parc Naturel Régional des Volcans d'Auvergne' – the Auvergne Volcano Park – is the largest natural park in France and is a protected environment for exceptional flora and fauna. The mountains provide three classified downhill ski resorts and excellent cross-country skiing and the ancient volcanoes have provided ten thermal spa areas, five of which are among the leading thermal resorts in France. For the sightseer the region offers beautiful Romanesque churches, medieval castles, ruined fortresses and stiff, black sculptures of the Madonna and child. It was once fairly isolated and inward looking but access is much improved and roads are well engineered and it is now realising its potential as a holiday area.

Cuisine of the region
Ham and andouille sausages, stuffed cabbage, and bacon with lentil are local specialities
Cèpes (mushrooms) and fresh river fish such as trout and pike are also much used
Excellent cheeses such as Cantal, St Nectaire and cabecou goat cheese
Aligot – purée of potatoes with Tomme de Cantal cheese, cream, garlic and butter
Friand Sanflorin – pork meat and herbs in pastry
Jambon d'Auvergne – a tasty mountain ham
Perdrix à l'Auvergnate – partridge stewed in white wine
Potée Auvergnate – a stew of vegetables, cabbage, pork and sausage
Le Puy is famed for its lentils and Vereine du Velay – yellow and green liqueurs made from over 30 mountain plants

Wine
Côtes Roannaises, Côtes d'Auvergne and Côtes du Forez – red wines to accompany meals, Saint Pourçain Rosé
Note: The area is well known for its bottled mineral water, eg. Vichy, Badoit, and Volvic

Places of interest
Aurillac – old town, wax museum, archeology museum
Clermont-Ferrand – old city centre, 11th and 12th century Notre Dame du Port Basilica,13th century cathedral; known as 'ville noire' for its houses built in local black volcanic rock
Le Mont-Dore – spa and winter sports, panoramic view
Montluçon – 15th and 15th century château with Vieux Château museum.
Moulins – Notre Dame cathedral with 15th century `triptyque' painting.
Puy-de-Dôme – Gallo/Roman site; televison tower and observatory
Royat – spa, St Leger church
Tronçais Forest – forest of ancient oak trees protected by Colbert
Vichy – spa, natural spring park, seat of the collaborationist government in 1940
Volvic – lava quarry; Volvic springs

Auvergne

0305 Camping-Caravaning La Petite Valette, Sazeret, Montmarault

Attractive, small, neat site with good facilities.

Originally a working farm, La Petite Valette has been transformed in recent years into a very attractive and peaceful campsite. The level grassy pitches are separated by new bushes and trees; as there are only a few older trees, as yet, there is little shade. A small fenced play area with a seat and 'brolly' for Mum will keep toddlers happy, whilst older children have table tennis, mountain bike hire and organised activities in July/August. A small lake is stocked with fish for anglers. Ponies and small animals keep the farm feeling alive. There is no shop but bread can be ordered. Meals and snacks are served all day in the farmhouse restaurant, also at outside tables in the cottage garden. A small swimming pool has a sunbathing area alongside. Montmarault is only 4 km and facilities for tennis, riding and sailing are in the area.

Directions: From the N145 Montmarault - Moulins road, turn right at first roundabout onto the D46 signed St Pourcain. Turn left at next roundabout onto unclassified road signed Deux-Chaises and La Valette. After 2.5 km. turn left at site sign (La Valette) and site is approx. 1 km.
Open: 1 April – 31 October.
Address: Sazeret, 03390 Montmarault. Tel: (0)4.70.07.64.57. Fax: (0)4.70.07.25.48.

RENTED ACCOMMODATION	MOBILE HOMES	CHALETS
Number of persons	2-4 persons	2-4 persons
Bedrooms	One bedroom: 1 x bunk beds	One bedroom: 1 x bunk beds
Living/Dining area	Table and seating, double sofa bed	Electric heating, table and seating, double sofa bed
Kitchen area	2 electric hot-plates, refrigerator, sink, utensils, crockery and cutlery	2 electric hot-plates, refrigerator, sink, utensils, crockery and cutlery
Bathroom/shower	Shower, washbasin; separate WC	Shower, washbasin, WC
Additional facilities	Terrace with garden furniture	Terrace with garden furniture
Bedding	Pillows and blankets provided	Pillows and blankets provided
Pets	Pets accepted	Pets accepted
Charges per week (98): From Ffr: *(low season)* to Ffr: *(high season)*	2 persons: Ffr 1,450 - 2,000	2 persons: Ffr 1,400 - 1,950
Amount/% of deposit	50%	50%

1504 Camping de Coursavy, Pont de Coursavy, nr Cassaniouze

Quiet site without bar and entertainment for relaxing holidays.

The owners cater for families who like to make their own amusements – hence there is no bar or organised entertainment. A play area, small swimming pool and table tennis are the only on site activities besides the river which is a big attraction for canoeing, swimming and also good fishing. Although there is no shop, the baker calls daily all season, the butcher weekly and a local lady brings home grown fresh vegetables. Reception is open 24 hrs but not manned. It houses a five language library, tables, chairs and a TV. The owner lives just across the road and there is a telephone link for emergencies. The toilet block is good and kept very clean with British style WCs, washbasins in cubicles with saloon type doors and controllable hot showers, which may be rather stretched in busy periods. The area is good for walking and mountain biking (bikes for hire). Tennis 2 km. and riding 6 km.

Directions: Use D920 south from Aurillac. After 10 km. turn right on D601 just south of Lafeuillade-en-Vézie. In 24 km. turn left signed Vieillevie and site is 800 m.

Open: 20 April - 30 September.

Address: 15340 Cassaniouze. Tel: (0)4.71.49.97.70. Fax: as phone.

RENTED ACCOMMODATION	CHALETS
Number of persons	2/4 persons
Bedrooms	One bedroom with 2 bunk beds
Living/Dining area	Electric heating, table and seating; double sofa bed
Kitchen area	4 ring gas hob (no oven), fridge/freezer, sink, utensils, crockery and cutlery
Bathroom/shower	No bathroom (chemical WC if required)
Additional facilities	Terrace with garden table and chairs
Bedding	Blankets and pillows provided
Pets	Pets accepted
Charges per week (98): From Ffr: *(low season)* to Ffr: *(high season)*	2 persons: Ffr 1,165 - 1,365; extra adult 165 - 195, child (under 14 yrs) 135 - 165; gas included but not electricity
Amount/% of deposit	33%

Auvergne

4303 Camping-Caravaning du Vaubarlet, Sainte-Sigolène

Spacious riverside site in beautiful location, with swimming pool.

This peacefully located family site of medium size is on level grass with perimeter shade. The main site is separated from the river (unfenced) by a large field which has the children's playground, volleyball net and acres of space for ball games. Organised activities in the main season include camp fire and music evenings, canoeing for children, pony riding and mini-motorbike motocross. Other facilities include a fenced swimming pool with children's pool, bicycle hire, table tennis, boules, trout fishing (licences available), birdwatching, walking and barbecues are loaned. There is a small shop (bread can be ordered) and a takeaway in high season. Two sanitary units have a baby room, laundry and two new family bathrooms (suitable for disabled people). An attractive site for a quieter late break in September, it can be warm and sunny with the swimming pool, rooftop sun-deck, delightful modern bar with covered terrace all open. Local attractions include a textile museum, an 'escargot' farm and the stunning scenery, châteaux and churches of the Haute-Loire.

Directions: Site is 6 km. southwest of Ste Sigolène on the D43.
Open: 1 May - 30 September.
Address: 43600 Sainte-Sigolène. Tel: (0)4.71.66.64.95. Fax: (0)4.71.75.04.04.

RENTED ACCOMMODATION	MOBILE HOMES *Type A*	BUNGALOW TENTS *'Trigano' BTM*
Number of persons	4 persons	4 persons
Bedrooms	Two bedrooms: 1 x double bed, 1 x twin beds	Two bedrooms: 1 x double bed, 1 x single beds (2)
Living/Dining area	Gas fire, table and chairs, double sofa bed	Tables and chairs
Kitchen area	4 ring gas hob, refrigerator, sink, utensils, crockery and cutlery	2 ring gas hob, refrigerator, utensils, crockery and cutlery (no sink)
Bathroom/shower	Shower, washbasin; separate WC	No bathroom
Additional facilities	Outdoor table and chairs, sunshade	Sunshade
Bedding	Pillows and duvets provided	Pillows and blankets provided
Pets	Pets accepted	Pets accepted
Charges per week (98): From Ffr: *(low season)* to Ffr: *(high season)*	Ffr 1,600 - 2,200	Ffr 1,000 - 1,800
Amount/% of deposit	Ffr 1,200 plus 130 fee	Ffr 1,200 plus 130 fee

6302 L'Etang de Flechat, Orcival, nr Clermont-Ferrand

Remote, rural site, yet close enough to some major attractions, with lake bathing.

L'Etang de Flechat takes some finding but a friendly welcome awaits. Set in hilly country, just southwest of the Puy de Dôme itself, it provides a good base for exploring this region, both countryside and town. A small site, it is arranged on hillside terraces or around the lake margins. The one modern toilet block includes a laundry room, general TV room and phone kiosk. The medium sized lake is available for bathing, fishing and boating (pedaloes for hire) and there is a beach with play area next to it so parents can supervise children while using the beach. A drinks terrace off the bar, snack bar (basic menu and lake trout) and takeaway, and the reception room overhang the water's edge. There are small shops (limited hours only), a children's playground, table tennis and some activities are organised. It is a pleasant quiet site.

Directions: Site is about 2 km. west/northwest of Orcival on an unmarked road linking the D555 (D27E) Gioux - Orcival road and the D74 east out of Rochefort-Montagne.

Open: 15 May - 15 September.

Address: Orcival, 63210 Rochfort-Montagne. Tel: (0)4.73.65.82.96. (winter: (0)4.50.77.53.52).

RENTED ACCOMMODATION	CHALETS
Number of persons	4-6 persons
Bedrooms	Two bedrooms: 1 x double bed, 1 x bunk beds
Living/Dining area	Double sofa bed, table and seating
Kitchen area	Hot-plates, refrigerator, sink, utensils, crockery and cutlery
Bathroom/shower	Shower, washbasin, WC
Additional facilities	Terrace with table and chairs
Bedding	Pillows and blankets provided
Pets	Pets accepted
Charges per week (98): From Ffr: *(low season)* to Ffr: *(high season)*	Ffr 1,600 - 2,300
Amount/% of deposit	25% plus Ffr 80 fee

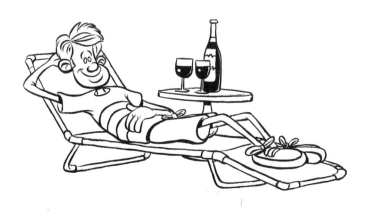

Auvergne

6303 Hotel de Plein Air L'Europe, Murol

Spacious, medium sized site with pool high in the Auvergne.

The site is a few minutes from the centre of the village, and just 15 minutes walk over the hill to the delightful Lac Chambon, with sandy beach and watersports. It has a swimming pool, with paddling pool, and a tennis court. There is a large football field and volleyball court at one end of the site. A small shop sells basics, some local specialities and bread. The takeaway service also operates from the shop, which abuts a bar/restaurant with pool-side terrace. The site is ideal for visits to the southern Auvergne, being only a short drive from St Nectaire, the Puy de Sancy, Le Mont Dore, or the pretty spa town of La Bourbolle – you could of course hike, since this is famous walking country, and a number of excursions are organised by the site. Fishing and bicycle hire 800 m and there are local markets. The site is used by tour operators.

Directions: Take exit 6 from the A75 motorway and drive through St Nectaire and on to Murol. The left turn towards the site is signed in the village.
Open: 25 May – 10 September.
Address: Rte de Jassat, 63790 Murol. Tel: (0)4.73.88.60.46 or (0)6.08.26.27.02 (low season).
Fax: (0)4.73.88.69.57.

RENTED ACCOMMODATION	MOBILE HOMES	CHALETS
Number of persons	4 persons	4/5 persons
Bedrooms	Two bedrooms: 1 x double bed, 1 x twin beds	Two bedrooms: 1 x double bed, 1 x bunk beds
Living/Dining area	Table and seating	Table and seating, convertible single bed
Kitchen area	Hot-plates, refrigerator, sink, utensils, crockery and cutlery	Hot-plates, refrigerator, sink, utensils, crockery and cutlery
Bathroom/shower	Shower, washbasin, WC	Shower, washbasin, WC
Additional facilities	Outdoor furniture, sunshade	Outdoor furniture, sunshade
Bedding	Pillows and blankets provided	Pillows and blankets provided
Pets	Pets accepted	Pets accepted
Charges per week (98): From Ffr: *(low season)* to Ffr: *(high season)*	Ffr 1,600 - 3,600; extra small tent 25 per day	Ffr 1,600 - 3,600; extra small tent 25 per day
Amount/% of deposit	25% plus Ffr 130 fee	25% plus Ffr 130 fee

Brittany

Major cities: Rennes, Brest
Départements: 22 Côtes d'Armor; 29 Finistère
35 Ille-et-Vilaine; 56 Morbihan

Strong Celtic roots provide this region with its own distinctive traditions, evident in the local Breton costume and music, the religious festivals and the cuisine, featuring crêpes and cider. Brittany offers 800 miles of rocky coastline with numerous bays, busy little fishing villages and broad sandy beaches dotted with charming seaside resorts. Inland you find wooded valleys, rolling fields, moors and giant granite boulders, but most impressive is the wealth of prehistoric sites, notably the Carnac standing stones. Many castles and manor houses, countless chapels and old villages provide evidence to Brittany's eventful history and wealth of traditions. The Bretons are proud of their culture, very different from the rest of France, and are determined to keep it so. If you are able to attend a 'Pardon' (a religious procession), you will understand some of the Breton history and piety, and see some beautiful traditional costumes. Brittany is a popular destination for families with young children or for those visiting France for the first time.

Cuisine of the region
Fish and shellfish are commonplace – lobsters, huitres, langoustes, various sorts of crabs, moules, prawns, shrimps, coquilles St Jacques, for example
Traditional 'crêperies' abound and welcome visitors with a cup of local cider
Other specialties are wafer biscuits and butter biscuits
Agneau de pré-salé – leg of lamb from animals pastured in the salt marshes and meadows
Beurre blanc – sauce for fish dishes made fron a reduction of shallots, wine vinegar and the finest butter (sometimes with dry white wine)
Cotriade – fish soup with potatoes, onions, garlic and butter
Crêpes Bretonnes – the thinnest of pancakes with a variety of sweet fillings
Galette – can be a biscuit, cake or pancake; the latter usually with fillings of mushrooms or ham or cheese or seafood, and called a Galette de blé noir (buckwheat flour)
Gâteau Breton – rich cake with butter, egg yolks and sugar
Poulet blanc Breton – free-range, fine quality, white Breton chicken

Wine
This is cider country! Crêperies serve cider in pottery type cups

Places of interest
Cancale – small fishing port famous for oysters
Carnac – 3,000 standing stones (menhirs), the last erected in 2,000 BC
Concarneau – fishing port, old walled town surrounded by ramparts
Dinan – historical walled town high above the River Rance
Perros-Guirec – leading resort of the 'Pink Granite Coast'
Quiberon – boat service to three islands: Belle Ile (largest of the Breton islands), Houat, Hoedic
Rennes – capital of Brittany, medieval streets, half timbered houses; Brittany Museum
St Malo – historical walled city, fishing port and yachting harbour
Tréguier – former Episcopal city, 13th-19th centuary St Tugdual cathedral

Brittany

2201 Camping Les Capucines, Trédrez, nr Lannion

Family run site, 1 km. from the beach and in good central location for touring Brittany.

Les Capucines is quietly situated 1 km. from the village of St Michel with its good, sandy beach and also very near Locquémeau, a pretty fishing village. This attractive, small site is on flat or slightly sloping ground with mature trees and hedges. There is a swimming pool with a small children's pool, solar heated and open from June. A small shop stocks essentials, with fresh bread to order. Amenities include a takeaway, bar and TV and a washing machine. There is a tennis court, minigolf, bicycle hire and a children's playground, plus a general room with table tennis and table football. A good value restaurant/crêperie can be found at Trédrez, with others at St Michel. A 'Sites et Paysages' member.

Directions: Turn off main D786 road northeast of St Michel where signed and 1 km. to site.
Open: 8 May – 10 September.
Address: Kervourdon, 22300 Trédrez. Tel: (0)2.96.35.72.28. Fax: as phone.

RENTED ACCOMMODATION	MOBILE HOMES	CHALETS
Number of persons	5-6 persons	5-7 persons
Bedrooms	Two bedrooms: 1 x double bed, 1 x twin beds plus 1 overhead bed	Two bedrooms: 1 x double bed, 1 x twin beds plus 1 overhead bed
Living/Dining area	Single sofa bed, gas heating, table and seating	Double sofa bed, electric convection heating, table and seating
Kitchen area	4 ring gas hob, refrigerator, sink, utensils, crockery and cutlery	2 ring gas hob, refrigerator, sink, utensils, crockery and cutlery
Bathroom/shower	Shower, washbasin, WC	Shower, washbasin, WC, electric heating
Additional facilities	Outdoor furniture	Covered terrace with garden furniture
Bedding	Pillows and blankets provided	Pillows and blankets provided
Pets	Pets not accepted	Pets not accepted
Charges per week (98): From Ffr: *(low season)* to Ffr: *(high season)*	Ffr 1,300 - 2,900; min. 1 week stay in high season	Ffr 1,600 - 3,300; min. 1 week stay in high season
Amount/% of deposit	30% plus Ffr 100 fee	30% plus Ffr 100 fee

2204 Camping Le Châtelet, St Cast le Guildo, nr St Malo

Pleasant site with views over the bay and steep path down to beach.

Carefully developed over the years, Le Châtelet is pleasantly and quietly situated with views over the estuary from many pitches. Of medium size, it is well laid out, mainly in terraces with a 'green' walking area around the lower edge. A little lake (unfenced) with some pitches around it can be used for fishing. An attractive, landscaped pool area has a heated swimming pool and children's pool (from 15 May) and there is a small children's play area. Amenities include a shop for basics, takeaway (also 15 May), bar lounge, general room with satellite TV and pool table, and a games room with table tennis and amusement machines. Games and activities are organised in season, plus dancing weekly in season. A path leads from the site directly down to a beach (about 150 m. but including steps). St Cast has a very long beach with opportunities for watersports. The site is used by tour operators.

Directions: Best approach is to turn off D786 road at Matignon towards St Cast; just inside St Cast limits turn left at sign for 'campings' and follow camp signs on C90.

Open: 10 April – 12 September.

Address: Rue des Nouettes, 22380 St Cast le Guildo. Tel: (0)2.96.41.96.33. Fax: (0)2.96.41.97.99.

RENTED ACCOMMODATION	MOBILE HOMES *Type B*
Number of persons	6 persons
Bedrooms	Two bedrooms: 1 x double bed, 1 x twin beds
Living/Dining area	Table and seating, double sofa bed
Kitchen area	4 hot-plates, refrigerator, sink, utensils, crockery and cutlery
Bathroom/shower	Shower, washbasin; separate WC
Additional facilities	Terrace with 2 sunbeds, sunshade
Bedding	Pillows and blankets provided
Pets	Pets not accepted
Charges per week (98): From Ffr: *(low season)* to Ffr: *(high season)*	Ffr 1,800 - 3,300
Amount/% of deposit	25%

45

Brittany

2212 Camping Le Cap Horn, Port-Lazo, Plouezec

Quiet, unsophisticated small site with marvellous views and satisfactory facilities.

In two distinct sections, Le Cap Horn provides some sheltered pitches in a small valley facing the sea with shade and mature trees, with newer ones on the hilltop with marvellous views of the islands out to sea. These pitches are semi-terraced and newly hedged, and this area now has its own modern toilet block with all facilities and direct gravel access roads. Many steps lead down to the bar, TV and games room and older, but modernised, toilet facilities in the valley. The blocks have hairdryers and facilities for babies and disabled people. There is a small shop for essentials (from 1 May). Amenities on the site include a small swimming pool and paddling pool (from 15 June), half-court, volleyball, table tennis and a simple children's play area. There is direct access to the secluded, quiet beach and good fishing and walking in the area.

Directions: Follow the D786 southeast and at Plouezec turn onto the D77 towards Port-Lazo; watch for site signs.

Open: 1 April – 30 September.

Address: Port-Lazo, 22470 Plouezec. Tel: (0)2.96.20.64.28. Fax: (0)2.96.20.63.88.

RENTED ACCOMMODATION	MOBILE HOMES *Type A*	MOBILE HOMES *Type B*
Number of persons	4 persons	6 persons
Bedrooms	Two bedrooms: 1 x double bed, 1 x twin beds	Two bedrooms: 1 x double bed, 1 x twin beds
Living/Dining area	Gas fire, table and seating	Gas fire, table and seating; double sofa bed
Kitchen area	4 hot-plates, refrigerator, sink, utensils, crockery and cutlery	4 hot-plates, refrigerator, sink, utensils, crockery and cutlery
Bathroom/shower	Shower, washbasin, WC	Shower, washbasin, WC
Additional facilities	Outdoor table and chairs	Outdoor table and chairs
Bedding	Pillows and blankets provided	Pillows and blankets provided
Pets	Pets accepted	Pets accepted
Charges per week (98): From Ffr: *(low season)* to Ffr: *(high season)*	Ffr 1,290 - 2,790; weekend rates available in low season; dog 150	Ffr 1,490 - 2,990; weekend rates available in low season; dog 150
Amount/% of deposit	25%	25%

2901 Castel Camping Ty Naden, Arzano, nr Quimperlé

Country site beside the River Ellé, with swimming pools.

Ty Naden, a medium sized site, is set deep in the countryside in the grounds of a country house some 18 km. from the sea. There are plenty of activities for young people here, including heated swimming pools, one with water slides and a children's paddling pool, a small beach on the river, tennis courts, table tennis, pool tables, archery and trampolines. Pony rides are offered and bicycles, skateboards, roller skates and boats can be hired. There is fishing, canoeing, a small roller skating rink and a BMX track. Guided mountain bike tours and canoeing trips (daily in season to Quimperlé, returning by bus). Restaurant (weekends only outside July/August), takeaway, bar and shop (all from 23 May). Across the road, by the attractive house and garden, is minigolf and, in converted Breton outbuildings, a TV room and delightful crêperie. Sanitary facilities of fair quality are in two blocks of unusual design.

Directions: Make for Arzano which is northeast of Quimperlé on the Pontivy road and turn off D22 just west of village at camp sign.
Open: 8 May – 5 September.
Address: Route d'Arzano, 29310 Locunolé. Tel: (0)2.98.71.75.47. Fax: (0)2.98.71.77.31.

RENTED ACCOMMODATION	MOBILE HOMES *Types A and B*	CHALETS	TENTS
Number of persons	Type A (21 sq.m): 4 persons, type B (25 sq.m.): 6 persons	6 persons	6 persons
Bedrooms	Two bedrooms: 1 x double bed, 1 x twin beds	Two bedrooms: 1 x double bed, 1 x twin beds	Two bedrooms: 1 x double bed, 4 x single beds
Living/Dining area	Table and seating; type B 2 x convertible beds	Table and seating, double sofa bed	Table, chairs, sofa
Kitchen area	Gas hot-plates, refrigerator, sink, utensils, crockery and cutlery	Electric hot-plates, refrigerator, sink, utensils, crockery and cutlery	Gas hot-plates, refrigerator, utensils, crockery and cutlery
Bathroom/shower	Shower, washbasin, WC	Shower, washbasin, WC	None
Additional facilities	Garden table and chairs, sunshade	Terrace with garden table and chairs, sunshade	Garden table and chairs, sunshade
Bedding	Blankets provided	Blankets provided	Blankets provided
Pets	Pets accepted	Pets accepted	Pets not accepted
Charges per week (98): From Ffr: *(low season)* to Ffr: *(highseason)*	Type A (4 persons) Ffr 1,200 - 3,100, type B (6 persons) 1,400- 3,400	Ffr 1,600 - 3,800	Ffr 900 - 2,600
Amount/% of deposit	30%, plus Ffr 150 fee	30%, plus Ffr 150 fee	30%, plus Ffr 150 fee

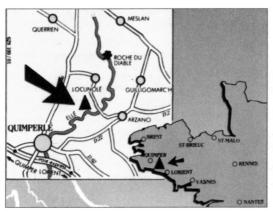

Brittany

2905 Castel Camping L'Orangerie de Lanniron, Quimper

Beautiful, quiet site in the mature grounds of a riverside and parkland estate.

This peaceful, family site of medium size, is set in 10 acres of a XVIIth century, 42 acre country estate on the banks of the Odet river, about 15 km. from the sea and beaches at Bénodet. The family are restoring the park, the original canal, fountains and ornamental Lake of Neptune. The original outbuildings have been attractively converted around a walled courtyard which includes a swimming pool with children's pool and a small play area. There is a shop, bar, snacks and takeaway, plus a restaurant in the beautiful XVIIth century Orangerie (open daily to the public). Activities include games and billiards rooms, a tennis court, minigolf, table tennis, fishing, archery and bicycle hire. There is a children's adventure playground and some farm animals. Animation is provided with a large room for indoor activities. The site is used by tour operators.

Directions: From Quimper follow 'Quimper Sud' signs, then 'Toutes Directions' and general camping signs, finally signs for Lanniron.
Open: 15 May – 12 September.
Address: Château de Lanniron, 29336 Quimper Cedex. Tel: (0)2.98.90.62.02. Fax: (0)2.98.52.15.56.
E-mail: lanniron@acdev.com. Internet: http://www.acdev.com/lanniron.

RENTED ACCOMMODATION	MOBILE HOMES	GITES *'Maisons du Bateau'*	*Maisons du Cocher, Champ, Ty-Kerbabic AND Canal*
Number of persons	4 + 2 persons + 1 child; (8.4 x 3 m)	One room (27 sq.m) over the river at high tide	4-8 persons + 1, according to property
Bedrooms	Two bedrooms: 1 x double bed, 1 x twin beds and 1 small bunk bed	2 + 1 persons, 1 x double bed, 1 x sofa bed	Two - three bedrooms: 1 x double bed, plus 1-3 x single beds
Living/Dining area	Table and seating, sofa bed (2 persons)	Tables and chairs	Tables and chairs, sofa bed
Kitchen area	4 electric hot-plates, fridge/freezer, microwave, sink, utensils, crockery and cutlery	2 electric hot-plates, refrigerator, microwave, sink, utensils, crockery and cutlery	4 ring hob, refrigerator, microwave, dishwasher (not du Cocher), washing machine in du Canal, sink, utensils, crockery and cutlery
Bathroom/shower	Shower, washbasin, WC	Shower, washbasin; separate WC	Shower, washbasin, WC or separate WC
Additional facilities	Private garden, garden furniture, barbecue	Garden furniture, barbecue	Garden furniture, barbecue
Bedding	Pillows and blankets provided; linen to rent	Pillows and blankets provided; linen to rent	Pillows and blankets provided; linen to rent
Pets	Pets not accepted	Pets not accepted	Pets not accepted
Charges per week (98): From Ffr: *(low season)* to Ffr: *(high season)*	Ffr 1,550 - 3,300	Ffr 1,500 - 2,940	Ffr 1,800 - 5,100, according to season and property
Amount/% of deposit	Ffr 1,000 plus 100 fee	Ffr 1,000 plus 100 fee	Ffr 1,000 plus 100 fee

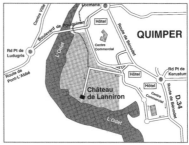

2906 Camping Caravaning Le Pil Koad, Poullan-sur-Mer, nr Douarnenez

Family run, attractive site just back from the sea in Finistère.

Pil Koad is on fairly flat ground, 6 km. from Douarnenez on the road to Pointe-du-Raz. It is 5 km. from the nearest sandy beach. On the medium sized site there is a heated swimming pool and paddling pool, an attractive sunbathing patio and a tennis court. A large room, the 'Woodpecker Bar', provides space for entertainment with discos and cabaret in July/August. A small shop stocks basic supplies and there is a takeaway food service in high season. There are restaurants in the village. Activities include a children's playground, table tennis, minigolf, volleyball, fishing and mountain bike hire with weekly outings organised. Clubs are arranged for children in season with a charge included in the tariff. The gates are closed 23.30 - 07.30 in high season.

Directions: Site is 500 m. from centre of Poullan on road towards Douarnenez. From Douarnenez take circular bypass route towards Audierne; if you see road for Poullan sign at roundabout, take it, otherwise there is a camping sign at turning to Poullan from the D765 road.

Open: 1 May – 26 September, mobile homes available from 4 April.

Address: Poullan, 29100 Douarnenez. Tel: (0)2.98.74.26.39. Fax: (0)2.98.74.55.97.

RENTED ACCOMMODATION	MOBILE HOMES	CHALET *'Rêve"*
Number of persons	6 persons (max)	6 persons (max)
Bedrooms	Two bedrooms: 1 x double bed, 1 x twin beds	Two bedrooms: 1 x double bed, 1 x two single beds
Living/Dining area	Table and seating, sofa bed (2 persons)	Tables and chairs, sofa bed (2 persons)
Kitchen area	Gas cooker, refrigerator, sink, utensils, crockery and cutlery	Hot-plates, refrigerator, sink, utensils, crockery and cutlery
Bathroom/shower	Shower, washbasin, WC	Shower, washbasin, WC
Additional facilities	Outdoor table and 6 chairs, barbecue	Covered terrace with table, 6 chairs and barbecue
Bedding	Pillows and blankets provided (not sheets)	Pillows and blankets provided
Pets	Pets not accepted	Pets not accepted
Charges per week (98): From Ffr: *(low season)* to Ffr: *(high season)*	Ffr 1,490 - 3,390; weekend and special rates available.	Ffr 1,590 - 3,790
Amount/% of deposit	25%, plus Ffr 120 fee	25%, plus Ffr 120 fee

Brittany

2908 Camping Le Panoramic, Telgruc-sur-Mer, nr Châteaulin

Family site in west Brittany, quite close to a good beach.

This medium sized, 10 acre site is situated on quite a steep hillside, arranged on flat terraces and with fine views along the coast. It is well tended and personally run by M. Jacq and his family who all speak good English. A good sandy beach is around 700 m. downhill by road, a bit less on foot. A heated swimming pool, children's pool and whirlpool with terraces are in the newer section of the site across the road (open 15 May – 7 Sept). A small shop is open 1 June – 7 Sept., plus a bar/restaurant with TV and good value takeaway food (July/August). Amenities include a sports ground with free tennis, volleyball, a children's playground, games room and children's club in season, and bicycle hire. There is fishing 700 m. away, a sailing school nearby and lovely coastal footpaths. The site is used by tour operators. A 'Sites et Paysages' member.

Directions: From Telgruc town centre, take road with signs to camp and Trez-Bollec-Plage and continue to site on right. Stop at property no. 130 to read the Panoramic information boards.

Open: 1 April – 30 September.

Address: Route de la Plage, 29560 Telgruc-sur-Mer. Tel: (0)2.98.27.78.41. Fax: (0)2.98.27.36.10.

RENTED ACCOMMODATION	MOBILE HOMES	FISHERMAN'S HOUSE	VILLA
Number of persons	6 persons	6 persons	9 persons
Bedrooms	Two bedrooms: 1 x double bed, 1 x twin beds	Three bedrooms: 2 x double beds, 1 x twin beds	Four bedrooms: 3 x double/twin beds, 1 x single bed
Living/Dining area	Gas fire, table and chairs, sofa bed (2 persons)	Fireplace, electric radiators, colour TV, sofas	Central heating, tables, chairs, sofas
Kitchen area	4 hot-plates, refrigerator, sink, utensils, crockery and cutlery	4 gas hot-plates, fridge, dishwasher, sink, utensils, crockery and cutlery	4 gas hot-plates, fridge, dishwasher, sink, utensils, crockery and cutlery
Bathroom/shower	Shower, washbasin; separate WC	Shower, washbasin; separate WC	Shower, washbasin; separate WC
Additional facilities	Outdoor sun-loungers, table and chairs	Outdoor sun-loungers, table and chairs	Outdoor sun-loungers, table and chairs
Bedding	Pillows and blankets provided	Pillows and blankets provided	Pillows and blankets provided
Pets	Pets accepted	Pets accepted	Pets accepted
Charges per week (98): From Ffr: (low season) to Ffr: (high season)	Ffr 1,600 - 3,200	Ffr 1,800 - 3,800	Ffr 2,200 - 4,200
Amount/% of deposit	25%, plus Ffr 150 fee/cancellation insurance	25%, plus Ffr 150 fee/cancellation insurance	25%, plus Ffr 150 fee/cancellation insurance

© Photographs Y.-R. CAOUDAL, Quimper

2910 Camping du Manoir de Pen-ar-Steir, La Forêt-Fouesnant, nr Concarneau

Charming, small site for a quiet stay, with few amenities but within village limits.

Manoir de Pen-ar-Steir will appeal to those who prefer a quiet place to stay without lots of amenities and entertainment on the site. It is arranged on terraces up the steep sides of a valley in the grounds of an old Breton house and has a picturesque, garden-like quality, with lots of well tended trees and flowers, including a pond and stream. There are some steep slopes to reach most of the pitches, but they are all on flat, grassy, terraces with hedges around them. The site has new mobile homes which are suitable for disabled people but there are also good, heated sanitary facilities which include facilities for the disabled in a small block which is part of the farmhouse. Washing machines and dryer are also there. The site has a tennis court, minigolf and a children's playground but no bar, restaurant or shop (baker 50 m.), however the facilities of the town are easily reached on foot.

Directions: Site is signed off the new roundabout at the northeast edge of La Forêt-Fouesnant.
Open: All year.
Address: 29940 La Forêt-Fouesnant. Tel: (0)2.98.56.97.75. Fax: (0)2.98.51.40.34.

RENTED ACCOMMODATION	MOBILE HOMES *Type B*	MOBILE HOMES *'Type Sovereign'* for people with physical disabilities
Number of persons	6 persons	6 persons (double glazing and central heating
Bedrooms	Two bedrooms: 1 x double bed, 1 x twin beds	Two bedrooms: 1 x double bed, 1 x bunk beds
Living/Dining area	Gas fire, table and seating, colour TV (Eurosport and Sky News); convertible double bed	Gas fire, table and seating, colour TV (Eurosport and Sky News); convertible double bed
Kitchen area	4 hot-plates, refrigerator, sink, utensils, crockery and cutlery	4 hot-plates, refrigerator, sink, utensils, crockery and cutlery
Bathroom/shower	Shower, washbasin; separate WC	Special bathroom– contact site for details
Additional facilities	Terrace	Terrace
Bedding	Pillows and blankets provided	Pillows and blankets provided
Pets	Pets accepted	Pets accepted
Charges per week (98): From Ffr: *(low season)* to Ffr: *(high season)*	Ffr 1,650 - 2,850	Ffr 2,100 - 3,200
Amount/% of deposit	Ffr 500	Ffr 500

Brittany

2912 Camping Manoir de Kerlut, Plobannalec, nr Pont l'Abbé

Developing site in grounds of manor house on river estuary.

Manoir de Kerlut is on the banks of a river estuary, 2 km. from the beaches of Lesconil and not far from the fishing and watersports opportunities offered by the southwest coast of Brittany. There are pleasant walks in the park and along the river bank. Of medium size and constructed on flat grass near the house, this site was opened in 1990 with strikingly modern buildings. One area is rather open with separating hedges planted, the other part being amongst mature bushes and some trees which provide shade. Site amenities are of good quality, with a large modern bar with TV (satellite) and entertainment in season, and two heated swimming pools with a children's pool. There is a small shop and takeaway. Activities include a sauna, solarium and small gym, tennis, volleyball, badminton, petanque, bicycle hire, a children's play area and games room. The gates are closed 22.30 - 7.30 hrs. The site is used by tour operators.

Directions: From Pont l'Abbé, on the D785, take the D102 road to Lesconil. Site is signed to the left, shortly after the village of Plobannalec.
Open: 1 May – 15 September.
Address: 29740 Plobannalec-Lesconil. Tel: (0)2.98.82.23.89 Fax: (0)2.98.82.26.49.

RENTED ACCOMMODATION	MOBILE HOMES	CHALETS
Number of persons	5/6 persons	6/7 persons
Bedrooms	Three bedrooms: 1 x double bed, 2 x twin beds	Two bedrooms: 1 x double bed, 1 x 3 single beds
Living/Dining area	Table and chairs	Table and chairs, double sofa bed
Kitchen area	4 hot-plates, oven, refrigerator, sink, utensils, crockery and cutlery	2 hot-plates, oven, refrigerator, sink, utensils, crockery and cutlery
Bathroom/shower	Shower, washbasin, WC	Shower, washbasin, WC
Additional facilities	Garden table and chairs, sunshade, barbecue	Terrace with garden table and chairs, sunshade, barbecue
Bedding	Pillows and blankets provided	Pillows and blankets provided
Pets	Pets accepted	Pets accepted
Charges per week (98): From Ffr: *(low season)* to Ffr: *(high season)*	Ffr 1,500 - 3,600	Ffr 1,800 - 4,000
Amount/% of deposit	30%, plus Ffr 120 fee	30%, plus Ffr 120 fee

3500 Ferme-Camping Le Vieux Chêne, Dol-de-Bretagne

Attractive, family owned farm site between St Malo and Mont St Michel for families.

This medium sized site has been developed in the grounds of a farmhouse which dates from 1638. It offers spacious rural surroundings on gently sloping grass. Centrally situated leisure facilities consist of an attractive pool complex with a medium sized, heated swimming pool, children's pool (from May), toboggans, slides, jacuzzi, etc., with a lifeguard during July/August. There is a TV room (satellite), table tennis and pool table. Other free facilities include a tennis court, trampolines (no safety matting), minigolf, giant chess and a children's play area. Riding is offered in July/August and bicycle hire is available. There is a bar, a café with a terrace overlooking the pools, takeaway, small shop (all from 1 June) and a supermarket 3 km. away in Dol. Fishing is possible in two of the three lakes on the site. Some entertainment is provided in high season, free for children. The site is used by tour operators.

Directions: Site is by the D576 Dol-de-Bretagne - Pontorson road, just east of Baguer-Pican. It can be reached from the new N176 following signs for Baguer-Pican, east of Dol.
Open: 15 April – 30 September.
Address: Baguer-Pican, 35120 Dol-de-Bretagne. Tel: (0)2.99.48.09.55. Fax: (0)2.99.48.13.37.

RENTED ACCOMMODATION	MOBILE HOMES *Type A*	CHALETS *Type A*
Number of persons	4 persons	5 persons
Bedrooms	Two bedrooms: 1 x double bed, 1 x twin beds	Two bedrooms: 1 x double bed, 1 x 3 single beds
Living/Dining area	Table and chairs	Table and chairs
Kitchen area	4 hot-plates, oven, refrigerator, sink, utensils, crockery and cutlery	2 hot-plates, oven, refrigerator, sink, utensils, crockery and cutlery
Bathroom/shower	Shower, washbasin, WC	Shower, washbasin, WC
Additional facilities	Terrace with garden table and chairs	Covered terrace with garden table and chairs
Bedding	Pillows and blankets provided	Pillows and blankets provided
Pets	Pets not accepted	Pets accepted
Charges per week (98): From Ffr: *(low season)* to Ffr: *(high season)*	Ffr 1,600 - 2,900; nightly and weekend rates available outside 4 July - 22 August	Ffr 1,800 - 3,200
Amount/% of deposit	50%	50%

The other titles in the ALAN ROGERS' series for independent campers and caravanners are:

- **Good Camps Guide – Britain & Ireland**

- **Good Camps Guide – France**

- **Good Camps Guide – Europe**

- **Camping & Caravanning All Year Round**

Brittany

3502 Castel Camping Domaine des Ormes, Epiniac, nr Dol-de-Bretagne

Impressive site on an estate of wooded parkland and lakes, with 18 hole golf course.

This site, about 30 km. from the old town of St Malo, has a pleasant atmosphere, busy in high season, almost a holiday village, but peaceful at other times, with a wide range of facilities. A marvellous `Aqua Park' with pink stone and palms and a variety of pools, toboggans, waterfalls and jacuzzi (free) is just above the small lake (pedaloes and canoes for hire). A pleasant bar and terrace overlooks the pools. The other traditional pools are sheltered by the restaurant building, parts of which are developed from the original, 600 year old water-mill. A particular feature is an 18 hole golf course, golf practice range and a beginners 5 hole course. There is a shop and takeaway. Other activities include minigolf, bicycle hire, 2 tennis courts, games room, fishing, paintball and archery. Horse riding and a cricket club are on site. A new hotel with adjacent apartments and its own pool and restaurant is now part of the complex. This is a popular site with British visitors and tour operators with organised entertainment in season.

Directions: Access road leads off the main D795 about 7 km. south of Dol-de-Bretagne, north of Combourg.
Open: campsite: 20 May - 10 September; apartments all year.
Address: 35120 Dol-de-Bretagne. Tel: (0)2.99.73.49.59. Fax: (0)2. 99.73.49.55.

RENTED ACCOMMODATION	APARTMENTS
Number of persons	4/6 persons
Bedrooms	One bedroom: 1 x double bed, plus 1 single folding bed
Living/Dining area	Table and chairs, 1 double sofa bed, 1 single sofa bed
Kitchen area	Electric hob and oven with filter hood, refrigerator, dishwasher, sink and crockery, cutlery and utensils
Bathroom/shower	Washbasin, bath, WC
Additional facilities	
Bedding	Blankets and pillows provided; sheets for hire
Pets	Pets accepted
Charges per week (98): From Ffr: *(low season)* to Ffr: *(high season)*	Ffr 2,000 - 3,900; bed and breakfast or half-board terms available
Amount/% of deposit	30% plus Ffr 100 fee

5602 Camping de la Plage, La Trinité-sur-Mer, nr Carnac

Family run, medium sized site with direct access to beach.

This area is popular with holidaymakers and La Plage has the great asset of direct access to a good sandy beach. There are also shops, takeaway and a site owned bar, seafood restaurant and crêperie very close, with a scenic outlook across the beach. La Trinité village is an hour's walk by the coastal path, 10 minutes or less by car. The site has a well established, mature feel, with a small, heated swimming pool (12 x 6 m.) and water slide and a good children's playground to add to the attractions of the beach. Other amenities include a play area for under 6s, two tennis courts, volleyball, basketball, table tennis, minigolf and a TV room with satellite and large screen for videos. Sail-boards and bicycles may be hired. Activities and entertainment are provided in July/August and tours organised on foot, by bicycle or by boat twice weekly in June and Sept. There is a shop open from 20 May. Only gas barbecues are allowed. The site is used by tour operators.

Directions: Site is signed in different places from the D186 coast road running from La Trinité to Carnac-Plage but entrance is easy to miss.
Open: 8 May – 12 September.
Address: 56470 La Trinité-sur-Mer. Tel: (0)2.97.55.73.28. Fax: (0)2.97.55.88.31.

RENTED ACCOMMODATION	MOBILE HOMES
Number of persons	6 persons
Bedrooms	Two bedrooms: 1 x double bed, 1 x twin beds
Living/Dining area	Gas heating, table and seating; convertible double bed
Kitchen area	4 gas hot-plates, refrigerator, coffee maker, sink, utensils, crockery and cutlery
Bathroom/shower	Shower, washbasin; separate WC
Additional facilities	Garden table and chairs, sunshade
Bedding	Pillows and blankets provided
Pets	Pets accepted
Charges per week (98): From Ffr: *(low season)* to Ffr: *(high season)*	Ffr 1,700 - 3,600
Amount/% of deposit	Deposit and fee required

Brittany

5604 Camping de Penboch, Arradon, nr Vannes

Quietly situated site on the Golfe du Morbihan with good facilities.

Penboch is 200 m. by footpath from the shores of the Golfe du Morbihan with its many islands, where there is plenty to do including watersports, fishing and boat trips. There are also old towns with weekly markets near and Arradon has a good range of shops and restaurants. The medium sized site is in a peaceful, rural area and is divided into two parts – one in woodland with lots of shade, and the other main part, across a minor road on more open ground with hedges and young trees. There is a friendly bar with satellite TV, snacks and takeaway, where basic food supplies are kept (all 16 May – 13 Sept) and a games room. A swimming pool with water slide toboggan and children's pool (also 16 May – 13 Sept) are in the centre of the site and a good children's playground with interesting play equipment. Barbecues are allowed. The site is popular with tour operators. A 'Sites et Paysages' member.

Directions: From the N165 at Auray or Vannes, take D101 road along northern shores of the Golfe du Morbihan; or leave N165 at D127 signed Ploeren and Arradon. Take turn to Arradon, and site is signed.
Open: 4 April – 20 September.
Address: Chemin de Penboch, 56610 Arradon. Tel: (0)2.97.44.71.29. Fax: (0)2.97.44.79.10.

RENTED ACCOMMODATION	MOBILE HOMES Type 1, 7 x 3 m	MOBILE HOMES Type 2, 7 x 3.7 m	MOBILE HOMES Type 3, 8.4 x 3.4 m
Number of persons	4 persons max.	5 persons max.	6 persons max.
Bedrooms	Two bedrooms: 1 x double bed, 1 x twin beds	Two bedrooms: 1 x double bed, 1 x twin beds	Two bedrooms: 1 x double bed, 1 x twin beds
Living/Dining area	Electric heating, table and seating	Electric heating, table and seating, convertible single bed	Electric heating, table and seating, convertible double bed
Kitchen area	3 ring gas hob (no oven or grill), refrigerator, sink, crockery, cutlery and utensils	3 ring gas hob (no oven or grill), refrigerator, sink, crockery, cutlery and utensils	4 ring gas hob (no oven or grill), refrigerator, sink, crockery, cutlery and utensils
Bathroom/shower	Shower, WC; separate WC	Shower, WC; separate WC	Shower, WC; separate WC
Additional facilities	Garden table and chairs, sunshade	Garden table and chairs, sunshade	Garden table and chairs, sunshade
Bedding	Blankets provided	Blankets provided	Blankets provided
Pets	Pets not accepted	Pets not accepted	Pets not accepted
Charges per week (98): From Ffr: (low season) to Ffr: (high season)	Ffr 1,400 - 3,200	Ffr 1,500 - 3,400	Ffr 1,700 - 3,600
Amount/% of deposit	30% plus Ffr 120 fee	30% plus Ffr 120 fee	30% plus Ffr 120 fee

Burgundy

Major city: Dijon
Départements: 21 Côte d'Or; 58 Nièvre
71 Saône-et-Loire; 89 Yonne

Burgundy (Bourgogne), in the rich heartland of France, is an historic region, once a powerful independent state and important religious centre. Its golden age is reflected in the area's magnificent art and architecture – the grand palaces and art collections of Dijon, the great pilgrimage church of Vézelay, the Cistercian Abbaye de Fontenay and the evocative abbey remains at Cluny, once the most powerful monastery in Europe. However Burgundy is best known for its wine including some of the world's finest, produced from the great vineyards of the Côte d'Or and Chablis, and perhaps for its rich cuisine including such dishes as 'Boeuf Bourguignon'. The area is criss-crossed by navigable waterways and also includes the 'Parc Régional du Morvan' good walking country. It is interesting to note that Dijon itself is only an hour and a half from Paris on the TGV.

Cuisine of the region
Many dishes are wine based, eg. 'Coq au Chambertin 'and 'Poulet au Meursault'
Dijon is known for its spiced honey-cake (pain d'épice) and spicy mustard
Boeuf Bourguignon – braised beef simmered in a red wine-based sauce
Charolais (Pièce de) – steak from the excellent Charolais cattle
Garbure – heavy soup, a mixture of pork, cabbage, beans and sausages
Gougère – cheese pastry based on Gruyère
Jambon persillé – parsley-flavoured ham, served cold in jelly
Matelote – fresh-water fish soup, usually based on a red wine sauce
Meurette – red wine-based sauce with small onions, used with fish or poached egg dishes

Wine
Burgundy is produced mainly from vineyards in the sheltered valleys that stretch south from Dijon to Lyon. The region is further subdivided into five main areas (from north to south): Chablis, Côte d'Or, Côte Chalonnaise, Mâconais and Beaujolais. It is the Côte d'Or region centred around Beaune that produces the great wines on which Burgundy's reputation depends

Places of interest
Autun – 12th century St Lazare cathedral.
Beaune – medieval town; its Hospices are a masterpiece of Flemish-Burgundian architecture; Museum of Burgundy Wine
Cluny – Europe's largest Benedictine abbey
Dijon – Palace of the Dukes, Fine Arts Museum, Burgundian Folklore Museum
Fontenay – Fontenay Abbey and Cloister
Joigny – medieval town
Mâcon – Maison des Vins (wine centre)
Paray-le-Monial – Romanesque basilica, pilgrimage centre
Sens – historic buildings, museum with fine Gallo-Roman collections
Vézelay – fortified medieval hillside, Magdalene Basilica

Burgundy

2100 Campings Lac de Panthier and Les Voiliers, Vandenesse en Auxois

'Two campsites, one system', attractively situated by a lake in Burgundy countryside.

Although officially two adjacent sites, these medium sized campsites are under the same ownership and are run as one. The older site, Lac de Panthier, is arguably the more attractive with a more mature appearance and this site is the base for most of the catering and entertainment facilities. The shared bar/restaurant, terrace and 'pub' are very attractive with a pleasant ambience. There is a swimming pool within Le Voiliers. Although the most obvious attraction is their proximity to the lake with its watersports facilities, these sites are in beautiful countryside and within easy reach of Dijon, Beaune and Autun, as well as being within 2 km. of the lovely Canal de Bourgogne, which links the Seine with the Saône. Boat excursions may be taken from Pouilly en Auxois which is about 8 km. A 'Sites et Paysages' member.

Directions: From the A6 use exit 24 (where the A6 joins the A38). Take the N81 towards Arnay Le Duc (back over the A6), then almost immediately turn left on D977 for 5 km. Fork left again for Vandenesse en Auxois. Continue through village on D977 for 2.5 km, turn left again and site is on left.
Open: 1 May – 30 September.
Address: 21320 Vandenesse en Auxois. Tel: (0)3.80.49.21.94. Fax: (0)3.80.49.25.80.

RENTED ACCOMMODATION	MOBILE HOMES
Number of persons	5 persons
Bedrooms	Two bedrooms: 1 x double bed, 1 x twin beds
Living/Dining area	Gas heating, table and seating, convertible double bed
Kitchen area	4 gas hot-plates, refrigerator, sink, crockery, cutlery and utensils
Bathroom/shower	Shower, WC
Additional facilities	Terrace and barbecue
Bedding	Blankets and pillows provided
Pets	Pets accepted
Charges per week (98): From Ffr: *(low season)* to Ffr: *(high season)*	Ffr 1,400 - 2,975
Amount/% of deposit	Ffr 1,500

Photograph: Jacques Thomas

5801 Camping Des Bains, Saint Honoré-les-Bains

Attractive family run site with pool, close to small spa-town.

This attractive small site incorporates a small 'village' of wooden chalets and is owned and run by the Luneau family who are keen to welcome British visitors. There are opportunities for horse riding, fishing, etc., or for 'taking the waters' which, combined with the clean, pollution free environment, are said to be very good for asthma sufferers (cures run for three week periods). The site has its own small swimming pool with a separate aqua slide (15 June – 15 Sept), a children's play area, and two small streams where children may fish, one of which is warm from the thermal springs. The actual thermal park is next door with added attractions for children. A traditional bar (all season) also provides food and takeaway (from 15 June). The semi-wooded site is within the town environs so it is possible to walk into the centre (uphill). A 'Sites et Paysages' member.

Directions: From the north approach via the D985 from Auxerre, through Clamecy and Corbigny to St Honoré-les-Bains, from where the site is signed 'Village des Bains'.
Open: Camping 1 May – 30 September; bungalows all year.
Address: BP 17, 15 Av. Jean Mermoz, 58360 Saint Honoré-les-Bains. Tel: (0)3.86.30.73.44. Fax: (0)3.86.30.61.88.

RENTED ACCOMMODATION	BUNGALOWS *Type A*
Number of persons	2-4 persons
Bedrooms	Two bedrooms: 1 x double bed, 1 x bunk beds
Living/Dining area	Electric heating, TV aerial point (no TV), table, chairs and seating
Kitchen area	2 hot-plates, mini-oven, refrigerator, sink, crockery, cutlery and utensils
Bathroom/shower	Electric heating, washbasin, shower, WC
Additional facilities	Terrace with garden furniture
Bedding	Blankets and pillows provided; sheets for hire
Pets	Pets accepted by prior arrangement
Charges per week (98): From Ffr: *(low season)* to Ffr: *(high season)*	Ffr 1,500 - 2,600
Amount/% of deposit	33%

Burgundy

5804 Le Village Européen, Montigny-en-Morvan

'Village vacances' near the banks of the Pannecière lake.

The original village was built some fifty years ago as accommodation for the manager and staff when building the barrage across the lake which forms a reservoir to provide water for Paris. The original stone houses have been converted into apartments, a restaurant, small hotel, etc. The village includes a wide variety of facilities and amenities, including a restaurant/bar, a large swimming pool with sunbathing area, two tennis courts, minigolf, pony and horse riding and watersports in July and August from the site's own marine base on the nearby lake. There are also plenty of amusements by way of pool, billiards and a well secluded disco and a theatre. The sanitary facilities comprise two blocks, both clean and functional, if fairly simple, with hot showers, basins in cabins and WCs. There are dishwashing facilities plus a laundry room. This fairly small village should appeal to those looking for value for money and an extensive range of activities for all the family.

Directions: Site is near the Barrage de Pannecière. From Château-Chinon, follow the D944 northward towards Montigny-en-Morvan and watch for site signs.

Open: 1 May – 31 October.

Address: Barrage de Pannecière, 58120 Montigny-en-Morvan. Tel: (0)3.86.84.79.00. Fax: (0)3.86.84.79.02.

RENTED ACCOMMODATION	APARTMENTS *Studio*	APARTMENTS *Duplex A and B*	BUNGALOW TENTS *'Trigano' Bengali*
Number of persons	4 persons	A: 4/6 persons, B: 6/8 persons	4 persons
Bedrooms	One bedroom: 1 double bed, 2 single beds	One or two bedrooms, plus mezzanine with twin beds	Two bedrooms: 1 x double bed, 1 x twin beds
Living/Dining area	Table and chairs, TV, telephone, cupboard	Table and chairs, TV, telephone, cupboard; type B: convertible single beds	Table, seating
Kitchen area	2 hot-plates, refrigerator, sink, crockery, cutlery and utensils	2 hot-plates, refrigerator, sink, crockery, cutlery and utensils	2 hot-plates, refrigerator, utensils, crockery and cutlery (no sink)
Bathroom/shower	Washbasin, bath; separate WC	Washbasin, bath; separate WC	None
Additional facilities	Terrace with garden furniture	Terrace with garden furniture	Table and chairs with awning
Bedding	Blankets and pillows provided; sheets for hire	Blankets and pillows provided; sheets for hire	Blankets and pillows provided; sheets for hire
Pets	Pets accepted	Pets accepted	Pets accepted
Charges per week (98): From Ffr: *(low season)* to Ffr: *(high season)*	Ffr 2,300 - 2,800; dog per day 15; weekend rates available	Duplex A 2,800 - 3,500, B 3,200 - 4,000; dog per day 15; weekend rates available	Ffr 1,790 - 2,390; dog per day 15
Amount/% of deposit	30% plus Ffr 100 fee	30% plus Ffr 100 fee	30% plus Ffr 100 fee

7105 Camping Moulin de Collonge, Saint-Boil

Well run, family site in the heart of the Burgundy countryside.

This small site offers an 'away from it all' situation, surrounded by sloping vineyards and golden wheat fields. Reception and the sanitary facilities are housed in a converted barn which is tastefully decorated and well kept. White tiled floors and whitewashed walls give it a very clean appearance and there is a washing machine and dryer inside. Hanging flower arrangements are in abundance and, like the shrubs and grounds, are constantly being attended to by the proprietor and his family. Beyond the stream which borders the site are a swimming pool, pizzeria and patio. Ices and cool drinks can be purchased but there is no food shop – baguettes and croissants arrive at 8.30 each morning. There is a freezer for campers' use. Other on-site activities are bicycle hire, table tennis, fishing and pony trekking. The 'Voie Vert', a 40 km. track for cycling or walking starts near the site.

Directions: From Chalon-sur-Saône travel 9 km. west on the N80. Turn south onto the D981 through Buxy (6 km). Continue south for 7 km. to Saint-Boil and site is signed at south end of the village.
Open: 15 May – 15 September.
Address: 71940 Saint-Boil. Tel: (0)3.85.44.00.40 or (0)3.85.44.00.32.

RENTED ACCOMMODATION	CHALET *Campitel*
Number of persons	5 persons
Bedrooms	Two bedrooms: 1 x double bed, 1 x double bed and 1 single bed
Living/Dining area	Table and seating
Kitchen area	Hot-plates, refrigerator, sink, utensils, crockery and cutlery
Bathroom/shower	Shower, washbasin; separate WC
Additional facilities	Covered terrace with garden table and chairs
Bedding	Pillows and blankets provided
Pets	Pets accepted
Charges per week (98): From Ffr: (low season) to Ffr: (high season)	Ffr 1,700 - 2,000
Amount/% of deposit	Details from site

Burgundy

7107 Castel Camping Château de l'Epervière, Gigny-sur-Saône

Enthusiastically run, rural site in the spacious grounds of a château.

Château de l'Epervière has undergone a transformation under its young owner Christophe Gay. Peacefully situated on the edge of the little village of Gigny-sur-Saône yet within easy distance of the A6 autoroute, it is in a natural woodland area near the Saône river. Sheltered, unheated outdoor pool, indoor pool for 1998, children's play area and paddling pool, and bicycle hire. Restaurant in the château with a distinctly French menu, shop for basics and takeaway in season. Perhaps the most striking feature of this attractive, fairly small site is the young owner's enthusiasm and the range of activities he lays on for visitors, which include wine tastings and regional tours. He is also the founder and driving force behind French Flavour Holidays, designed to provide an insight into French culture by special theme tours and activities. The site is used by tour operators.

Directions: From the N6 between Châlon-sur-Saône and Tournus, turn east onto the D18 (just north of Sennecey-le-Grand) and follow site signs for 6.5 km. From the A6, exit Châlon-Sud from the north, or Tournus from the south.

Open: 1 May – 30 September for campsite, shop, restaurant, wine cellars, etc., apartments available all year.
Address: 71240 Gigny-sur-Saône. Tel: (0)3.85.94.16.90. Fax: (0)3.85.94.16.93.

RENTED ACCOMMODATION	APARTMENTS
Number of persons	2-5 persons
Bedrooms	Two bedrooms: 1 x double bed, 1 x bunk beds and 1 single bed
Living/Dining area	Open fireplace, colour TV, sofa, telephone, table and chairs
Kitchen area	4 hot-plates, oven, refrigerator, dishwasher, sink, crockery, cutlery and utensils
Bathroom/shower	Washbasin, bath; separate WC
Additional facilities	Terrace with chairs and table, sunbeds, barbecue
Bedding	Blankets and pillows provided; sheets for hire
Pets	Pets not accepted
Charges per week (98): From Ffr: *(low season)* to Ffr: *(high season)*	Ffr 1,600 - 3,600
Amount/% of deposit	20%

LES CASTELS
Camping & Caravaning

The 'Castels' group comprises 49 campsites which have been created in the grounds of chateaux and mature country estates. They are individually owned and this contributes to their individuality, although they all conform to the high standards which are the main criteria for membership of this well known chain. This is evidenced by the fact that most of the Castels sites have been selected for the Alan Rogers' Good Camps Guide for France.

The majority of owners have opened their estates and residences and have created a variety of sport and leisure facilities, swimming pools, bars, restaurants and entertainment programmes for adults and children, making them among the finest holiday sites in France.

Côte d'Azur

Major cities: Nice, Cannes, Monte Carlo (Monaco)
Départements: 06 Alpes-Maritime

The Côte d'Azur, perhaps better known as the French Riviera, is a beautiful stretch of coast studded with sophisticated towns such as Monte Carlo, Nice, and Cannes or more discreet villages such as Beaulieu, Menton or Cap Ferrat. This popular region epitomises the pleasures of sun, sea and hedonism. The quaint harbours and fishing villages have become chic destinations, now full of pleasure yachts and crowded summertime beaches. The famous resorts of Juan-les-Pins and Cap d'Antibes attract the stylish jet set, but up in the hills are quieter tiny medieval villages of winding streets and white-walled houses with terracotta roofs, unchanged for centuries. In St Paul-de-Vence visitors can browse through shops and galleries set on narrow winding cobblestone streets, and in Grasse, the perfume capital of the world, one can learn how French perfumes are made. However, there are also post-modern museums, art collections including museums dedicated to Matisse and Picasso and celebrated film and jazz festivals.

Cuisine of the region
The Riviera shares its cuisine with Provence enjoying the same vegetables and fish dishes.
Aïgo Bouido – garlic and sage soup with bread (or eggs and cheese)
Aïgo saou – fish soup served with 'rouille'
Aïoli (ailloli) – a mayonnaise sauce with garlic and olive oil
Anchoïade – anchovy
Bouillabaisse – a dish of Mediterranean fish soup served with 'rouille', safron (saffron) and aïoli
Bourride – a creamy white fish soup, thickened with aïoli and flavoured with crawfish.
Brandade (de morue) à huile d'olive – a mousse of salt cod with cream, olive oil and garlic.
Pain Bagna – bread roll with olive oil, anchovies, olives, onions, etc.
Pissaladière – Provencal bread dough with onions, anchovies, olives, etc.
Pistou (Soupe au) – vegetable soup bound with 'pommade'
Pommade – a thick paste of garlic, basil, cheese and olive oil
Ratatouille – aubergines, courgettes, onion, garlic, red pepper and tomatoes in olive oil
Rouille – orange coloured sauce with hot peppers, garlic and saffron
Salade Niçoise – tomatoes, beans, potatoes, black olives, anchovy, lettuce and olive oil and sometimes tuna fish

Wine
Anise flavoured pastis is said to be the Riviera's favourite drink

Places of interest
Antibes – 17th century ramparts, 12th century castle with 16th century tower, old city
Cannes – popular for conventions and festivals, Cannes Film Festival, la Croisette, old city
Grasse – Capital of perfume industry, cathedral, Art and History of Provence Museum
Menton – warmest of coastal cities, year-round, Cocteau Museum, Promenade de Soleil
Monte Carlo – main city of Monaco, casinos, gardens, Napoleon Museum. motorsport circuit
Nice – Promenade des Anglais, fine arts museum, Matisse Museum, Ruhl Casino
Roquebrune – château, Ste Marguerite church
Saint Paul-de-Vence – medieval village, Maeght Foundation
Saint Raphael – Archeological museum, old port, church

63

Côte d'Azur

0605 Camping La Vieille Ferme, Villeneuve Loubet Plage, nr Antibes

Family owned site with good facilities, open all year.

Family owned and medium sized, La Vieille Ferme is in a popular resort area. In high season there is a shop, at other times bread and milk may be ordered. A drinks, sweets and ices machine is in the TV room. The swimming pool is heated and covered in winter (closed mid Nov–mid Dec) and beside it is a sunbathing area, children's pool and jacuzzi. Bicycle hire, table tennis and boules are provided with games and competitions organised in July/August. English is spoken and the place has a friendly feel to it. Restaurants nearby and a 1km walk towards Antibes brings you to the railway station, giving access to all the towns along the coast.

Directions: From west take Antibes exit from Esterel autoroute and turn left towards Nice when joining the N7 outside Antibes. After 3½ km. on N7 turn left for site. From east take N7 towards Antibes and turn right after Villeneuve Loubet Plage. The turning off the N7, though signed, is not easy to see particularly at busy times but, coming from Antibes, it is on the left, more or less between the Bonne Auberge and the Parc de Vaugrenier. Site is 150 m. on right. (Note: avoid N98 Route du Bord de Mer.)
Open: All year.
Address: Bvd. des Groules, 06270 Villeneuve Loubet Plage. Tel: (0)4.93.33.41.44. Fax: (0)4.93.33.37.28.

RENTED ACCOMMODATION	CHALETS *6 models*
Number of persons	2-6 persons
Bedrooms	One to two bedrooms according to model; at least 1 x double bed, plus bunk beds
Living/Dining area	Table and seating, colour TV; heating at extra cost
Kitchen area	Gas cooker, oven, refrigerator, sink, utensils, crockery and cutlery
Bathroom/shower	Shower, washbasin, WC
Additional facilities	Terrace (smallest model with sunshade, remainder covered) with garden table and chairs
Bedding	Bolsters and blankets provided; sheets for hire
Pets	Pets accepted
Charges per week (98): From Ffr: *(low season)* to Ffr: *(high season)*	Ffr 1,200 - 3,200; heating (October – March) 120; animal 70; nightly rates available in low season
Amount/% of deposit	25% plus Ffr 120 fee; min. 1 week in high season

Franche-Comté

Major city: Besançon
Départements: 25 Doubs; 39 Jura
79 Haute-Saône; 90 Tre.de Belfort

Geographically Franche-Comté is really two regions. The high valley of the Saône is wide, gently rolling country with a certain rustic simplicity, while the Jura mountains are more rugged with dense forests, sheer cliffs, deep gorges and torrents of water. In winter this means cross-country skiing over 2,000 km of marked trails and, in the summer, rafting along the gentle Lison and Loue rivers or the more challenging Saône or Doubs. Nature lovers can climb, bike and hike in the mountains or explore the hills honeycombed with over 4,000 caves. The streams and lakes provide world-class fishing. The spa towns of Salin les Bains and Besançon offer relaxation and a chance to 'take the waters'. The Region's position, bordering Switzerland and close to Germany, is reflected in its culture and the great diversity of architectural style in the many fine buildings.

Cuisine of the region
Freshwater fish such as trout, grayling, pike and perch are local specialities
Brési – wafer-thin slices of dried beef; many local hams
Jésus de Morteau – fat pork sausage smoked over pine and juniper
Poulet au vin jaune – chicken, cream and 'morilles' (chestnuts) cooked in 'vin jaune'
Gougère – hot cheese pastry based on the local 'Comté' cheese

Wine
The region has a rare wine known as 'vin de paille' as well as vin jaune, (deep yellow and very dry) and vin du jura, Jura wine
Pontarlier – aniseed liqueur
Kirsh – cherry flavoured liqueur

Places of interest
Arbois – Pasteur Family Home and Museum, Museum of Wine and Wine Growing
Belfort – sandstone lion sculpted by Bartholdi; castle and Vauban fortifications; Memorial and Museum of the French Resistance
Champlitte – Museum of Folk Art and Franche Comté Traditions
Dole – lovely old town, Louis Pasteur's birthplace
Gray – Baron Martin Museum
Luxeuil-les-Bains – Tour des Echevins Museum and Abbey
Morez – Eyeglass Museum
Morteau – Watch Museum
Morains-en-Montagne – the House of Toys
Ornans – Gustave Courbet birthplace and museum
Ronchamp – Chapel of Notre-Dame du Haut de Ronchamp designed by Le Corbusier
Saline – Royale d'Arc et Senans Royal Salt Works
Salins-les-Bains – Salt mines and tunnels
Sochaux – Peugeot Museum

Franche-Comté

2503 Camping du Bois de Reveuge, Huanne-Montmartin

New, medium sized, hill-side site with summer activities.

Bois de Reveuge still has a new look about it and there is little shade yet from the young trees. The enthusiastic owner has installed a good solar heated swimming pool which has a 'Swim Master' during the summer who, as well as acting as a lifeguard, offers swimming lessons. Being on a hillside, the terraced pitches have good views across the surrounding countryside and leading down to two lakes which may be used for fishing and canoeing. The site has private use of a 10 hectare lake 10 km. away where there is a watersport school. In high season there is a kiosk for basic food supplies and a restaurant with terrace. There is a high season 'baby club' with a large tent for wet weather, some music and other entertainment for adults. A package deal includes use of canoes, sailing boats and sailboards as well as archery, fishing and pedaloes. For an extra charge, rock climbing, potholing in nearby caves and rowing on the river Ognon can be organised, as well as bicycle hire.

Directions: Site is well signed from the D50 road. From A36 autoroute south of the site, take exit for Baume-les-Dames and head north on D50 towards Villersexel for about 12 km. to camp signs.
Open: 25 April – 19 September.
Address: 25680 Huanne-Montmartin. Tel: (0)3.81.84.38.60. Fax: (0)3.81.84.44.04.

RENTED ACCOMMODATION	MOBILE HOMES *Type B*
Number of persons	5-7 persons
Bedrooms	Two bedrooms: 1 x double bed or 2 single beds, 1 x 3 single beds
Living/Dining area	Table and seating, double sofa bed
Kitchen area	4 ring gas hob, refrigerator, sink, crockery, cutlery and utensils
Bathroom/shower	Washbasin, shower; separate WC
Additional facilities	Garden table and chairs, barbecue
Bedding	Blankets and pillows provided
Pets	Pets not accepted
Charges per week (98): From Ffr: *(low season)* to Ffr: *(high season)*	5 persons: Ffr 1,140 - 3,300; extra person 100
Amount/% of deposit	Ffr 1,000 plus 70 fee

Languedoc-Roussillon

Major cities: Montpellier, Perpignan, Nîmes, Carcassonne
Départements: 11 Aude; 30 Gard; 34 Hérault
48 Lozère; 66 Pyrénées-Orientales

Once an independent duchy, the ancient land of Languedoc combines three distinct regions: the mountains and gorges of the Cévennes; the vineyards of the Corbières and Minervois; and the coastal plain stretching from the Rhône to the Spanish border. Much of the region is rugged and unspoilt and there is ample evidence of the dramatic past. Ruins of the former Cathar castles can be seen throughout the region. The walled city of Carcassonne with its towers, dungeons, moats and drawbridges is one of the most impressive examples of medieval France. Today, Languedoc and Roussillon (the area between Narbonne and the Pyrénées) are wine and agricultural regions. Languedoc, with considerable success, is a producer of much of the nation's cheap table wine. On the coast the vast sandy beaches/resorts are being promoted as an alternative to the more famous Mediterranean stretches of the Côte d'Azur, for example La Grande Motte, Cap d'Agde and Canet. It is interesting to note that this far south there is a strong Spanish influence – in the look of the people, their culture, accent and in their language too. The local tongue, the ancient 'Occitan' is still spoken in rural areas, while down the coast in the Roussillon area, Catalan is spoken almost as much as French.

Cuisine of the region
Cooking is Provençal, characterised by garlic and olive oil with sausages and smoked hams
Fish is popular along the coast – fish soup bourride in Sète
Aïgo Bouido – garlic soup; the garlic is boiled so its impact is lessened; served with bread
Boles de picoulat – small balls of chopped-up beef and pork, garlic and eggs, served with tomatoes and parsley
Bouillinade – a type of bouillabaisse with potatoes, oil, garlic and onions
Boutifare – a sausage-shaped pudding of bacon and herbs
Cargolade – snails, stewed in wine
Ouillade – heavy soup of bacon, 'boutifare' (see above), leeks, carrots, and potatoes
Touron – a pastry of almonds, pistachio nuts and fruit

Wine
Wines include the reds of Corbières, Minervois, and the sweet Banyuls and Muscat

Places of interest
Aigues-Mortes – medieval city
Béziers – wine capital of the region, St Nazaire cathedral, Canal du Midi
Carcassonne – largest medieval walled city in Europe
Limoux – medieval town, Notre Dame de Marseilla Basilica, St Martin church
Montpellier – famous for universities, Roman sites; Gothic cathedral
Nîmes – Roman remains and amphitheatre, Pont du Gard
Perpignan – Kings Palace; Catalan characteristics
Pézenas – Molière's home
Villeneuve-les-Avignon – Royal City and residence of popes in 14th century

67

Languedoc-Roussillon

1106 Camping-Caravaning Au Pin d'Arnauteille, Montclar, nr Carcassonne

Peaceful, spacious, developing site with superb views to the Corbières and beyond.

Enjoying some of the best and most varied views of any we have visited, this rather unusual small site is ideally situated for exploring, by foot or car, the little known Aude département, the area of the Cathars and for visiting the walled city of Carcassonne. The site is set in 115 hectares of farmland on hilly ground. A swimming pool with children's pool and paved sunbathing area is in a hollow basin. A restaurant in a converted stable block provides plat du jour, grills and takeaway and there is a shop (both 15 May – 15 Sept; out of season the site is a little out of the way). Activities include table tennis, volleyball and riding, with fishing, rafting and canoeing near, and many walks with marked paths. This is a developing site with riding stables on site (note: the French are more relaxed about hard hats, etc).

Directions: Using the D118 from Carcassonne, after bypassing the small village of Rouffiac d'Aude, there is a small section of dual carriageway. Before the end of this, turn right to Montclar up a rather narrow road for 3 km. Site is signed sharp left and uphill before the village.
Open: 1 April – 30 September.
Address: 11250 Montclar. Tel: (0)4.68.26.84.53. Fax: (0)4.68.26.91.10.

RENTED ACCOMMODATION	MOBILE HOMES	CHALETS
Number of persons	6 persons	7 persons
Bedrooms	Two bedrooms: 1 x double bed, 1 x twin beds	Two bedrooms: 1 x double bed plus 1 single bed, 1 x double bed
Living/Dining area	Electric heating, table, chairs, easy chair, double sofa bed	Electric heating, colour TV, table, chairs, double sofa bed
Kitchen area	4 ring gas hob, refrigerator, sink, crockery, cutlery and utensils	2 ring gas hob (no oven or grill), refrigerator, sink, crockery, cutlery and utensils
Bathroom/shower	Washbasin, shower; separate WC	Washbasin, shower; separate WC
Additional facilities	Terrace with pergola and furniture	Terrace with roof and furniture
Bedding	Blankets and pillows provided	Blankets and pillows provided
Pets	Pets accepted	Pets accepted
Charges per week (98): From Ffr: *(low season)* to Ffr: *(high season)*	Ffr 1,500 - 2,850	Ffr 1,700 - 3,500
Amount/% of deposit	25% plus Ffr 150 fee	25% plus Ffr 150 fee

3000 Camping Domaine de Gaujac, Anduze

Woodland holiday site, with lively atmosphere and swimming pool.

This fairly large site is enthusiastically run by the energetic and friendly Holley family. It has a well stocked shop, takeaway and crêperie, bar and restaurant (open main season, on demand at other times). The fenced swimming pool and children's pool have a lifeguard in high season. Organised activities in main season include a children's club, plus cabaret, disco, buffet parties and even cinema shows. There are two tennis courts, minigolf, a children's playground plus a sports field for football, volleyball etc. Just across the lane is the river with a small beach where one can swim, boat or fish, and pony riding is available 150 m. from the site. Attractions in the region include the mining museum at Alès, steam trains run between Anduze and St Jean-du-Gard, and a number of spectacular caverns and grottoes. Four sanitary units are clean and practical rather than luxurious, providing mostly British style WCs, washbasins and free showers.

Directions: From Alès take N110 towards Montpellier. At St Christol-lès-Alès fork right on D910 towards Anduze, and in Bagard turn left on D246 to Boisset et Gaujac. Site is signed from village.
Open: 1 April – 30 September.
Address: Boisset et Gaujac, 30140 Anduze. Tel: (0)4.66.61.80.65. Fax: (0)4.66.60.53.90.

RENTED ACCOMMODATION	MOBILE HOMES	BUNGALOWS	CHALETS *Types A and B*
Number of persons	4-6 persons	2-4 persons	4-6 persons
Bedrooms	Two bedrooms: 1 x double bed, 1 x twin beds	One bedroom with double bed	Type A: two bedrooms - 2 x double beds. Type B: two bedrooms - 1 x double bed, 2 x bunk beds
Living/Dining area	Sofa bed (2 persons), table and seating	Table, seating, plus bunk beds	Table, seating
Kitchen area	4 ring gas hob, refrigerator, sink, utensils, crockery and cutlery	2 ring gas hob, refrigerator, sink, utensils, crockery and cutlery	2 ring gas hob, refrigerator, sink, utensils, crockery and cutlery
Bathroom/shower	Shower, washbasin, WC	Only washbasin with cold water, WC	Shower, washbasin, WC (separate WC in type A)
Additional facilities	Garden table and chairs	Terrace with garden furniture	Terrace with garden furniture
Bedding	Pillows and blankets provided	Pillows and blankets provided	Pillows and blankets provided
Pets	Pets accepted	Pets accepted	Pets accepted
Charges per week (98): From Ffr: *(low season)* to Ffr: *(high season)*	Ffr 1,300 - 2,900, weekend rates available outside 4 July - 29 August	Ffr 1,000 - 2,600, weekend rates available outside 4 July - 29 August	Type A Ffr 1,500 - 3,200, B 1,400 - 3,000; weekend rates available outside 4 July - 29 August
Amount/% of deposit	30% plus Ffr 80 fee	30% plus Ffr 80 fee	30% plus Ffr 80 fee

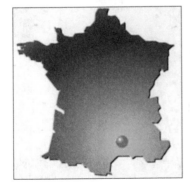

Languedoc-Roussillon

3009 Castel Camping Château de Boisson, Les Fumades, Allègre, nr Alès

Quiet site in peaceful surroundings, with outstanding pool complex.

A château in the grounds, an imposing church and a sleepy village as neighbours guarantee peace, tranquillity and pleasing views. The bar, TV and pool room at this medium sized site are set near the château, along with a terraced restaurant and takeaway (1 May–15 Sept). There is a small shop with the nearest towns being St Ambroix (4 km) and Alès (20 km). The 'jewel in the crown' is undoubtedly the pool complex, comprising an outdoor pool (1 May–15 Sept), a heated indoor pool (all season), toddlers' pool, flume and sun terrace. Entertainment is organised in July/August, plus photography and painting courses. Tennis, table tennis, boules and volleyball. Convenient for exploring the Camargue, Ardèche and the coast, the area has good riding, walking and river pursuits, including gold panning.

Directions: Site is about 17 km. northeast of Alès. Take D16 from Alès through Salindres. Continue for 8 km. staying on D16 as it turns sharp right over the Auzon river and then turn left almost immediately. The site and village can be seen on the right after 500 m.
Open: 1 April – 31 October.
Address: Boisson, Les Fumades, 30500 Allègre. Tel: (0)4.66.24.85.61. Fax: (0)4.66.24.80.14.

RENTED ACCOMMODATION	MOBILE HOMES *Types A and B*	APARTMENTS *Types A and B*
Number of persons	Type A: 2 persons, type B: 4 persons	Type A: 2 persons, type B: 4 persons
Bedrooms	Two bedrooms: 1 x double bed, 1 x twin beds	Type A: 1 x twin beds; type B: 2 x twin beds
Living/Dining area	Heating, table and seating	Table and seating, armchairs, telephone
Kitchen area	Gas hot-plates (no oven), refrigerator, sink, crockery, cutlery and utensils	Gas hob (no oven), refrigerator, sink, crockery, cutlery and utensils
Bathroom/shower	Washbasin, shower, WC	Washbasin, shower; separate WC
Additional facilities	Garden furniture and sunshade	Shared balcony with some flats with garden table and chairs, sunshade
Bedding	Pillows provided	Blankets and pillows provided
Pets	Cats accepted, some dogs in low season	Cats accepted (no dogs)
Charges per week (98): From Ffr: *(low season)* to Ffr: *(high season)*	Type A: Ffr 1,505 - 2,520, type B 2,016 - 3,360	Type A: Ffr 1,890 - 2,394, type B 2,520 - 3,500
Amount/% of deposit	25% plus Ffr 100 fee	25% plus Ffr 100 fee

3012 Camping TCS L'Ile des Papes, Villeneuve lès Avignon

New, very well equipped site run by the Touring Club Suisse.

L'Ile des Papes is only two years old and, as yet, is under used. From the moment you walk into reception you realise you have come to a site of quality. Everywhere at this medium sized site looks so neat and tidy due, no doubt, to the fact that it is Swiss owned. The swimming pool area is extensive with two pools for adults and one for children and with plenty of sunbathing areas. All is overlooked by the terrace of the bar and restaurant. At the height of the season there are organised games and competitions. A play area will keep children happy and the lake is used for fishing and water-cycles. The list of activities includes archery, tennis, table tennis, volleyball, minigolf, basketball, pony rides, dances, aquarobics (all free) and bicycle hire (charged). The shop is well stocked. If all this fails to keep you occupied, Avignon and its museums is only 8 km.

Directions: Take N100 Nîmes road out of Avignon towards Bagnoles-sur-Cèze and turn right after crossing the Rhône. Turn left along the river bank and follow signs for Roquemaure (D980). In 6 km. turn right onto D228 signed Barrage de Villeneuve and site is 1 km.
Open: 10 April – 2 November.
Address: 30400 Villeneuve lès Avignon. Tel: (0)4.90.15.15.90. Fax: (0)4.90.15.15.91.

RENTED ACCOMMODATION	CHALETS
Number of persons	2-4 persons
Bedrooms	Two bedrooms; 1 x double bed, 1 x twin beds
Living/Dining area	Electric heating, table and seating
Kitchen area	2 electric hot-plates, refrigerator, sink, crockery, cutlery and utensils
Bathroom/shower	Shower, washbasin, WC
Additional facilities	Terrace with garden furniture
Bedding	Sheets, pillows and blankets provided
Pets	Pets accepted
Charges per week (98): From Ffr: *(low season)* to Ffr: *(high season)*	4 persons: Ffr 1,980 - 2,980, plus cleaning fee 200; pet 10
Amount/% of Deposit	Details from site

Languedoc-Roussillon

3014 Camping Caravaning Soubeyranne, Remoulins

Medium size, quiet campsite near Pont du Gard.

This family run site is well positioned for visiting the Pont du Gard, Nîmes and Uzès, famed for their Roman connections. Varied and plentiful trees provide shade and keeping the 4.5 hectares watered involves over 5 km. of hose pipe, with the greenness bearing out this dedication. A small shop sells basic provisions, although Remoulins is only 1.5 km. The swimming pool comprises a 20 x 10 m. pool and a smaller, toddlers' pool (unsupervised), with paved sunbathing surrounds. Even the pool is partly shaded – greatly appreciated in the heat of the day. Overlooking the pool from an attractive terrace are the restaurant, bar and takeaway. There is a play area, including trampoline, climbing frame, swings, table tennis, boules, tennis and volleyball court. An animation programme (July/August) is mainly for young children; teenagers may find it rather quiet.

Directions: From Uzès take D981 to Remoulins, turn right at lights over river bridge, left at roundabout, then left (signed D986 Beaucaire). Site is 1.5 km. further on left.
Open: 11 April – 14 September.
Address: Route de Beaucaire, 30210 Remoulins. Tel: (0)4.66.37.03.21. Fax: (0)4.66.37.14.65.

RENTED ACCOMMODATION	CHALETS
Number of persons	4 persons (max)
Bedrooms	One bedroom with double bed, mezzanine with twin beds
Living/Dining area	Table, chairs, sofa
Kitchen area	Gas hob, refrigerator, sink, crockery, cutlery and utensils
Bathroom/shower	Shower, washbasin, WC
Additional facilities	Terrace with garden furniture and barbecue
Bedding	Pillows and blankets provided
Pets	Pets accepted
Charges per week (98): From Ffr: *(low season)* to Ffr: *(high season)*	4 persons: Ffr 1,600 - 2,500
Amount/% of deposit	20% plus Ffr 80 fee

3403 Camping Club International Le Napoleon, Vias Plage

Family site bordering the Mediterranean at Vias Plage.

The town of Vias is in the wine-growing area of the Midi, an area which includes the Camargue, Béziers and popular modern resorts such as Cap d'Agde. The single street that leads to Vias Plage is hectic in season, but once through the entrance to Le Napoleon, the contrast is marked – tranquillity, yet still only a few yards from the beach and other attractions. Not that the medium sized site itself lacks vibrancy, with its own pool, bar and extensive entertainment programme, but thoughtful planning and design ensure that the camping area is quiet, with good shade from the many tall trees. The site has a supermarket and there are plenty of other shops and restaurants are immediately adjacent. Facilities include volleyball, bicycle hire, boules and TV. Fishing nearby. A new Californian style swimming pool opened in '97. Most amenities are available from May. In addition to the accommodation below, Trigano (Bengali) tents may be rented.

Directions: From Vias town, take the D137 towards Vias Plage. Site is on the right near the beach.
Open: 1 April – 30 September.
Address: Farinette Plage, 34450 Vias sur Mer. Tel: (0)4.67.01.07.80. Fax: (0)4.67.01.07.85.

RENTED ACCOMMODATION	MOBILE HOMES	CHALETS 'Gitotel'	APARTMENTS Types 1 and 2
Number of persons	4/6 persons	4/6 persons	4/6 persons or 4/8 persons
Bedrooms	Two bedrooms: 1 x double bed, 1 x twin beds	Two bedrooms: 1 x double bed, 1 x twin beds and 2 bunk beds	Type 1: two bedrooms: 1 x double bed, 1 x twin beds; type 2: plus 1 x bunk beds
Living/Dining area	Table and seating, convertible double bed	Table and seating	Table and seating
Kitchen area	Hot-plates, refrigerator, sink, crockery, cutlery and utensils	Hot-plates, refrigerator, sink, crockery, cutlery and utensils	Hob, refrigerator, sink, crockery, cutlery and utensils
Bathroom/shower	Washbasin, shower, WC	Washbasin, shower, WC	Washbasin, shower; separate WC
Additional facilities	Garden furniture and sunshade	Covered terrace with garden furniture	Terrace with garden table and chairs, sunshade
Bedding	Blankets and pillows provided	Blankets and pillows provided	Blankets and pillows provided
Pets	Pets accepted	Pets accepted	Pets accepted
Charges per week (98): From Ffr: *(low season)* to Ffr: *(high season)*	4 persons: Ffr 1,000 - 3,350; extra person per day (over 3 yrs) 18 - 30; dog 15 - 20; nightly and w/end rates available in low seasons	4 persons: Ffr 1,200 - 3,500; extra person per day (over 3 yrs) 18 - 30; dog 15 - 20; nightly and w/end rates available in low seasons	Type 1 (4 persons) Ffr 1,200 - 3,600, type 2 (4 persons) 1,500 - 3,900; extra person per day (over 3 yrs) 18 - 30; dog 15 - 20; nightly and w/end rates available in low seasons
Amount/% of deposit	30% plus Ffr 170 fee	30% plus Ffr 170 fee	30% plus Ffr 170 fee

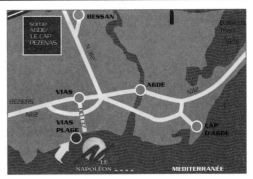

Languedoc-Roussillon

3404 Camping Lou Village, Valras-Plage, nr Béziers

Family owned, good value large site with direct access to beach.

Valras is perhaps smarter and is certainly larger than nearby Vias and it has a good number of campsites. Lou Village has direct access to a sandy beach and is a busy site with lots of facilities. The swimming pool, children's paddling pool, restaurant, bar (both 8 May – 15 Sept) and shops all form part of the 'village centre' where most of the site's activity takes place. There is a raised stage for entertainment, children's club, supermarket, bakery, takeaway, bazaar with papers and hairdressing salon. The bar has a large screen for TV and a terrace overlooking the pool. It is a busy area with a pleasant ambience. Other facilities include a children's playground, football field, bicycle hire, minigolf, volleyball, tennis, etc. There is lots to do off the site - sailing, windsurfing, riding, canoeing, river fishing, bike rides and the history of the Languedoc to discover. English is spoken.

Directions: Site is south of Béziers. From autoroute, take Béziers-Ouest exit for Valras Plage and continue for 13-14 km. Follow 'Casino' signs and site is 1 km south of centre of Valras Plage in the direction of Vendres.
Open: 24 April – 19 September.
Address: BP 30, 34350 Valras-Plage. Tel: (0)4.67.37.33.79. Fax: (0)4.67.37.53.56.

RENTED ACCOMMODATION	MOBILE HOMES *Type A*	MOBILE HOMES *Type B*	CHALETS
Number of persons	4 persons	6 persons	6 persons
Bedrooms	Two bedrooms: 1 x double bed, 1 x twin beds	Two bedrooms: 1 x double bed, 1 x twin beds	Two bedrooms: 1 x double bed, 1 x twin beds
Living/Dining area	Table and seating	Table and seating, double sofa bed	Table and seating, double sofa bed
Kitchen area	4 ring gas hob, refrigerator, sink, crockery, cutlery and utensils	4 ring gas hob, refrigerator, sink, crockery, cutlery and utensils	2 ring gas hob, refrigerator, sink, crockery, cutlery and utensils
Bathroom/shower	Washbasin, shower, WC	Washbasin, shower, WC	Wwashbasin, shower; separate WC
Additional facilities	Paved terrace with garden furniture	Paved terrace with garden furniture	Covered terrace with garden furniture
Bedding	Pillows and blankets provided	Pillows and blankets provided	Pillows and blankets provided
Pets	Small pets accepted	Small pets accepted	Small pets accepted
Charges per week (98): From Ffr: *(low season)* to Ffr: *(high season)*	Ffr 1,000 - 2,800	Ffr 1,700 - 3,300	Ffr 1,800 - 3,750
Amount/% of deposit	Contact site for details	Contact site for details	Contact site for details

N3405 Camping Naturiste Le Mas de Lignieres, Cesseras, nr Olonzac

Small, rural naturist site with pool in the hills of the Minervois.

Only 3 km. from the medieval town of Minerve, parts of this site enjoy some marvellous views to the Pyrénées, the Corbières and the coast at Narbonne. There is some shade, although the many trees are mainly young (but growing) and there is a variety of flora including four types of orchid. Within the site there are some good walks with superb views and, although the camping area is actually quite small, the very large pitches and young trees and hedges give an impression of spaciousness, creating a very relaxing ambience and a nice introduction to naturist camping. The attractive swimming pool (June – Sept) has a paved sunbathing area and a children's paddling pool. Tennis, volleyball and boules are free. A small shop sells essentials including bread to order and local specialities (15 June – 15 Sept). At present there is only a bar/snackbar (July/August); a restaurant is planned. Facilities for sailing, riding and canoeing are near.

Directions: From A61 autoroute take Lezignan-Corbières exit, through the town via the D611 to Homps, then via the D190 to Olonzac. Go through village following the signs to Cesseras, from where site is signed.
Open: 1 April – 31 October.
Address: Cesseras-en-Minervois, 34210 Olonzac. Tel: (0)4.68.91.24.86. Fax: as phone.

RENTED ACCOMMODATION	MOBILE HOMES	BUNGALOWS
Number of persons	4 persons	2-4 persons
Bedrooms	Two bedrooms: 1 x double bed, 1 x twin beds	Two bedrooms: 1 x double bed, 1 x twin beds
Living/Dining area	Table and seating, double sofa bed	Table and seating, double sofa bed
Kitchen area	4 ring gas hob, refrigerator, sink, crockery, cutlery and utensils	4 ring gas hob, refrigerator, sink, crockery, cutlery and utensils
Bathroom/shower	Washbasin, shower, WC	Washbasin, shower, WC
Additional facilities	Terrace (28 sq.m) with table and chairs	Terrace (12 sq.m) with table and chairs
Bedding	Pillows and blankets provided	Pillows and blankets provided
Pets	Only cats accepted	Only cats accepted
Charges per week (98): From Ffr: *(low season)* to Ffr: *(high season)*	Ffr 1,700 - 2,600	Ffr 1,200 - 2,400
Amount/% of deposit	25%	25%

The other titles in the ALAN ROGERS' series for independent campers and caravanners are:

• **Good Camps Guide – Britain & Ireland**

• **Good Camps Guide – France**

• **Good Camps Guide – Europe**

• **Camping & Caravanning All Year Round**

Languedoc-Roussillon

3406 Hotel de Plein Air L'Oliveraie, Laurens

Site with many attractive features at the foot of the Cevennes, open all year.

This lively, fairly small site has a lot to offer in terms of activities, particularly for youngsters, including plenty of evening entertainment in the high season, but can be comfortable and quiet at other times. The large leisure area includes a good sized pool and children's pool (1 June – 30 Sept), with an attractive paved sunbathing area, a tennis court and tennis practice wall, volleyball, basketball, minigolf, children's play area and adjoining riding stables. There are also good facilities for archery which is quite a feature of the site. Overlooking these facilities is a large terrace with a bar/restaurant serving simple grills in the high season. At other times there is an indoor bar, also used for films and activities for younger children. The two sanitary blocks, the one on the lower level being more modern and well equipped, provide hot showers, washbasins in cabins, British WCs, dishwashing areas and a washing machine. A small shop is well stocked. A 'Sites et Paysages' member.

Directions: Site is signed 2 km. north of Laurens off the D909 (Béziers - Bédarieux) road.
Open: All year.
Address: 34480 Laurens. Tel: (0)4.67.90.24.36. Fax: (0)4.67.90.11.20.

RENTED ACCOMMODATION	MOBILE HOMES *Type A*	MOBILE HOMES *Type B*	BUNGALOWS *Type HLL*
Number of persons	4 persons	6 persons	6 persons
Bedrooms	Two bedrooms: 1 x double bed, 1 x twin beds	Two bedrooms: 1 x double bed, 1 x bunk beds, 1 x folding bed (2 persons)	Two bedrooms: 1 x double bed, 1 x bunk beds, 1 x folding bed (2 persons)
Living/Dining area	Doubles as bedroom	Table and seating	Table and seating
Kitchen area	Gas hob, refrigerator, sink, crockery, cutlery and utensils	4 ring gas hob, refrigerator, fan, coffee machine, sink, crockery, cutlery and utensils	Gas hob, refrigerator, coffee machine, sink, crockery, cutlery and utensils
Bathroom/shower	None	Washbasin, shower, WC	Washbasin, shower, WC
Additional facilities	Terrace with garden furniture and sunshade	Covered terrace, table, chairs, sunbeds and sunshade	Covered terrace, table, chairs, sunbeds and sunshade
Bedding	Duvets and pillows provided (not covers)	Duvets and pillows provided (not covers)	Duvets and pillows provided (not covers)
Pets	Pets accepted	Pets accepted	Pets accepted
Charges per week (98): From Ffr: *(low season)* to Ffr: *(high season)*	Only available 1 June - 30 Sept; Ffr 1,235 - 1,900	Ffr 1,460 - 2,650	Ffr 1,460 - 2,650
Amount/% of deposit	Ffr 1,200 plus 80 fee	Ffr 1,200 plus 80 fee	Ffr 1,200 plus 80 fee

3407 Camping Village Le Sérignan Plage, Sérignan

Unusual, well equipped site with indoor pool and direct access to sandy beach.

This is a large, but very comfortable site, built in a genuinely unique style. Perhaps the most remarkable aspect is the cluster of attractive buildings which form the central amenity area, amongst which is a small indoor heated swimming pool. This is not intended for use in the high season, when the beach and sea offer a better alternative but, even so, a large outdoor pool complex is also planned. These attractive buildings are virtually a small village, with bar, restaurant, takeaway, disco, small amphitheatre, supermarket, newsagent/tobacconist, an outdoor market and even a roof-top bar – all with an international, lively atmosphere. The site has direct access to a large sandy beach and to the adjoining naturist beach, both of which slope very gently and offer safe bathing at most times (lifeguard in high season). There is a sailing and windsurfing school.

Directions: From the A9 take exit 35 (Béziers Est) and follow signs for Sérignan on the D64 (9 km). Don't go into Sérignan, but take sign for Sérignan Plage for 4 km. At first camping sign turn right (one way) for 500 m. Bear left past two naturist sites.
Open: 15 April – 15 September.
Address: 34410 Sérignan. Tel: (0)4.67.32.35.33. Fax: (0)4.67.32.26.36.

RENTED ACCOMMODATION	MOBILE HOMES	COTTAGES
Number of persons	6 persons	6 persons
Bedrooms	Two bedrooms: 2 x twin beds	Two bedrooms: 1 x twin beds, 1 x twin beds and 2 bunk beds
Living/Dining area	Table and seating	Table and seating
Kitchen area	Gas hob, refrigerator, sink, crockery, cutlery and utensils	Gas hob, refrigerator, sink, crockery, cutlery and utensils
Bathroom/shower	Shower, washbasin, WC	Shower, washbasin, WC
Additional facilities	–	–
Bedding	Blankets provided	Blankets provided
Pets	Pets not accepted	Pets not accepted
Charges per week (98): From Ffr: *(low season)* to Ffr: *(high season)*	Ffr 1,450 - 3,600	Ffr 1,600 - 3,800
Amount/% of deposit	25% plus Ffr 100 fee	25% plus Ffr 100 fee

Languedoc-Roussillon

6601 Camping-Caravaning California, Le Barcarès, Perpignan

Family owned site with swimming pool, not far from beach.

This small site is attractively laid out with much green foliage (formerly an orchard) on flat ground. Cool and shaded, the medium sized site now has a mature look with an attractive terraced pool bar area and an efficient reception area built in local materials. The site is about 900 m. from a sandy beach. It has a swimming pool of 200 sq.m. and children's pool (from 1 May), with a free water slide (July/August) in a small separate pool. A pleasant, good value restaurant and bar with takeaway, shop (all open 20 June – 4 Sept), wine store and pizzeria are at the rear entrance to the site. Activities include tennis, a TV room, small multi-gym, archery, mountain bikes for hire and a BMX track on site. There are facilities for river fishing 500 m. Children's animation is organised in season and some evening entertainment. Only gas or electric barbecues are allowed.

Directions: Site is on the D90 coast road 2 km. southwest of Le Barcarès centre.
Open: 25 May – 25 September.
Address: Route de St Laurent, 66420 Le Barcarès. Tel: (0)4.68.86.16.08. Fax: (0)4.68.86.18.20.

RENTED ACCOMMODATION	MOBILE HOMES *Types A and B*	CHALETS *Campitel Confort*	BUNGALOWS
Number of persons	Type A: 4 persons, type B: 6 persons	6 persons	6 persons
Bedrooms	Two bedrooms: 1 x double bed, 1 x twin beds	Two bedrooms: 1 x double bed, 1 x double and 2 single beds	Two bedrooms: 1 x double bed, 1 x twin beds
Living/Dining area	Table and seating; type B double sofa bed	Table and seating	Table and seating, double sofa bed
Kitchen area	3 ring gas hob, refrigerator, sink, crockery, cutlery and utensils	3 ring gas hob, refrigerator, sink, crockery, cutlery and utensils	3 ring gas hob, refrigerator, sink, crockery, cutlery and utensils
Bathroom/shower	Shower, washbasin, WC	Shower, washbasin, WC	Shower, washbasin, WC
Additional facilities	Garden table and chairs, sunshade	Garden table and chairs, sunshade	Garden table and chairs, sunshade
Bedding	Blankets only provided	Blankets only provided	Blankets only provided
Pets	Pets accepted	Pets accepted	Pets accepted
Charges per week (98): From Ffr: *(low season)* to Ffr: *(high season)*	Type A: Ffr 1,150 - 2,400; type B: 1,250 - 2,950; animal 70; gas (not included) 55; weekend rates available outside 27 June - 29 August	Ffr 1,400 - 3,250; animal 70; gas (not included) 55; weekend rates available outside 27 June - 29 August	Ffr 1,400 - 3,250; animal 70; gas (not included) 55; weekend rates available outside 27 June - 29 August
Amount/% of deposit	Ffr 1,200 plus 80 fee	Ffr 1,200 plus 80 fee	Ffr 1,200 plus 80 fee

6602 Camping Club Ma Prairie, Canet, nr Perpignan

Excellent site 3 km. back from sea among the vineyards, with various amenities.

The Gil family provide a warm welcome and pleasant atmosphere at Ma Prairie. It lies some 3 km. back from the sandy Canet beaches, with two swimming pools – one for children and one for adults, across a small road from the camping area. The pitches are on flat grassy ground with trees and bushes separating them and providing shade (possible road noise). A large bar overlooks the terraced pool area and satellite TV has been installed, with table tennis, billiards and amusement machines; discos and dancing are held about three times weekly, with daily animation in season. There is a shop for basics and a covered snack bar and open air restaurant are next to reception. Tennis and bicycle hire are available and a children's play area. Bus/tram services run to the modern resort of Canet, where there are first class restaurants, including one owned by the same family. The attractive, old 'Canet Village' is within walking distance and has all amenities. The medium sized site is used by tour operators and there is a busy atmosphere.

Directions: Site access is from the D11 Perpignan road close to the junction with D617 in Canet-Village.
Open: 10 May – 20 September.
Address: 66140 Canet en Roussillon. Tel: (0)4.68.73.26.17. Fax: (0)4.68.73.28.82.

RENTED ACCOMMODATION	MOBILE HOMES *Type A*	MOBILE HOMES *Type B*
Number of persons	4 persons	6 persons
Bedrooms	Two bedrooms: 1 x double bed, 1 x bunk beds (children under 15 yrs)	Two bedrooms: 1 x double bed, 1 x twin beds
Living/Dining area	Fireplace, table, sofa and seating	Fireplace, table and seating, convertible double bed
Kitchen area	4 ring gas hob, oven or grill in some, refrigerator (some have freezer), sink, crockery, cutlery and utensils	4 ring gas hob, oven or grill in some, refrigerator (some with freezer), sink, crockery, cutlery and utensils
Bathroom/shower	Shower, washbasin, WC	Shower, washbasin, WC
Additional facilities	Outdoor table and 4 chairs	Outdoor table and 6 chairs
Bedding	Blankets and pillows provided	Blankets and pillows provided
Pets	Pets accepted	Pets accepted
Charges per week (98): From Ffr: *(low season)* to Ffr: *(high season)*	Ffr 1,430 - 2,860; dog 15 per day	Ffr 1,640 - 3,280; dog 15 per day
Amount/% of deposit	Ffr 1,150 and 150 fee	Ffr 1,150 and 150 fee

Languedoc-Roussillon

6607 Camping-Caravaning Le Brasilia, Canet Plage en Roussillon

Excellent, well run site beside beach with wide range of facilities.

We were impressed with La Brasilia – it is pretty, neat and well kept with a wide range of facilities and activities. A large site, it does not seem so, with a range of shade from mature pines, flowering shrubs and neat access roads. The sandy beach is busy, with a club (windsurfing boards to hire). There is also a large pool (1 May – 30 Sept), with sunbathing areas and bar. A sports field is beside the tennis courts and there are activities such as aqua gym, aerobics, football, etc. plus a games and video room (club card required in high season), bicycle hire and fishing. The village area with shops, bars and restaurant is busy, providing meals, entertainment (including a night club) and a range of shops. In fact you do not need to stir from the site which is almost a resort in itself. It has a lively atmosphere but is orderly and well run. The site is used by tour operators. English is spoken.

Directions: Site is north of Canet Port. From Canet Plage follow signs for Port, then 'Campings', and then follow site signs (near the American Park).

Open: 4 April – 3 October.

Address: BP 204, 66141 Canet Plage en Roussillon. Tel: (0)4.68.80.23.82. Fax: (0)4.68.73.32.97. E-mail: brasilia@mnet.fr.

RENTED ACCOMMODATION	MOBILE HOMES	BUNGALOWS	CHALETS
Number of persons	4 persons	4 persons	5 persons
Bedrooms	Two bedrooms: 1 x double bed, 1 x twin beds	Two bedrooms: 1 x double bed, 1 x twin beds or bunk beds	Two bedrooms: 1 x double bed, 1 x 3 single beds
Living/Dining area	Table, seating and chairs	Table, seating and chairs; double sofa bed	Table, seating and chairs
Kitchen area	2 gas hot-plates, refrigerator, sink, utensils, crockery and cutlery	2 electric hot-plates and oven, refrigerator, sink, utensils, crockery and cutlery	2 gas hot-plates, refrigerator, sink, utensils, crockery and cutlery
Bathroom/shower	Shower, washbasin, WC	Shower, washbasin, WC (or separate WC)	Shower, washbasin, WC
Additional facilities	Patio with garden furniture	Patio with garden furniture	Patio with garden furniture
Bedding	Pillows and blankets provided	Pillows and blankets provided	Pillows and blankets provided
Pets	Pets accepted	Pets accepted	Pets accepted
Charges per week (98): From Ffr: (low season) to Ffr: (high season)	Ffr 1,400 - 3,200; weekend rates available in low season	Ffr 1,600 - 3,500; weekend rates available in low season	Ffr 1,600 - 3,500; weekend rates available in low season
Amount/% of deposit	Ffr 800 per week plus 100 fee	Ffr 800 plus 100 fee	Ffr 800 plus 100 fee

Limousin

Major cities: Limoges, Brive-la-Gaillarde
Départements: 19 Corrèze; 23 Creuse
87 Haute-Vienne

Limousin is an unspoilt, thinly populated region on the western side of the Massif Central. With hills and gorges and lush green meadows grazed on by the Limousin breed of cattle, numerous ancient village churches dot the landscape as well as more imposing abbey churches and fortresses. Its moorland has made the region popular with horse breeders. The Anglo-Arab horse originated from the famous studs at Pompadour. The city of Limoges, synonymous with porcelain, produced the finest painted enamelware of Europe in the 16th and 17th centuries and today remains the porcelain capital of France, and Aubusson is known for its beautiful and intricate tapestries. But Limousin's appeal is more than anything the freedom of the countryside and it has not as yet been discovered, except by the discriminating traveller. It is said that in Limousin a discovery awaits you at the end of every path and we consider this to be a fairly accurate description.

Cuisine of the region
Limousin is known for a soup called 'bréjaude', eaten with rye bread, and so thick with cabbage and other vegetables that a spoon will stand up in it
Traditional dishes include a varity of stews such as potée, cassoulet, beans and pork and sauced dishes accompanied by chestnuts or rye pancakes
The beef (Limousin) of the region is extremely tender and full of flavour
Desserts include thick home-made cakes, almond cake of the Creuse, galette Corrézienne,
Clafoutis – a pancake batter poured over fruit for example:
Gargouillau – a clafoutis of pears and Milliard (millat) (milla) – a clafoutis of cherries

Places of interest
Aubusson – long tradition of tapestry making, Hotel de Ville tapestry collections
Grimel-les-Cascades – a pretty hamlet set in a deep gorge
Gueret – built around a monastery founded in the 8th century; the municipal museum houses a fine collection of porcelain
Limoges – porcelain, enamel and faience work, château, church of St Michel-de-Lions, cathedral of St Etienne
Noirlac – abbey
Solignac – the Abbatiale church
Segur-le-Château – picturesque village dominated by its fortified château, Henri IV's house
Treignac – Rocher des Folles with a view of the Vézères gorges
Tulle – 12th century cathedral, City museum, Maison de Loyac, cathedral cloister
Uzerche – site of a famous 8th century siege by the Sarazins

Limousin

2301 Castel Camping Le Château de Poinsouze, Boussac-Bourg

Well designed, high quality site, set in a beautiful château parkland.

Le Château de Poinsouze is a newly developed, fairly small site arranged on the open, gently sloping, grassy park to one side of the château's main drive – a beautiful oak tree avenue. The château (not open to the public) lies across the lake and the exceptionally well restored outbuildings on the opposite side of the drive house the well stocked shop, takeaway and a comfortable bar. These surround the attractively designed swimming pool with water slide, children's pool and terrace. Other amenities include bicycle hire, free lake fishing; boats and lifejackets can be hired. Table tennis, pool table and table football games. The site has a friendly family atmosphere, there are organised activities in main season including dances, children's games and crafts, family triathlons, and there are marked walks around the park and woods. A large area is set aside for football, volleyball, badminton, and other games. All facilities open from 15 May, although times may vary. Boussac (2.5 km.) has a market every Thursday. Young trees have been planted to provide shade.

Directions: Site entrance is 2.5 km north of Boussac on the D917 (towards La Châtre).
Open: 1 May - 20 September; Gîte all year.
Address: Route de la Châtre, 23600 Boussac-Bourg. Tel: (0)5.55.65.02.21. Fax: (0)5.55.65.86.49.

RENTED ACCOMMODATION	MOBILE HOMES *Types A and B*	MOBILE HOMES *Type C*	GÎTE
Number of persons	Type A (26 sq.m) and type B (34 sq.m): 4/5 persons	6/7 persons (44 sq.m)	8/9 persons
Bedrooms	Two bedrooms: 1 x double bed, 1 x twin beds	Three bedrooms: 1 x double bed, 2 x twin beds	Three bedrooms: 2 x double beds, 1 x 5 single beds
Living/Dining area	Gas heater, table and seating, coffee maker; single sofa bed	Gas heater, table and seating, coffee maker; single sofa bed	Table and seating, TV
Kitchen area	4 ring gas hob, oven in type B, fridge/freezer, sink, crockery, cutlery and utensils	4 ring gas hob, fridge, large freezer, sink, crockery, cutlery and utensils	Gas hob, electric oven, refrigerator, dishwasher, washing machine, sink, crockery, cutlery and utensils
Bathroom/shower	Shower, washbasin; separate WC	Shower, washbasin; separate WC	Two bathrooms: 1 x bath, shower, washbasin and separate WC, 1 x shower, WC
Additional facilities	Garden table and chairs, sunshade	Garden table and chairs, sunshade; washing machine	Garden table and chairs, sunshade
Bedding	Blankets and pillows provided; sheets for hire	Blankets and pillows provided; sheets for hire	Blankets and pillows provided; sheets for hire
Pets	Pets not accepted	Pets not accepted	Pets not accepted
Charges per week (98): From Ffr: *(low season)* to Ffr: *(high season)*	Type A: Ffr 1,800 (2 persons 1,500) - 2,900; type B: 2,200 - 3,400; extra gas bottle in low season (first included) 120	Ffr 2,500 - 3,800; extra gas bottle in low season (first included) 120	Ffr 2,800 - 3,700
Amount/% of deposit	Ffr 1,000 or 1,800	Ffr 1,800	Ffr 1,800

Loire Valley

Major cities: Orléans, Tours
Départements: 18 Cher; 28 Eure-et-Loir; 36 Indre; 37 Indre-et-Loire; 41 Loir-et-Cher; 45 Loiret

For centuries the Loire Valley was frequented by French royalty and the great River Loire winds its way past some of France's most magnificent châteaux. Known as the Garden of France, it is a most productive and lush area with large farms and a mild climate making it a favourite with visitors. Well known for its wines, over 100 different ones are produced from vineyards stretching along the 1,000 km (620 mile) course of the River Loire. Imposing abbeys, troglodyte caves, tiny Romanesque churches, woodlands such as the Sologne and sleepy, picturesque villages reward exploration. Cities like Blois and Tours are elegant with fine architecture and museums and Paris is only one hour by the TGV.

Cuisine of the region
Wild duck, pheasant, hare, deer, and quail are classics and fresh water fish such as salmon, perch and trout are favourite. A tasty 'beurre blanc' is the usual sauce with fish. The Sologne is famous for asparagus, frogs, game, fungi, lake and river fish and wildfowl.
For dessert, this is the home of Tarte Tatin – upside down tart of caramelised apples and pastry
Tarte a la citrouille – pumpkin tart
Bourdaines – apples stuffed with jam and baked

Wine
Loire Valley wines are earthy, flinty Sancerre (both the outstanding white and the lesser-known red), the light red Chinon and the lightly sparkling Vouvray, all good choices. Most Loire wines, even the reds, should be served chilled.

Places of interest
Amboise – château by the river, Clos Lucé and Leonardo da Vinci museum with scale models of his inventions
Azay-le-Rideau – Renaissance château
Blois – château with architecture from Middle Ages to Neo-Classical periods
Chambord – Renaissance château, park and terraces, grandiose creation of François I
Chartres – cathedral with famous stained glass windows
Chenonçeau – château with great gallery and bridge
Cheverny – delightful privately owned château
Chinon – old town, Pavillon de l'Horloge, Joan of Arc museum
Langeais – château and tapestry collection
Loches – old town, château and its fortifications
Orléans – Holy Cross cathedral, house of Joan of Arc
Tours – Renaissance and Neo-Classical mansions, cathedral of St Gatien, museums of archeology and modern art
Vendôme – Tour St Martin, La Trinité
Villandry – famous renaissance gardens.
Vouvray – wine cellars

Loire Valley

3701 Camping de la Mignardière, Ballan-Miré, nr Tours

Pleasant little site quietly situated just southwest of Tours.

The situation of this little site may appeal to many – only 8 km. from the centre of the city of Tours, yet in a peaceful spot within easy reach of several of the Loire châteaux, notably Azay-le-Rideau, and with various sports activities on or very close to the site. Amenities on the site include a shop, two unheated, large swimming pools (15 May – 15 Sept) with sunbathing terrace, a good tennis court, table tennis and bicycle hire. There is a bar, restaurant and crêperie with takeaway nearby (all 15 May - 15 Sept). Just outside the site is a small 'parc de loisirs' with pony rides, minigolf, small cars, playground and some other amusements. An attractive lake catering particularly for windsurfing is 300 m. (boards can be hired or use your own) and there is a family fitness run. Fishing 500 m. The barrier gates are operated by card, closed 22.30 - 07.30 hrs.

Directions: From Chinon along A751, follow signs to site on entering Ballan-Miré. From Tours take D751 towards Chinon. Just after Joué-les-Tours look for and turn right at Campanile Hotel – follow signs to site.
Open: 4 April – 3 October.
Address: Ave des Aubépines, 37510 Ballan-Miré. Tel: (0)2.47.73.31.00. Fax: (0)2.47.73.31.01.
Internet: www.france-campings.com.mignardiere. E-mail: mign@france-campings.com

RENTED ACCOMMODATION	MOBILE HOMES *Type A and B*	CHALETS *'Gitotel'*
Number of persons	Type A: 4 persons, type B: 6 persons	4-6 persons
Bedrooms	Two bedrooms: 1 x double bed, 1 x twin beds	Two bedrooms: 1 x double bed, 1 x double bed plus twin beds
Living/Dining area	Gas fire, table and seating; type B double sofa bed	Table and seating
Kitchen area	4 hot-plates, refrigerator, sink, utensils, crockery and cutlery	2 hot-plates, refrigerator, microwave, sink, utensils, crockery and cutlery
Bathroom/shower	Shower/bath, washbasin; separate WC	Shower/bath, washbasin; separate WC
Additional facilities	Table and chairs, 2 sunbeds, barbecue	Terrace with table, chairs, 2 sunbeds, barbecue
Bedding	Pillows and blankets provided; sheets and towels for hire	Pillows and blankets provided; sheets and towels for hire
Pets	One pet only accepted	One pet only accepted
Charges per week (98): **From Ffr:** *(low season)* **to Ffr:** *(high season)*	Type A: Ffr 1,000 - 2,400, type B 1,200 - 2,800; daily rates or long stay discounts available in low season	Ffr 1,400 - 3,000; daily rates or long stay discounts available in low season
Amount/% of deposit	30%	30%

4101 Le Parc du Val de Loire, Mesland, nr Blois

Family owned site with swimming pools, between Blois and Tours.

This quite large site is quietly situated away from the main roads and towns, but is nevertheless centrally placed for visits to the châteaux; Chaumont, Amboise and Blois (21 km.) are the nearest in that order. There are three swimming pools, the newest with a sunbathing area and heated all season, a smaller pool with slide and a children's pool. Activities include tennis, good children's playgrounds with skateboard facilities, bicycle hire, table tennis, minigolf, BMX track, tennis training wall, football pitch and basketball. Pony rides and some sports and competitions are organised in July/August. A bar is adjacent to pools, with a restaurant, snack service and TV room, plus a pizzeria with takeaway and a large shop. There are weekly wine tasting opportunities and a coach to Paris each week, plus local walks on marked footpaths. Barbecue area.

Directions: The village of Mesland is 5 km. northwest of Onzain, from A10 autoroute take Château-Renault/Amboise exit and D31 to Autrèche. Continue 5 km, then left at La Hargardière at camp sign and 8 km to site.

Open: 6 April – 15 September.

Address: 41150 Mesland. Tel: (0)2.54.70.27.18. Fax: (0)2.54.70.21.71.

RENTED ACCOMMODATION	MOBILE HOMES *Type B*	CHALETS *'Gitotel' Type A*	CHALETS *'Gitotel' Type B*
Number of persons	6 persons max.	6 persons	4 persons
Bedrooms	Two bedrooms: 1 x double bed, 1 x twin beds	Three bedrooms: 1 x double bed, 2 x twin beds	Two bedrooms: 1 x double bed, 1 x twin beds
Living/Dining area	Table and seating; double sofa bed	Table and seating, double sofa	Table and seating, double sofa
Kitchen area	4 ring gas hob, refrigerator, sink, utensils, crockery and cutlery	4 ring gas hob, refrigerator, sink, utensils, crockery and cutlery	4 ring gas hob, refrigerator, sink, utensils, crockery and cutlery
Bathroom/shower	Shower, washbasin; separate WC	Shower, washbasin: separate WC	Shower, washbasin: separate WC
Additional facilities	Garden table and chairs, sunshade, barbecue	Terrace with garden table and 6 chairs, sunshade, barbecue	Terrace with garden table and 4 chairs, sunshade, barbecue
Bedding	Pillows and blankets provided; sheets for hire	Pillows and blankets provided; sheets for hire	Pillows and blankets provided; sheets for hire
Pets	Pets accepted	Pets accepted	Pets accepted
Charges per week (98): From Ffr: (low season) to Ffr: (high season)	2 persons Ffr 1,150 - 3,300, 3/4 persons 1,350 - 3,300, 5/6 persons 1,550 - 3,300; nightly rates available outside 4 July - 22 August	2/4 persons Ffr 2,100 - 3,500, 5/6 persons 2,450 - 3,500; nightly rates available outside 4 July - 22 August	2 persons Ffr 1,300 - 3,300, 3/4 persons 1,500 - 3,300; nightly rates available outside 4 July - 22 August
Amount/% of deposit	Ffr 500 plus 100 fee	Ffr 500 plus 100 fee	Ffr 500 plus 100 fee

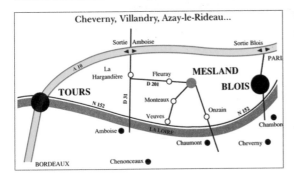

Loire Valley

4103 Sologne Parc des Alicourts, Pierrefitte sur Sauldre

Secluded 21 hectare site in the heart of the forest with many sporting facilities.

This medium sized site is in a very secluded, forested area midway between Orléans and Bourges, about 20 km. east of the A10. There is a restaurant using fresh produce and traditional cuisine (from 25 May) plus a takeaway in a pleasant bar with terrace. The shop (also 25 May) has a good range of produce in addition to the basics (the nearest good-sized town is some distance). Leisure facilities are exceptional: an inviting swimming pool complex with two pools (one heated), a spa and two water slides, a 7 hectare lake with fishing, bathing, canoes, pedaloes and children's play area, 5 hole golf course, football pitch, volleyball, tennis, minigolf, table tennis, boules, cyclo-cross and mountain bikes and a way-marked path for walking and cycling. Competitions are organised and, in high season, a club for children with an entertainer twice a day, a disco once a week and a dance for adults. The site is used by tour operators.

Directions: Site is on a back road, 5 km. from Pierrefitte sur Sauldre and is well signed from this village. From A71 take Lamotte-Beuvron exit.

Open: 1 May – 12 September.

Address: Domaine des Alicourts, 41300 Pierrefitte sur Sauldre. Tel: (0)2.54.88.63.34. Fax: (0)2.54.88.58.40.

RENTED ACCOMMODATION	MOBILE HOMES *Type B*	CHALETS *'Gitotel' two models*
Number of persons	6 persons	4 or 6 persons
Bedrooms	Two bedrooms: 1 x double bed, 1 x twin beds	Two or three bedrooms: 1 x double bed, 1 or 2 x twin beds
Living/Dining area	Gas fire, table and seating; double sofa bed	Electric heating, table and seating
Kitchen area	2 hot-plates, refrigerator, sink, utensils, crockery and cutlery	2 hot-plates, refrigerator, sink, utensils, crockery and cutlery
Bathroom/shower	Shower, washbasin; separate WC	Shower, washbasin, WC (6 person: separate WC)
Additional facilities	Terrace with garden table and chairs	Terrace with garden table and chairs
Bedding	Pillows and blankets provided; sheets for hire	Pillows and blankets provided; sheets for hire
Pets	Pets not accepted	Pets not accepted
Charges per week (98): From Ffr: *(low season)* to Ffr: *(high season)*	Ffr 800 - 3,400; daily rates (min. 2) or long stay discounts in low season	4 persons: Ffr 750 - 3,200, 6 persons 1,050 - 3,990; daily rates (min. 2) or long stay discounts in low season
Amount/% of deposit	25% plus Ffr 100 fee	25% plus Ffr 100 fee

4501 Les Bois du Bardelet, Gien

Attractive, lively family run site with lake and pool complex in eastern Loire.

In a rural setting, this medium sized site is well situated for exploring the less well known eastern part of the Loire Valley. A lake and pools have been attractively landscaped in 20 acres of former farmland blending old and new with natural wooded areas and more open 'field' areas with rural views. The communal areas are based on attractively converted former farm buildings. The range of leisure facilities includes two swimming pools (an indoor pool is planned), archery, a lake for canoeing and fishing, tennis, minigolf, boules, table tennis and bicycle hire (some activities high season only). A family club card can be purchased to make use of these activities on a daily basis. There is a shop for basics only (from 1 July, supermarket 5 km), a snack bar and restaurant (July/August), pizzeria and takeaway (1 June - 15 Sept), plus a pleasant terraced bar. Various excursions are organised, including to Paris on Wednesdays. A 'Sites et Paysages' member.

Directions: From Gien take D940 towards Bourges. After some 5 km. turn left just before Peugeot garage – follow signs to site for 1.5 km. (narrow road and turning from main road).

Open: 1 April – 30 September.

Address: Route de Bourges, Poilly, 45500 Gien. Tel: (0)2.38.67.47.39. Fax: (0)2.38.38.27.16.

RENTED ACCOMMODATION	MOBILE HOMES
Number of persons	4/6 persons
Bedrooms	Two bedrooms: 1 x double bed, 1 x twin beds
Living/Dining area	Table and seating, double sofa bed
Kitchen area	Gas hot-plates and oven, refrigerator, coffee maker, sink, utensils, crockery and cutlery
Bathroom/shower	Shower, washbasin, WC
Additional facilities	Covered terrace or sunshade, table and chairs, sunbed, barbecue
Bedding	Blankets provided
Pets	Pets not accepted
Charges per week (98): From Ffr: *(low season)* to Ffr: *(high season)*	Ffr 1,390 - 3,060
Amount/% of deposit	Ffr 500 per week booked plus 150 fee

Midi-Pyrénées

Major city: Toulouse
Départements: 09 Ariège; 12 Aveyron; 31 Haute-Garonne; 32 Gers; 46 Lot; 65 Hautes-Pyrénées; 81 Tarn; 82 Tarn-et Garonne

Home of Armagnac, Rugby and the Three Musketeers, the Midi-Pyrénées is the largest region of France, extending from the Dordogne in the north to the Spanish border. It is a region blessed by bright sunlight and a fascinating range of scenery. High chalk plateaux, majestic peaks, tiny hidden valleys and small fortified sleepy villages, which seem to have changed little since the Middle Ages, contrast with the high-tech, industrial and vibrant university city of Toulouse; also rich in art and architecture. Lourdes is one of the most visited pilgrimage sites in the world. The Canal du Midi which links Bordeaux to the Mediterranean was commissioned by Louis XIV in 1666 and is still in working order to day.

Cuisine of the region
The cuisine of the Midi-Pyrénées is rich and strongly seasoned, making generous use of garlic and goose fat
Foie Gras – specially preserved livers of goose and duck
Cassoulet – a hearty stew of duck, sausages and beans
Confit de Canard (d'oie) – preserved duck meat (goose)
Magret de canard – duck breast fillets
Poule au pot – chicken simmered with vegetables
Seafood such as oysters, salt-water fish, or piballes from the Adour river
Ouillat (Ouliat) – Pyrénées soup: onions, tomatoes, goose fat, garlic
Tourtière Landaise – a sweet of Agen prunes, apples and Armagnac
Grattons (Graisserons) – a mélange of small pieces of rendered down duck, goose, and pork fat; served as an appetiser – very filling

Wine
There are some excellent regional wines, such as full-bodied red Cahors and, of course, Armagnac to follow the meal. Try 'Floc', a mixture of Armagnac and grape juice

Places of Interest
Albi – birthplace and Museum of Toulouse-Lautrec, imposing Ste Cécile cathedral
Collonges-la-Rouge – picturesque village of Medieval and Renaissance style mansions and manors in red sandstone
Conques – 11th century Ste Foy Romanesque church
Cordes – medieval walled hilltop village
Foix – 11th/12th century towers on rocky peak above town; 14th century cathedral.
Lourdes – famous pilgrimage site where Ste Bernadette is said to have spoken to the Virgin Mary in a grotto; 12th century cloisters nearby at Moissac
Rocamadour – cliffside medieval pilgrimage site
Saint Cirq-La Popie – medieval village perched on a cliff

0906 Camping Le Pré Lombard, Tarascon-sur-Ariège

Well managed site in popular area and 600m. walk from town.

This busy, medium sized site is beside the river on the outskirts of the town, with a supermarket a 300m. stroll. It is well run, with a lively bar and takeaway, opened according to demand. Playgrounds are provided for toddlers and older children, plus games machines, table tennis, table football, boules and volleyball. An outdoor pool is open when weather permits. A programme of entertainment and activities is offered in the main season. A gate in the fence provides access to the river bank for fishing (licences required). As this is a town site there is some traffic noise during the day and evening. At Tarascon itself you can go underground at the Parc Pyrénéen de l'Art Préhistorique to view prehistoric rock paintings, or the really adventurous can take to the air for para-gliding, hang-gliding or micro-lighting. Six sanitary units provide mostly British style WCs, washbasins, free showers and facilities for disabled people.

Directions: Site is 600 m. south of the town centre adjacent to the river. Turn off the main N20 into the town centre and watch closely for camp signs – these can be hard to spot amongst many other signs.
Open: 1 February –1 November.
Address: 09400 Tarascon-sur-Ariège. Tel: (0)5.61.05.61.94. Fax: (0)5.61.05.78.93.

RENTED ACCOMMODATION	MOBILE HOMES *Types 1 and 2*	CHALETS	BUNGALOW TENTS *'Trigano' Bengali*
Number of persons	4-6 persons	5 persons	4 persons
Bedrooms	Two bedrooms: 1 x double bed, 2 x single beds	Two bedrooms: 1 x double bed, 1 x 3 single beds	Two bedrooms: 1 x double bed, 1 x two single beds
Living/Dining area	Sofa bed (2 persons), table, seating and stools	Table, seating	Table, seating
Kitchen area	2 gas hot-plates, refrigerator, sink, utensils, crockery and cutlery	2 ring gas hob, refrigerator, sink, utensils, crockery and cutlery	2 gas hot-plates, refrigerator, utensils, crockery and cutlery (no sink)
Bathroom/shower	Shower, washbasin, WC	Shower, washbasin; separate WC	None
Additional facilities	Terrace with garden furniture and sunshade	Covered terrace with garden furniture	Terrace with awning
Bedding	Pillows and blankets provided; sheets for hire	Pillows and blankets provided; sheets for hire	Pillows and blankets provided; sheets for hire
Charges per week (98): From Ffr: *(low season)* to Ffr: *(high season)*	Ffr 1,100 - 3,000, according to type, number of persons and season; electricity in low season 150; nightly rates available outside 4 July - 21 August	4 persons Ffr 1,500 - 2,600, 5 persons Ffr 1,600 - 2,800; electricity in low season 150; nightly rates available outside 4 July - 21 August	Available 2 May - 25 September: Ffr 1,400 - 2,000; nightly rates available outside 4 July - 21 August
Amount/% of deposit	Ffr 500, cancellation insurance 90 and fee 100 (total 690)	Ffr 500, cancellation insurance 90 and fee 100 (total 690)	Ffr 500, cancellation insurance 90 and fee 100 (total 690)

Midi-Pyrénées

1202 Les Rivages, Millau

Fairly large site on town outskirts close to Tarn Gorges with good sporting facilities.

This well organised site is very popular, being close to the high limestone 'Causses' and the various river Gorges, particularly the Tarn, and their associated attractions, such as caves, remote villages, wildlife refuges, etc. It occupies flat ground adjacent to the Dourbie river and there is safe bathing from the river beach. On site are indoor and outdoor tennis courts, two badminton courts, two squash courts, football, volleyball, basketball and two swimming pools, table tennis, petanque and a cyclo-cross track. Activities on the river, mountain biking, walking, bird watching, fishing and many more are organised, all exclusively for campers in high season. There is a children's play area and entertainment, with child minding (3-6 yrs). Shop (15 May – 15 Sept), snack bar and restaurant/bar (all season). Sanitary facilities are good, the four modern blocks providing washbasins in cabins, showers and toilets, dishwashing sinks, plus rooms for disabled people.

Directions: Site is on the Nant (D991) road out of Millau.
Open: 1 May – 30 September.
Address: Avenue de l'Aigoual, Route de Nant, 12100 Millau. Tel: (0)5.65.61.01.07. Fax: (0)5.65.59.03.56.

ACCOMMODATION	MOBILE HOMES	BUNGALOW TENTS
Number of persons	4 persons	4 persons
Bedrooms	Two bedrooms: 1 x double bed, 1 x twin beds	Two bedrooms: 1 x double bed, 1 x two single beds
Living/Dining area	Table and seating	Table, seating
Kitchen area	Gas hot-plates, refrigerator, sink, crockery, cutlery and utensils	Gas hot-plates, refrigerator, utensils, crockery and cutlery (no sink)
Bathroom/shower	Shower, washbasin; separate WC	None
Additional facilities	Garden table and chairs, sunshade	Awning
Bedding	No bedding provided	No bedding provided
Pets	Pets accepted	Pets accepted
Charges per week (98): From Ffr: *(low season)* to Ffr: *(high season)*	High season per week, 4 persons: Ffr 3,000, other times per night 2 persons 200, 4 persons 300	High season per week, 4 persons: Ffr 2,200, other times per night 2 persons 150, 4 persons 230
Amount/% of deposit	25% plus Ffr 100 fee	25% plus Ffr 100 fee

1207 Camping La Grange de Monteillac, Sévérac L'Église

Modern well equipped site, close to beautiful, well preserved small village.

This is a small, but spacious, newly developed site set in 4.5 hectares near the wild, open spaces of the Causses and a nearby forest. At reception you will find plenty of local tourist information, and the owner will advise you about the visits to a château evening with candlelight banquet, an angora farm and a local pottery. Music and groups feature in the site's bar. A children's club is organised and archery lessons, fishing or riding can be arranged. Adventure courses including pot-holing, caving and climbing are led by qualified personnel. The swimming pool and sun terrace has a pool-side snack bar (main season) serving pizzas, grills, etc. There is a well equipped children's playground, plus plenty of grassy space. An evening stroll around this delightful village is a must, and Sévérac Le Château (21 km), Rodez (28 km), and the many other pretty towns and villages in the region should satisfy all shopping, sightseeing and cultural needs.

Directions: Site is on the edge of Sévérac L'Église, just off N88 Rodez – Sévérac Le Château road. From the A75 use exit 42.
Open: all year.
Address: 12310 Sévérac L'Église. Tel: (0)5.65.70.21.00. Fax: (0)5.65.70.21.01.

RENTED ACCOMMODATION	CHALETS
Number of persons	4-6 persons
Bedrooms	Two bedrooms: 1 x double bed, 1 x twin beds
Living/Dining area	Table and seating, convertible double bed
Kitchen area	Electric hot-plates, oven, refrigerator, sink, utensils, crockery and cutlery
Bathroom/shower	Shower, washbasin; separate WC
Additional facilities	Terrace with table, chairs, barbecue and sunshade
Bedding	Pillows and blankets provided (sheets for hire)
Pets	Pets accepted
Charges per week (98): From Ffr: *(low season)* to Ffr: *(high season)*	Ffr 1,800 - 3,500
Amount/% of deposit	25% plus Ffr 100 fee

Midi-Pyrénées

3201 Le Camp de Florence, La Romieu

Attractive site on edge of historic village in pleasantly undulating Gers countryside.

A warm welcome awaits at Camp de Florence from its Dutch owners who have converted the old farmhouse buildings to provide facilities for the medium sized site. There is a restaurant which includes local specialities, a swimming pool, paddling pool (supervised July/August), adventure play area, games and pets areas. Activities include a games room, tennis, table tennis, volleyball, petanque and bicycle hire. Clay pigeon shooting, video shows, discos, picnics, musical evenings and excursions are organised. Bread is available on site in season (shop in the village). The 13C village of La Romieu is on the Santiago de Compostela pilgrim route and the collegiate church is worth a visit. Fishing and riding are nearby and the site arranges walking tours. Two toilet blocks (mixed) have British style toilets, free hot water, showers and washbasins, some in cabins.

Directions: Site is signed from the D931 Agen – Condom road. Turn left at Ligardes (signed) and follow D36 for 1 km. and take right turn for La Romieu (signed). Otherwise continue until outskirts of Condom and take D41 left to La Romieu and pass through village to site.

Open: 1 April – 31 October; Trigano tents 1 May - 30 September.

Address: 32480 La Romieu. Tel: (0)5.62.28.15.58. Fax: (0)5.62.28.20.04.

RENTED ACCOMMODATION	MOBILE HOMES	BUNGALOWS *Types A, B and C*	BUNGALOW TENTS *'Trigano' Bengali*
Number of persons	6 persons	6 persons max.	4/5 persons
Bedrooms	Two bedrooms: 1 x double bed, 1 x two single beds	Types A and B: Two bedrooms: 1 x 2 single beds, 1 x 1 single bed or bunk beds Type C: Two bedrooms: 1 x 3 single beds, 1 x 1 single bed	Two bedrooms: 1 x double or 2 single beds, 1 x two single beds
Living/Dining area	Gas or electric fire, table and seating, double sofa bed	Heating, table and seating, convertible sofa bed	Table and seating (concrete floor)
Kitchen area	4 gas hot-plates, refrigerator, utensils, sink, crockery and cutlery	4 gas hot-plates, refrigerator, sink, utensils, crockery and cutlery	2 gas hot-plates, refrigerator, utensils, crockery and cutlery; no running water (tap next to tent)
Bathroom/shower	Shower, washbasin, WC	Shower, washbasin, WC	None
Additional facilities	Garden table and chairs, sunshade	Balcony with table and chairs, 2 sunbeds, sunshade	Awning
Bedding	Pillows and blankets provided: sheets for hire	Pillows and blankets provided; sheets for hire	Pillows and blankets provided; sheets for hire
Pets	Pets accepted	Pets accepted	Pets accepted
Charges per week (98): From Ffr: *(low season)* to Ffr: *(high season)*	Low season per night (2 persons) Ffr 180, high season per week 2,930 - 3,255	Low season per night (2 persons) Ffr 180, high season per week 3,140 - 3,465	Low season (4 persons) Ffr 1,590, high season 2,090 - 2,300; extra person (on request with extra bed) plus 10%
Amount/% of deposit	Ffr 700 per week booked plus 100 fee and 50 cancellation insurance	Ffr 700 per week booked plus 100 fee and 50 cancellation insurance	Ffr 700 per week booked plus 100 fee and 50 cancellation insurance

3207 Camping-Caravaning Les Angeles, Cézan

Peaceful small site in unspoiled Gascony countryside.

Enjoying attractive rural views, Les Angeles is a peaceful, family run site in a quiet corner of the Gers countryside. On one side of a shallow valley, the pitches are arranged on grass terraces and, whilst all are separated by hedging, there are varying amounts of shade, which could be important in this area. In high season there is a small shop. The site is family oriented with a varied programme of activities which includes walks, various competitions, etc., all on a quite small scale and probably best suited to families with younger children rather than teenagers. Activities available include mountain bike hire, fishing in the small, well stocked lake, a mini-sized football pitch and volleyball. Golf and tennis are within easy reach by car. The pleasant, small swimming pool and children's pool are supervised in high season. A takeaway restaurant (with seating to eat in if you prefer) serves a dish of the day and `floc'!

Directions: From Fleurance follow the D103 (signed Jegun) southwest for 6 km. Then branch west on the D303 for Réjaumont and pick up camp signs. The final 1 km. is on an unmade, but perfectly satisfactory track.
Open: 1 April – 30 September.
Address: 32410 Cézan. Tel: (0)5.62.65.29.80.

RENTED ACCOMMODATION	MOBILE HOMES	CHALETS
Number of persons	4/6 persons	2/5 persons
Bedrooms	Two bedrooms: 1 x double bed, 1 x bunk beds	One bedroom: 1 double bed, 2 bunk beds
Living/Dining area	Table and seating, double sofa bed	Table and seating, convertible double bed
Kitchen area	3 hot-plates, refrigerator, sink, crockery, cutlery and utensils	2 hot-plates, refrigerator, sink, crockery, cutlery and utensils
Bathroom/shower	Shower, washbasin, WC	Shower, washbasin, WC
Additional facilities	Garden table and chairs, sunshade	Garden table and chairs, sunshade
Bedding	Pillows and blankets provided; sheets for hire	Pillows and blankets provided; sheets for hire
Pets	Pets accepted	Pets accepted
Charges per week (98): From Ffr: *(low season)* to Ffr: *(high season)*	High season 5/6 persons Ffr 2,490; other times 2/3 persons 1,390, 4/6 persons 1,590	High season 2/4 persons Ffr 2,350, 5 persons 2,490; other times 2/3 persons 1,390, 4/5 persons 1,590
Amount/% of deposit	25% plus Ffr 60 fee	25% plus Ffr 60 fee

Midi-Pyrénées

4603 Camping Les Pins, Payrac-en-Quercy

Medium size site in wooded parkland, suitable for a Dordogne holiday.

Camping Les Pins, named after its magnificent pine trees, has impressive views. A heated swimming pool with sunbathing area and a smaller children's paddling pool are on site and a separate, small leisure park (Aqua Follies) adjoins the site with water chute, jacuzzi pool, contra-current pool and trampoline (access is free for campers). There is a shop (1 June – 31 August), TV and library. Sports facilities include a good quality tennis court, table tennis, pétanque and volleyball. A good value bar/restaurant provides views over the surrounding countryside, reasonably imaginative menus, and a good range of takeaway food. Equally imaginative are the site's new options of half-board and full-board tariffs. There is some entertainment in season, including weekly family discos. Nearby activities include fishing, riding and canoeing on the Dordogne. The three recently modernised toilet blocks are very well maintained, providing British WCs, showers and washbasins in cabins.

Directions: Site entrance is on the western carriageway of the N20 just south of Payrac-en-Quercy, 16 km. from Souillac.

Open: 1 April – 15 September.

Address: 46350 Payrac. Tel: (0)5.65.37.96.32. Fax: (0)5.65.37.91.08. In UK: (01722) 322583.

RENTED ACCOMMODATION	MOBILE HOMES *Type A*	MOBILE HOMES *Type B*
Number of persons	2-4 persons	2-6 persons
Bedrooms	Two bedrooms: 1 x double bed, 1 x twin beds	Two bedrooms: 1 x double bed, 1 x twin beds
Living/Dining area	Table and seating	Table and seating, convertible double bed
Kitchen area	4 hot-plates, refrigerator, sink, crockery, cutlery and utensils	4 hot-plates, refrigerator, sink, crockery, cutlery and utensils
Bathroom/shower	None	Shower, washbasin, WC
Additional facilities	Garden table and 4 chairs	Garden table and 6 chairs, 2 sunbeds
Bedding	Pillows and blankets provided; sheets and extra blankets for hire	Pillows and blankets provided; sheets and extra blankets for hire
Pets	Pets accepted	Pets accepted
Charges per week (98): From Ffr: *(low season)* to Ffr: *(high season)*	20 June - 28 August: Ffr 1,750 - 2,160, other times per night Ffr 130	20 June - 28 August: 2-4 persons Ffr 2,250 - 3,250, other times per night Ffr 180; 5 persons Ffr 2,460 - 3,480, other times per night Ffr 220; extra person 32
Amount/% of deposit	25% plus Ffr 100 fee	25% plus Ffr 100 fee

‚4605 Camping Le Rêve, Le Vigan

Very peaceful, small, clean site with pool far from the madding crowd.

Le Rêve is in the heart of rolling countryside where the Perigord runs into Quercy. The site is divided by shrubs and a variety of attractive trees provide some shade. There is plenty of space and some pitches are very large. The small swimming pool is very clean, with a large separate children's paddling pool with 'mushroom' fountain. The reception area houses a small shop, pleasant bar, restaurant and takeaway, serving snacks and more substantial dishes. A small shaded children's playground, boules area, table tennis and volleyball complete the amenities. Le Rêve continues to impress us with its tranquillity and the young Dutch owners are keen to develop the site in such a way that this will not be lost. It is a site particularly suitable for families with very young children. The modern toilet block also provides cubicles for disabled people and a baby room.

Directions: Follow the N20 from Souillac towards Cahors. About 3 km. south of Payrac, turn right onto the D673 (signed Le Vigan and Gourdon). After 2 km, Le Rêve is signed on the right down a small lane and the site is 3 km. further on.
Open: 25 April – 23 September.
Address: 46300 Le Vigan. Tel: (0)5.65.41.25.20. Fax: (0)5.65.41.68.52.

RENTED ACCOMMODATION	CHALETS
Number of persons	4-6 persons
Bedrooms	Two bedrooms: 1 x double bed, 1 x twin beds
Living/Dining area	Heater, table and seating; double sofa bed
Kitchen area	2 ring gas hob, fridge/freezer, sink, utensils, crockery and cutlery
Bathroom/shower	Shower, washbasin, WC
Additional facilities	Patio with garden furniture
Bedding	Pillows and blankets provided
Pets	Pets not accepted
Charges per week (98): From Ffr: *(low season)* to Ffr: *(high season)*	Ffr 1,000 - 2,500
Amount/% of deposit	30%

Midi-Pyrénées

8101 Camping Relais de l'Entre Deux Lacs, Teillet, nr Albi

Small, quiet, family run site between the Rassisse and Bancalié lakes.

This is a lovely little site, run by the Belgian family of Lily and Dion Heijde-Wouters. Situated in part meadow, part semi-cleared woodland, with a small farm alongside, the site offers a range of amenities including a swimming pool and an excellent bar/restaurant specialising in Belgian cuisine (both 1 May – 30 Sept. It serves a range of no less than 30 different Belgian beers, as well as French wine. Lily is developing a reputation for her very good recipes using the Belgian beers and is also attracting local French people to eat at the restaurant. Family attractions include a weekly barbecue, children's activity programme and 'It's a Knockout' contests. A small library in reception includes some English books and board games. Other activities include volleyball, table tennis, boules and bicycle hire. There is a children's farm and canoes may be hired on the Rassisse lake. Bread to order, with a shop in the village. Guided hikes and free guided tours of Albi or a Gaillac wine cellar are arranged.

Directions: From the Albi ring-road, take the D81 going southeast to Teillet (approx. 20 km). Continue through the village on the D81 and site is on the right.

Open: All year.

Address: 81120 Teillet. Tel: (0)5.63.55.74.45. Fax: (0)5.63.55.75.65.

RENTED ACCOMMODATION	CHALETS
Number of persons	6 persons (max)
Bedrooms	Two bedrooms: 1 x double bed, 1 x 2 pairs bunk beds
Living/Dining area	Gas fire, table and seating; sofa bed (2 persons)
Kitchen area	4 ring gas hob (no oven or grill), refrigerator, sink, crockery, cutlery and utensils
Bathroom/shower	Washbasin, shower, WC
Additional facilities	Terrace with garden table and chairs
Bedding	Duvets and pillows provided
Pets	Pets not accepted
Charges per week (98): From Ffr: *(low season)* to Ffr: *(high season)*	Ffr 2,830; low season less 20-40% according to number of persons; nightly rates available in low season
Amount/% of deposit	50% plus Ffr 80 fee

© Photograph: D. Morel

Normandy

Major cities: Caen, Rouen
Départements: 14 Calvados; 27 Eure; 50 Manche; 61 Orme; 76 Seine Maritime

Normandy is a pastoral region – or, in fact, the dairy of France providing rich cream, butter, and fine cheeses such as Camembert and 'Pont l'Evêque'. Contented cows graze the apple orchards – the apples are used in producing cider and the well known 'Calvados', Normandy's apple brandy. Normandy also has a superb coast line including the Cotentin Peninsula, the cliffs of the Côte d'Albâtre and the fine beaches and fashionable resorts of the Côte Fleurie. The history of Normandy is closely linked with our own as in 1066 the Norman Duke William defeated the Saxon King Harold in the battle of Hastings and was crowned King of England, his exploits well chronicled on the famous Bayeux Tapestry. In more recent times, June 1944, the Allied Forces landed on the Normandy coast. Many museums, exhibitions, sites and monuments, including the Caen Memorial Museum, commemorate operations that took place between 6 June and August of 1944.

Cuisine of the region
Andouillette de Vire – small chitterling (tripe) sausage
Barbue au cidre – brill cooked in cider and Calvados
Douillons de pommes à la Normande – baked apples in pastry
Escalope (Vallée d'Auge) – veal sautéed and flamed in Calvados and served with cream and apples
Ficelle Normande – pancake with ham, mushrooms and cheese
Marnite Dieppoisse – fish soup with some or all of the following: sole, turbot, rouget, moules, crevettes, onions, white wine, butter and cream
Poulet (Vallée d'Auge) – chicken cooked in the same way as Escalope Vallée d'Auge
Tripes à la Mode de Caen – stewed beef tripe with onions, carrots, leeks, garlic, cider and Calvados

Wine
Cider usually accompanies a meal
Trou Normand Calvados – a 'dram' drunk in one gulp, between courses; claimed to restore the appetite

Places of interest
Alençon – famous for lace, fine art museum, birthplace of Ste Thérèse
Bagnoles-de-l'Orne – spa resort and casino, guided tours of Arthurian land of Lancelot
Bayeux – home to the famous tapestry; 15th-18th century houses, cathedral, museums
Caen – feudal castle, Museum of Normandy, Museum for Peace
Omaha Beach – D-Day beaches, Landing site monuments commemorating the Allied Forces, American Cemetery
Deauville – internationally famous seaside resort and horse racing centre
Giverny – home of impressionist painter Claude Monet, Monet Museum
Honfleur – picturesque port city with old town and bridge
Lisieux – pilgrimage site, shrine of Ste Thérèse, Basilic and Carmelite convent
Mont St Michel – world famous abbey on island which becomes isolated by incoming tide
Rouen – Joan of Arc Museum; Gothic churches, cathedrals, abbey, clock tower

Normandy

5000 Camping L'Etang des Haizes, St Symphorien-le-Valois, La Haye-du-Puits

Attractive, informal site with small heated pool and pretty lake.

L'Etang des Haizes is set in a mixture of conifers and orchard, beside an attractive lake. The lake offers good coarse fishing for huge carp (we are told!), swimming (with a long slide), pedaloes, a small beach and, believe it or not, a turtle can sometimes be seen on a fine day! Other facilities include a heated swimming pool, an attractive bar with terrace overlooking the lake and pool (both 20 May – 5 Sept), two children's play areas, bicycle hire, table tennis, TV lounge, pool table, pétanque, volleyball and archery, plus ducks and goats. Only milk, bread and snacks (takeaway) are available on site, but a supermarket is in La Haye-du-Puits (1 km). The small site is 8 km. from a sandy beach and a 25 km. drive from the Normandy landing beaches.

Directions: From Cherbourg follow N13 (Mont St Michel) road as far as Valognes, then the D2 to St Sauveur-le-Vicomte. Continue on the D900 for La Haye-du-Puits, go straight on at new roundabout on the outskirts of town and site is signed almost immediately on the right.
Open: Mobile homes 1 April – 30 September; chalets 1 March – 30 November.
Address: 50250 La Haye-de-Puits. Tel: (0)2.33.46.01.16. Fax: (0)2.33.47.23.80.

RENTED ACCOMMODATION	MOBILE HOMES	CHALETS *Rêve*
Number of persons	4/6 persons	4/6 persons
Bedrooms	Two bedrooms: 1 x double bed, 1 x two single beds	Two bedrooms: 1 x double bed, 1 x two single beds
Living/Dining area	Sofa bed (2 persons), gas fire, table and seating	Sofa bed (2 persons), table and seating
Kitchen area	4 ring gas hob, refrigerator, sink, crockery, cutlery and utensils	4 ring gas hob, refrigerator, sink, crockery, cutlery and utensils
Bathroom/shower	Washbasin, shower, WC	Washbasin, shower, WC
Additional facilities	Picnic table and sunshade	Balcony with picnic table and sunshade
Bedding	Blankets and pillows provided	Blankets and pillows provided (sheets for hire)
Pets	Pets not accepted	Pets not accepted
Charges per week (98): From Ffr: *(low season)* to Ffr: *(high season)*	Ffr 1,650 - 2,900	Ffr 1,815 - 3,190
Amount/% of deposit	25%	25%

5003 Castel Camping Lez Eaux, Granville

Family site with swimming pools just back from sea on Cotentin coast.

Set in the spacious grounds of a château, Lez Eaux lies in a rural situation just off the main route south, under 2 hours from Cherbourg. The nearest beach is 3 km, St Pair is 4 km. and Granville 7, and it is a very pleasant situation from which to explore this corner of the Cotentin peninsula. However, because of its location, the medium sized site receives much 'en-route' trade, both from tour operator clients and independent campers on their way further south. A small heated swimming pool is supplemented by an attractive fun pool with slide and water slide (from 15 May). There is a shop, small bar and snacks and takeaway with a set meal each night to order in advance (also from 15 May). Activities include an adventure play area, good tennis (charged in high season) a games room with table tennis, jacuzzi, fishing in the lake and a TV room. Washing machine and dryer. Torches are required at night.

Directions: Site access is signed west about 7 km. southeast of Granville on main D973 road to Avranches.
Open: 1 May – 15 September.
Address: 50380 St Pair-sur-Mer. Tel: (0)2.33.51.66.09. Fax: (0)2.33.51.92.02.

RENTED ACCOMMODATION	CHALETS
Number of persons	6 persons
Bedrooms	Two bedrooms: 1 x double bed, 1 x twin beds
Living/Dining area	Table and seating, 2 single convertible beds
Kitchen area	2 ring gas hot-plates, microwave, refrigerator, sink, crockery, cutlery and utensils for 6 persons
Bathroom/shower	Shower, washbasin, WC
Additional facilities	Terrace with garden table, chairs and barbecue
Bedding	Blankets and pillows provided
Pets	Pets accepted
Charges per week (98): From Ffr: *(low season)* to Ffr: *(high season)*	Ffr 1,900 - 3,200
Amount/% of deposit	25%

Normandy

5005 Camping Le Cormoran, Ravenoville-Plage, nr Sainte-Mère-Eglise

Neat, seaside site on eastern Cotentin coast, 5 km. north of Utah Beach.

Set in a flat and open landscape and only separated from the beach by the coast road, Le Cormoran is ideal for a holiday or short break, with the Landing Beaches close by. With a narrow frontage decorated with flags and a fountain, it is a fairly long site with most of the amenities at the entrance. These include reception, a small shop, bar with snacks (all season) and takeaway, with an entertainment and games room opposite. There is a small swimming pool with paved surrounds, tennis, boules and a small children's play area. Adjacent to the site are a sports field and storage for boats. Activities such as archery are organised and day trips to the Channel Islands or riding arranged. Bicycles and shrimp nets may be hired and a hairdresser calls weekly. There is a communal barbecue. This is a well run, family managed medium sized site. A 'Sites et Paysages' member.

Directions: From the N13 take Ste Mère Eglise exit and in the centre of the town take road to Ravenoville (6 km), then Ravenoville-Plage (3 km). Just before the beach turn right and site is 500 m.
Open: 3 April – 27 September.
Address: Ravenoville-Plage, 50480 Ste Mère Eglise. Tel: (0)2.33.41.33.94. Fax: (0)2.33.95.16.08.

RENTED ACCOMMODATION	MOBILE HOMES *Type A*	MOBILE HOMES *Type B*	MOBILE HOMES *Type CP3*
Number of persons	4 persons	4 persons	6 persons
Bedrooms	Two bedrooms: 1 x double bed, 1 x junior beds	Two bedrooms: 1 x double bed, 1 x junior beds	Three bedrooms: 1 x double bed, 2 x junior beds
Living/Dining area	Gas heating	Gas heating, colour TV	Gas heating, colour TV
Kitchen area	Electric or gas hot-plates, sink, crockery, cutlery and utensils for 6 persons	Gas cooker, sink, crockery, cutlery and utensils for 6 persons	Gas cooker, sink, crockery, cutlery and utensils for 6 persons
Bathroom/shower	Bath or shower, washbasin, WC	Bath or shower, washbasin, WC	Bath or shower, washbasin, WC
Additional facilities	Garden table, chairs and sunshade	Garden table, chairs and sunshade	Garden table, chairs and sunshade
Bedding	Two blankets and two duvets provided; bed linen hire available	Two blankets and two duvets provided; bed linen hire available	Two blankets and two duvets provided; bed linen hire available
Pets	Pets accepted	Pets not accepted	Pets not accepted
Charges per week (98): **From Ffr:** *(low season)* **to Ffr:** *(high season)*	Ffr 1,500 - 2,700; weekend and daily rates available	Ffr 1,600 - 3,000; weekend and daily rates available	Ffr 1,700 - 3,200; weekend and daily rates available
Amount/% of deposit	25%	25%	25%

Paris/Ile-de-France

Major cities: Paris, Versailles, Ivry, Melun, Nanterre, Bobigny, Creteil, Pontoise

Départements: 75 Paris, 77 Seine-et-Marne, 78 Yvelines, 91 Essone, 92 Hauts-de-Seine, 93 Seine-St-Denis, 94 Val de Marne, 95 Val d'Oise

How many millions of words have been written about Paris? Quite simply, it is a marvellous place of infinite variety – the list of things to do is virtually endless and could easily fill many holidays – window shopping, the Eiffel Tower, Montmartre, the Louvre, trips on the Seine, pavement cafés, the Moulin Rouge, etc, etc! Both the bus and Metro systems are efficient and reasonably priced, so there is no need to take a car into the centre.

The history, customs and language of the Ile-de-France region have merged with those of Paris, and spread throughout the whole country. The destiny of France was played out in the Ile-de-France, in the magnificent castles of Fontainebleau, Compiègne, Provins, Saint-Germain and Versailles. This `garden of kings' is in fact made up of many smaller regions whose names – Valois, Beauvaisis, Vexin, Brie, Gatinais, Hurepoix – irresistibly evoke royal banners and the pageantry of past years. Square bell towers in gentle valleys, white silos on endless plains of wheat: subtle and harmonious landscapes painted and praised by Racine, La Fontaine, Corot and all the landscape painters. Paris is surrounded by forests: Fontainebleau, Compiègne, St-Germain-en-Laye, attracting Parisians in their thousands each weekend.

Cuisine of the region
Although without a specific cuisine of its own, Paris and Ile de France offer a wide selection of dishes from all the regions of France. Paris also has a wide choice of foreign restaurants, such as Vietnamese and North African.

Places of interest
Auvers-sur-Oise – Van Gogh museum
Fontainebleau – château and national museum, history of Napoléon from 1804-1815
Malmaison – château and museum devoted to the story of Napoléon and Joséphine
Meaux – agricultural centre, Gothic cathedral, chapter house and palace
Rambouillet – château and park with national sheep farm and Queen's Dairy
St Denis – basilica, Funeral Art museum, tombs of the Kings of France
St Germain-en-Laye – château, Gallo-roman and Merovingian archeological museum.
Sèvres – ceramics museum, history of fine china and pottery
Versailles – the most famous Royal Castle in the world, Royal Apartments, Hall of Mirrors, Chapel, Royal Opera and French History Museum. Park with statues, fountains, the Grand Trianon, the Petit Trianon, the Temple of Love
Vincennes – château (fortified castle) and museum

Leisure Parks
Parc Astérix (April-October) – Discover the world of the Gauls with Astérix and Obélix.
Euro Disneyland – the 'magic kingdom'
France Miniature (April-October) – 150 historic monuments, 20 typical villages, countryside, scenes from everyday life.
Mer de Sable (April-September) – a page out of the history of the American West.
Saint-Vrain (April-October) – A prehistoric world with wild animals. Boat-safari.
Thoiry – château and Parc Zoologique, park with gardens and African animal reserve

Paris/Ile de France

7704 Le Parc de la Colline, Torcy

Mature 2 star site, open all year, with easy access to Paris and Disneyland.

This family owned and run site provides a minibus service to the local metro station from where Disneyland is 10 minutes away, Paris 20 minutes and Versailles 45 minutes; ticket information and even booking are possible on the site. The well developed pitches are terraced on a sloping hillside and shaded with a variety of mature trees and shrubs. Primroses and violets were in abundance when we visited in spring time. Access is via tarmac or concrete roads with a security barrier after reception. A small shop for bread and basics operates all year round and a snack bar opens in the summer. Minigolf and a children's play area are provided. This is an attractive campsite offering competitive terms and arrangements for visiting Disneyland or Paris.

Directions: From A4 Paris – Reims autoroute take the A104 north towards Lille and Roissy and site is signed from exit 10 (900 m). From the A1 going south, follow Disneyland signs after Charles de Gaulle airport and take A104 for approx. 24 km. to exit 10.
Open: All year.
Address: Route de Lagny, 77200 Torcy. Tel: (0)1.60.05.42.32. Fax: (0)1.64.80.05.17.
E-mail: camping.parc.de.la.colline@wanadoo.fr.

RENTED ACCOMMODATION	CHALETS *Néva*	MOBILE HOMES *Coline*	COTTAGES
Number of persons	4 persons	6 persons	6 persons
Bedrooms	Two bedrooms: 1 x double bed, 1 x bunk beds	Two bedrooms: 1 x double bed, 1 x twin beds	Two bedrooms: 1 x double bed, 1 x twin beds
Living/Dining area	Table and seating, TV to hire	Table and seating, sofa bed (2 persons), TV to hire	Table and seating, sofa bed (2 persons), telephone, TV to hire
Kitchen area	2 electric hot-plates (no oven or grill), fridge/freezer, sink, utensils, crockery and cutlery	2 electric hot-plates (no oven or grill), fridge/freezer, sink, utensils, crockery and cutlery	3 ring gas hob (no oven or grill), fridge/freezer, sink, utensils, crockery and cutlery
Bathroom/shower	Shower, washbasin, WC	Shower, washbasin; separate WC	Shower, washbasin; separate WC
Additional facilities	Terrace with barbecue to hire	Terrace with barbecue to hire	Terrace with barbecue to hire
Bedding	Pillows, sheets and blankets provided; towels for hire	Pillows, sheets and blankets provided; towels for hire	Pillows, sheets and blankets provided; towels for hire
Pets	Pets accepted	Pets accepted	Pets accepted
Charges per week (98): From Ffr: *(low season)* to Ffr: *(high season)*	Ffr 450, from 4th night 400	Ffr 550, from 4th night 500	Charges per night (98): Ffr 500, from 4th night 480
Amount/% of deposit	25% plus Ffr 50 booking fee	25% plus Ffr 50 booking fee	25% plus Ffr 50 booking fee

Picardy

Major city: Amiens
Départements: 02 Aisne, 60 Oise, 80 Somme

Picardy tends to be a region most people travel through, either to or from a ferry or to or from the north. This was the invaders' route as well as the tourist route. Evidence of this is visible in the 17th century defensive citadels designed by Vauban at the end of a long period of conquests by English kings and Burgundian dukes; and from a more recent age, acres of immaculately tended war graves are a sobering reminder of two Great Wars. At Vimy Ridge near Arras, First World War trenches have been preserved intact, a most poignant sight; while almost every village between Arras and Amiens has its memorial. Picardy is also the birthplace of Gothic architecture with six cathedrals, Amiens, Laon and Beauvais the better known, and Amiens arguably the grandest in France. However, the region is still predominantly rural with deep river valleys, forests of mature beech and oak, peaceful lakes and sandy beaches providing plenty of contrast.

Cuisine of the region
Fresh fish and seafood is popular, as is chicory flavored coffee
Carbonnade de Boeuf à la Flamande – braised beef with beer, onions and bacon
Caudière (Chaudière, Caudrée) – versions of fish and potato soup
Ficelles Picardes – ham pancakes with mushroom sauce
Flamiche aux poireaux – puff pastry tart with cream and leeks
Gaufres – yeast waffles
Hochepot, pepperpot (pot au feu) – a stew of mutton, pork, beer and vegetables
Soupe courquignoise – soup with white wine, fish, moules, leeks and Gruyère cheese
Tarte aux Maroilles – a hot creamy tart based on Maroilles cheese
Waterzooï – a cross between soup and stew, usually of fish or chicken

Places of interest
Abbeville – Church of St Vulfran, Bagatelle Château, Somme Bay nature reserve
Amiens – Notre Dame cathedral, impressive for its size and the richly sculpted facade and the wood and stone carvings of the choir; monument to 1918 Battle of the Somme
Aisne – surrounded by 60 fortified churches
Chantilly – Horse capital of the world; Château Thierry medieval castle, WW1 American Cemetery; credited with the invention of whipped cream!
Laon – 12th century cathedral, WW1 trenches, Vauclair Abbey
Saint Quentin – 11th-18th century basilica, 16th century town hall
Soissons – cathedral of St Jean des Vignes, National museum of the Franco-American Co-operation in the Blérancourt Château
Senlis – Gothic cathedral

103

Picardy

8004 Caravaning du Royon, Fort-Mahon-Plage

Busy holiday site with pleasant atmosphere and good range of activities.

This family run, medium sized site, some 2 km. from the sea, has an excellent friendly clubroom and bar which serves all types of drinks and ices, sells bread and newspapers and has the usual games machines. A mobile takeaway calls each evening in July/August with a good selection of dishes. Also on the site are a small shop (open July/August), table tennis, children's playground, plus a swimming pool (16 x 8 m) and children's pool. Entertainment is organised for adults and children in July and August. Nearby there are opportunities for fishing, golf, windsurfing, sailing, sand yachting, canoeing, swimming, climbing, riding and shooting. The site is close to a cinema, disco and casino and the Baie de L'Authie which is an area noted for migrating birds.

Directions: Site is on outskirts of Fort Mahon Plage, on D32 towards Quend.
Open: 13 March – 31 October.
Address: 1271 Route du Quend, 80790 Fort-Mahon-Plage. Tel: (0)3.22.23.40.30. Fax: (0)3.22.23.65.15.

RENTED ACCOMMODATION	MOBILE HOMES	CHALETS 'Giitotel"
Number of persons	4-5 persons	6 persons
Bedrooms	Two bedrooms: 1 x twin beds, 1 x bunk beds	Three bedrooms: 2 x twin beds, 1 x bunk beds
Living/Dining area	Fireplace, table, sofa	Colour TV, fireplace, table, chairs and sofa
Kitchen area	4 hot-plates, refrigerator, sink, utensils, crockery and cutlery	2 hot-plates, refrigerator, sink, utensils, crockery and cutlery
Bathroom/shower	Bath, shower, WC	Bath, shower; separate WC
Additional facilities	Terrace	Patio with garden furniture
Bedding	Pillows and blankets provided; sheets for hire	Pillows and blankets provided; sheets for hire
Pets	Pets accepted	Pets accepted
Charges per week (98): From Ffr: (low season) to Ffr: (high season)	Ffr 1,800 - 2,800	Ffr 2,300 - 3,400
Amount/% of deposit	30%	30%

8007 Caravaning La Ferme des Aulnes, Fresne, Nampont Saint Martin

Small countryside site on a restored 17th century farm in village location.

This peaceful site has been developed on the grassy meadows of a small farm on the edge of the village, with the reception and facilities being housed in the restored outbuildings, arranged around a central courtyard. Sanitary fittings are smart, modern and well maintained, with a large cubicle available for disabled people. The pitches are divided by small hedges, but there is little shade from trees as yet. There is a small bar and a shop for necessities (high season only), TV, playground for small children, and boules. However, since our visit the owners have added a heated pool, fitness room and archery facilities. Fishing is available in the river 200 m. from the site and there is a golf course 3 km. away.

Directions: At Nampont Saint Martin, turn off the N1 on to the D85E (site is signed), towards Fresne, site is on right after about 3 km.
Open: Easter – 31 October.
Address: Fresne, 80120 Nampont Saint Martin. Tel: (0)3.22.29.22.69 or (0)3.22.29.97.08. Fax: as phone.

RENTED ACCOMMODATION	MOBILE HOMES *Type A*
Number of persons	4 persons
Bedrooms	Two bedrooms: 1 x double bed, 1 x twin beds
Living/Dining area	Gas fire, table and seating
Kitchen area	4 hot-plates, refrigerator, sink, utensils, crockery and cutlery
Bathroom/shower	Shower/bath, washbasin; separate WC
Additional facilities	Garden table and chairs, sunshade
Bedding	Pillows and blankets provided; sheets for hire
Pets	Pets not accepted
Charges per week (98): From Ffr: *(low season)* to Ffr: *(high season)*	From Ffr 2,550; weekend rates available in low season
Amount/% of deposit	Ffr 1,000

Poitou-Charentes

Major cities: Poitiers, La Rochelle, Cognac
Départements: 16 Charente, 17 Charente-Maritime,
79 Deux Sèvres, 86 Vienne

On the Atlantic coast, between the châteaux of the Loire
Valley and the Bordeaux vineyards, lies
Poitou-Charentes, one of the sunniest parts of
the French western coast. Its mild climate –
2,250 hours of sunshine per year –
makes it popular to visit from early
spring to late autumn. Three
hundred miles of coastline with fine
sandy beaches, backed by fragrant
pine forests, lively resorts such as
La Rochelle, Royan and the islands
of Oléron, Aix and Ré attract tourists,
particularly the French themselves. The
scenery inland is in marked contrast, vast
horizons and wooded valleys, the vineyards
of Cognac, the valley of Vienne and the
foothills of Charente. Poitiers, associated
with the Black Prince, has an interesting
history and La Rochelle was once a
famous trading port with Canada. Today
the Futuroscope theme park near Poitiers
offers visitors a glimpse into future technology
and media.

Cuisine of the region
Fish predominates, both fresh water (eel, trout, pike), and sea
water (shrimps, mussels etc), and 'huitres' – oysters!
Bouilliture (bouilleture) – eel stew with shallots, prunes in Sauvignon white wine
Boulaigou – thick sweet or savoury pancake
Bréjaude – cabbage, leek and bacon soup
Cagouilles – snails from Charentes
Casserons en matelote – squid in red wine sauce with garlic and shallots
Cèpes – fine, delicate, flap mushrooms (worth trying)
Chaudrée – ragout of fish cooked in white wine, shallots and butter
Chevrettes – local name for crevettes (shrimps)
Clafoutis – pancake batter poured over fruit (usually black cherries) and baked
Farcidure – a dumpling either poached or sautéed
Farci Poitevin – pâté of cabbage, spinach and sorrel, encased in cabbage leaves
Mouclade – mussels cooked in wine, egg yolks and cream, served with Pineau des Charentes
Soupe de moules à la Rochelaise – soup of various fish, mussels, saffron, garlic, tomatoes,
onions and red wine
Sourdons – cockles from the Charentes

Wine
Light fruity wines from Haut-Poitou, Deux-Sèvres and Charente
Very popular – Cognac and Pineau des Charentes (an aperitif of grape juice and Cognac)

Places of interest
Angoulême – Hill-top town surrouded by ramparts; cathedral, Renaissance château
Cognac – the most celebrated `eau de vie' in the world, cellars, Valois Castle
Marais Poitevin – marshes known as the `Green Venice'
Poitiers – Palais de Justice, Notre-Dame-la-Grande romanesque church, old city
La Rochelle – port, Porte de la Grosse Horloge (clock gate), Museum of the New World
Saint Savin – 17th century abbey, mural painting

1708 Camping Les Chirats, Angoulins-sur-Mer, nr La Rochelle

Quiet site with first class amenities and swimming pool, near La Rochelle.

Good quality sites near large towns or cities are hard to find and so we were pleased to locate such a site about 15 minutes drive from the centre of La Rochelle. Only 50 m. from the beach at Angoulins (bathing only possible at high tide but with no sand then), this medium sized site is divided into two parts. The more open, new extension also provides a spacious reception area and parking on the opposite side of the quiet road. The original part, still fairly new, has some shade now as trees and hedges grow. There is a good heated swimming pool with water slide and children's pool (from 15 May). A fitness centre has a sauna, gym, solarium and jacuzzi. Snacks, takeaway and a bar open in high season. There is a children's play area on grass, plus boules, minigolf, a games room and table tennis. Essential supplies are kept in the bar. Entertainment is organised in season. The gates are locked at night in July/August.

Directions: From the N137 La Rochelle - Rochefort road, take exit for Angoulins-sur-Mer. Follow signs for 'Port' and 'Plage' avoiding village centre, then signs to site.
Open: all year.
Address: Route de la Platère, 17690 Angoulins-sur-Mer. Tel: (0)5.46.56.94.16. Fax: (0)5.46.56.65.95.

RENTED ACCOMMODATION	CHALETS	CHALETS
Number of persons	2 persons	5-6 persons
Bedrooms	One bedroom with twin beds	Two bedrooms: 2 x twin beds
Living/Dining area	Table and seating	Table and seating, double sofa bed
Kitchen area	Electric hot-plates, fridge/freezer, sink, utensils, crockery and cutlery	Gas hob, oven, fridge/freezer, sink, utensils, crockery and cutlery
Bathroom/shower	Shower, washbasin; separate WC	Shower, washbasin; separate WC
Additional facilities	Covered terrace with garden furniture	Covered terrace with garden furniture
Bedding	Pillows and blankets provided	Pillows and blankets provided
Pets	Pets accepted	Pets accepted
Charges per week (98): From Ffr: (low season) to Ffr: (high season)	Ffr 1,400 - 2,000; special off season rate (October - March) Ffr 1,500 per month	Ffr 2,800 - 3,200; special off season rate (October - March) Ffr 2,600 per month
Amount/% of deposit	Ffr 1,000	Ffr 1,500

Poitou-Charentes

1713 Camping-Caravaning L'Ile Blanche, La Flotte de Ré

Good quality wooded site with covered pool on the beautiful Ile de Ré.

In a popular holiday area and used by families, L'Ile Blanche is a fairly small, good quality site. Arranged under medium sized, mixed trees, it is a shady and pleasant environment with hard access roads. Smart, modern buildings by the entrance provide reception, a small shop (July/August) and a large restaurant and bar which is open all season and also provides snacks and takeaway. The restaurant overlooks the swimming pool, which is cleverly protected in poor weather by a sliding glass cover, and a children's pool, both with paved surrounds, plus a large, sandy children's play area. Entertainment is organised in season and the beaches and little villages of the Ile de Ré are within easy driving distance and there is a network of cycle paths in the area. There are some tour operator pitches.

Directions: Cross the bridge to the Ile de Ré and follow signs for St Martin de Ré on the D735. Bypass La Flotte and site is signed on left after several roundabouts. The turning is quite narrow and sharp.
Open: 1 April – 11 November.
Address: Déviation de La Flotte, 17630 La Flotte de Ré. Tel: (0)5.46.09.52.43. Fax: (0)5.46.09.36.94.

RENTED ACCOMMODATION	MOBILE HOMES *Type A*	MOBILE HOMES *Type B*
Number of persons	4 persons	5 persons
Bedrooms	Two bedrooms: 1 x double bed, 1 x twin beds	Two bedrooms: 1 x double bed, 1 x twin beds
Living/Dining area	Electric fire, table and seating	Electric fire, table and seating, convertible bed
Kitchen area	3 hot-plates, refrigerator, sink, crockery, cutlery and utensils.	3 hot-plates, refrigerator, sink, crockery, cutlery and utensils.
Bathroom/shower	Shower, washbasin, WC	Shower, washbasin, WC
Additional facilities	Terrace with furniture and barbecue	Terrace with furniture and barbecue
Bedding	Blankets and pillows provided	Blankets and pillows provided
Pets	Pets accepted	Pets accepted
Charges per week (98): From Ffr: *(low season)* to Ffr: *(high season)*	Ffr 1,750 - 3,450	Ffr 1,950 - 3,800; pet 150.
Amount/% of deposit	Ffr 1,000 plus fee 160	Ffr 1,000 plus fee 160

7902 Camping de Courte Vallée, Airvault

Small, pretty, British-run family site on the Route d'Or.

This small site is strategically situated in a river valley on the outskirts of Airvault, on the Route d'Or from Dieppe to Bordeaux, and convenient for Futuroscope. Since our first visit the owners, Richard and Wendy Curtis from Jersey, have added an attractive swimming pool and the site has matured very nicely, with small trees and an abundance of flowers and shrubs providing more shade and better separation of the pitches. There are, in fact, just 41 pitches on gently sloping grass. Apart from the swimming pool and facilities to purchase essentials, the site has few amenities but the town of Airvault is only 10-15 minutes walk away. There are restaurants within walking distance. Fishing 300 m. There is plenty to see and do in this little known area.

Directions: Site is 50 km. south of Saumur, signed off the D938 road to Airvault. Watch for 'Courte Vallée' signs with logo.
Open: 1 May – 30 September.
Address: 79600 Airvault. Tel: (0)5.49.64.70.65. Fax: as phone.

RENTED ACCOMMODATION	MOBILE HOMES *Type B*
Number of persons	4 persons, plus 2
Bedrooms	Two bedrooms: 1 x double bed, 1 x twin beds
Living/Dining area	Gas fire, table and seating; sofa bed (2 persons)
Kitchen area	4 hot-plates, refrigerator, sink, crockery, cutlery and utensils
Bathroom/shower	Bath, shower, washbasin; separate WC
Additional facilities	Outdoor area with furniture and barbecue
Bedding	Pillows only provided
Pets	Pets not accepted
Charges per week (98): From Ffr: *(low season)* to Ffr: *(high season)*	Ffr 1,500 - 2,750; no smoking permitted
Amount/% of deposit	Ffr 500

Poitou-Charentes

8604 Camping Le Futuriste, St Georges Les Baillargeaux, nr Poitiers

Purpose built site on a hill overlooking Futuroscope, open all year.

On raised ground with panoramic views over the strikingly modern buildings and night-time bright lights that comprise the popular attraction of Futuroscope, Le Futuriste is a neat, fairly small modern site. It is ideal for a short stay to visit the park which is only 1.5 km. away and, with a busy, 'short-stay' atmosphere, there are naturally early departures and late arrivals, but you will probably be amongst them! Reception opens 8 am. - 11 pm. The grassy pitches are separated by growing trees and shrubs which are beginning to break up the very open site (possibly windy), and accessed by gravel roads. If you have time to spend on the site, there are two outdoor pools, one with a slide, with paved surrounds, a children's play area and a TV/games room. A small shop provides essentials (order bread the night before); there are plenty of supermarkets near. Of course, the area has other attractions and details are available from reception.

Directions: From either A10 autoroute or the N10, take Futuroscope exit. Site is signed (together with others) at various roundabouts near the park entrance. It is east of both roads, off the D20 to St Georges.
Open: All year.
Address: 86130 St Georges Les Baillargeaux. Tel: (0)5.49.52.47.52. Fax: as phone.

RENTED ACCOMMODATION	CHALETS
Number of persons	2-6 persons
Bedrooms	Two or three bedrooms: 1 or 2 x double bed, 1 x twin beds
Living/Dining area	Heating, table and seating, colour TV
Kitchen area	2 electric hot-plates, fridge/freezer, sink, crockery, cutlery and utensils.
Bathroom/shower	Shower, washbasin; separate WC
Additional facilities	Terrace with outdoor furniture
Bedding	Pillows and blankets provided
Pets	Pets not accepted
Charges per week (98): From Ffr: *(low season)* to Ffr: *(high season)*	4 persons Ffr 1,350 - 1,700, 6 persons 1,650 - 2,500; nightly and weekend rates available
Amount/% of deposit	Ffr 500

Provence

Major city: Marseille
Départements: 04 Alpes-de-Haute-Provence, 05 Hautes-Alpes 13 Bouches-du-Rhône, 83 Var, 84 Vaucluse

The mention of Provence immediately draws to mind lavender fields and olive groves; it is a sunny bright region of mountains and glittering coastline. The Romans settled in the region and their legacy remains in the great amphitheatres and monuments of Arles, Nîmes and Orange. Later it became the site of the papal court and the Palais des Papes at Avignon is a spectacular construction. The scents and colours with an amazing intensity of light, have encouraged such artists and writers as Cézanne, Picasso, Zola and Pagnol to settle amidst the sleepy villages, with narrow streets and ancient dwellings topped with sun-baked terracotta tiles, where the air is fragrant with the smell of wild herbs. A marked contrast to the spectacularly beautiful (and sometimes spectacularly busy!) coastline, including such famous resorts as St Tropez and Fréjus.

Cuisine of the region (see also Côte d'Azur region).
Cuisine emphasizes seasonings, such as herbs and garlic, and fish

Aigo Bouido -garlic and sage soup with bread (or eggs and cheese)
Aigo saou – fish soup with 'rouille', an orange-coloured sauce with peppers, garlic and saffron
Aïoli (ailloli) – a mayonnaise sauce with garlic and olive oil
Bouillabaisse – fish soup served with 'rouille' (see above), safran (saffron) and aïoli (see above)
Bourride – a creamy fish soup (usually made with big white fish), thickened with aïoli and flavoured with crawfish
Brandade (de morue) à l'huile d'olive – a mousse of salt cod with cream, olive oil and garlic
Pain Bagna – bread roll with olive oil, anchovies, olives, onions, etc.
Pissaladière – Provencal bread dough with onions, anchovies, olives, etc.
Pollo pépitora – Provencal chicken fricassée thickened with lemon-flavoured mayonnaise
Ratatouille- aubergines, courgettes, onions, garlic, red peppers and tomatoes in olive oil
Tian – Provencal earthenware dish

Wine
The Côtes de Provence wine region is mainly known for its dry, fruity rosé wines: Bandol, Bellet, Palette, Cassis. Red wines include Côtes du Rhône and Châteauneuf-du-Pape.

Places of interest.
Aix-en-Provence – old town with 17th/18th century character; Paul Cézanne and Tapestry museums
Arles – Roman capital (arena, theatre remains), major medieval religious centre
Avignon – ramparts, old city, Papal Palace, old palace, Calvet museum
La Camargue – Rhône delta region famous for its white horses, black bulls and pink flamingos
Orange – Roman city, gateway to the Midi, Colline St Europe
Saint Rémy-de-Provence – Arc of Triumph, Van Gogh's convalescent home
Tarascon – made famous by Alphonse Daudet's Tartarin apple pie and fabrics, 13th century castle of King René, 10th century St Marthe Church, Tartarin's house
Vaison la Romaine – Roman city, the French Pompei

Provence

0401 Hotel de Plein Air L'Hippocampe, Volonne, nr Sisteron

Attractive, friendly site with good pool complex and sports opportunities.

This large site is set in one of the most beautiful and unspoilt regions of France, Haute-Provence. The air is clear and the smells of thyme, lavender and other wild herbs have to be experienced to be believed. Olives and cherry trees make an attractive setting and provide welcome shade. The site has a bar, self service restaurant, takeaway and pizzeria (15 May – 15 Sept) and a small shop (July/August). The toilet blocks of varying design have British style WCs, free hot water and washbasins in cabins. The attractive swimming pool complex is heated from 1 May. entertainment, games and competitions are organised in high season and good sports facilities include tennis, table tennis, fishing and archery. The village is 600 m. The Gorge du Verdon is a sight not to miss and there are many lesser known gorges and mountains waiting to be explored. Rafting and canoeing expeditions are arranged. A very busy site, there is lots going on for teenagers.

Directions: Approaching from the north turn off N85 across river bridge to Volonne, then right to site. From the south right on D4 1 km. before Château Arnoux.

Open: 28 March – 30 September; Bengali tents 1 June – 30 September only.

Address: Route Napoléon, 04290 Volonne. Tel: (0)4.92.33.50.00. Fax: (0)4.92.33.50.49.

RENTED ACCOMMODATION	MOBILE HOMES *Type A*	MOBILE HOMES *Type B*	BUNGALOW TENTS *'Trigano' Bengali*
Number of persons	4 persons max.	6 persons max.	4-5 persons
Bedrooms	Two bedrooms: 1 x double bed, 1 x twin beds	Two bedrooms: 1 x double bed, 1 x twin beds	Two bedrooms: 1 x double bed and 1 single bed, 1 x twin beds
Living/Dining area	Table, sofa and chairs, telephone, satellite TV	Table, sofa and chairs, satellite TV, telephone, double sofa bed	Table and chairs
Kitchen area	4 ring gas hob (no oven or grill), fridge/freezer, coffee machine, sink, utensils, crockery and cutlery	4 ring gas hob (no oven or grill), fridge/freezer, coffee machine, sink, utensils, crockery and cutlery	2 ring gas hob (no oven or grill), fridge/freezer, utensils, crockery and cutlery (no sink)
Bathroom/shower	Shower, washbasin, WC	Shower, washbasin, WC	None
Additional facilities	Garden furniture	Garden furniture	Awning with table and chairs
Bedding	Pillows and blankets provided	Pillows and blankets provided	Pillows and blankets provided
Pets	Pets accepted	Pets accepted	Pets accepted
Charges per week (98): From Ffr: *(low season)* to Ffr: *(high season)*	Ffr 1,260 - 3,100; charge for TV in July/August (free other times); special offers in low seasons	Ffr 1,400 - 3,400; charge for TV in July/August (free other times); special offers in low seasons	4 persons Ffr 790 - 2,600, 5 persons 790 - 2,860
Amount/% of deposit	25%, plus Ffr 100 fee	25%, plus Ffr 100 fee	25%, plus Ffr 100 fee

0402 Castel Camp du Verdon, Castellane

Good site with swimming pool close to 'Route des Alpes' and Gorges du Verdon.

The neat and tidy air at Camp du Verdon is very striking. This is a very popular holiday area, the gorge, canoeing and rafting being the main attractions. Two heated swimming pools and numerous on-site activities help to keep non-canoeists here. It is a large level site, part meadow, part wooded. The restaurant is very popular and a takeaway opens twice daily. A pizzeria/crêperie has a terrace and a bar including a room with a log fire for cooler evenings. Two heated swimming pools open all season and a small fishing lake for children is restocked regularly. Younger children have playgrounds. A wide variety of activities includes archery, minigolf, volleyball, bicycle hire and table tennis. Entertainers provide games and competitions in July/August. Dances and discos suit all age groups. With the facilities open all season, the site is very popular and is used by tour operators. The river Verdon runs along one edge of the site, so watch children carefully.

Directions: From Castellane take D952 westwards in direction of Gorges du Verdon and Moustiers. Site is 1 km. on left.
Open: 15 May - 15 September.
Address: Domaine de la Salaou, 04120 Castellane. Tel: (0)4.92.83.61.29. Fax: (0)4.92.83.69.37.

RENTED ACCOMMODATION	MOBILE HOMES	BUNGALOWS
Number of persons	4-6 persons	4-5 persons
Bedrooms	Two bedrooms: 1 x double bed, 1 x twin beds	Two bedrooms: 1 x double bed, 1 x bunk beds
Living/Dining area	Table and seating, sofa bed (2 persons)	Table and seating, sofa bed (1 person)
Kitchen area	4 ring gas cooker, refrigerator, sink, crockery, cutlery and utensils.	4 ring electric cooker, refrigerator, sink, crockery, cutlery and utensils.
Bathroom/shower	Bath, shower, washbasin and WC	Shower, washbasin, WC
Additional facilities	Outdoor terrace with sun shade	Small wooden outdoor terrace with table, chairs
Bedding	Pillows and covers provided, but not sheets, pillow cases and towels	Pillows and covers provided, but not sheets, pillow cases and towels
Pets	Pets accepted	Pets accepted
Charges per week (98): From Ffr: *(low season)* to Ffr: *(high season)*	4 persons Ffr 1,750 - 3,500; extra person 30 - 38; car or tent 20 - 30; dog 15 (high season prices include Carte d'Or discount)	Ffr 1,960 - 3,710; sixth person 30 - 38; extra car or tent 20 - 30; dog 15
Amount/% of deposit	Ffr 600 per week plus 130 fee (high season only)	Ffr 600 per week plus 130 fee (high season only)

LES CASTELS
Camping & Caravaning

LES CASTELS

The 'Castels' group comprises 49 campsites which have been created in the grounds of chateaux and mature country estates. They are individually owned and this contributes to their individuality, although. they all conform to the high standards which are the main criteria for membership of this well known chain. This is evidenced by the fact that most of the Castels sites have been selected for the Alan Rogers' Good Camps Guide for France.

The majority of owners have opened their estates and residences and have created a variety of sport and leisure facilities, swimming pools, bars, restaurants and entertainment programmes for adults and children, making them among the finest holiday sites in France.

Provence

0403 Camping Lac du Moulin de Ventre, Niozelles, Forcalquier

Small, peaceful lakeside site, close to the Luberon.

In the heart of Haute-Provence, near Forcalquier, a busy French town, this is an attractive site situated beside a small lake offering opportunities for swimming (supervised in season), canoeing or for hiring a pedalo and 28 acres of wooded, hilly land available for walking. Trees and shrubs are labelled and the herbs of Provence can be found growing wild. A nature lover's delight – birds and butterflies abound. The site has a bar/restaurant with waiter service, takeaway meals, themed evenings (high season) and a pizzeria. There is a shop for essentials (supermarket 5 km). Activities are organised in high season and there is a children's playground, library and facilities for fishing. The swimming pool has a large shallow area (open from 1 May). Barbecues are permitted in a special area only. The site is well situated to visit Mont Ventoux, the Luberon National Park and the Gorges du Verdon. A 'Sites et Paysages' member.

Directions: From A51 autoroute take exit for village of Brillanne and follow N100 east for 3 km. Site is signed near Forcalquier, 3 km. east/southeast of Niozelles.

Open: 15 March – 31 October (bungalows: 1 January – 19 December).

Address: Niozelles, 04300 Forcalquier. Tel: (0)4.92.78.63.31. Fax: (0)4.92.79.86.92.

RENTED ACCOMMODATION	MOBILE HOMES	BUNGALOWS	CHALETS
Number of persons	6 persons	4 persons	6 persons
Bedrooms	Two bedrooms: 1 x double bed, 1 x twin beds	One bedroom with double bed	Two bedrooms: 1 x double bed, 1 x twin beds
Living/Dining area	Electric fire, table and seating, double sofa bed	Electric fire, table and 4 chairs, twin beds	Electric fire, table and seating, double sofa bed
Kitchen area	3 hot-plates, refrigerator, sink, crockery, cutlery and utensils.	2 hot-plates, refrigerator, sink, crockery, cutlery and utensils	3 hot-plates, refrigerator, sink, crockery, cutlery and utensils.
Bathroom/shower	Shower, washbasin; separate WC	Shower, washbasin, WC	Shower, washbasin, WC
Additional facilities	Patio with table and 6 chairs	Open terrace with table and 4 chairs	Terrace with table and 6 chairs
Bedding	Pillows and covers provided; sheets for hire	Pillows and covers provided; sheets for hire	Pillows and covers provided; sheets for hire
Pets	Pets accepted	Pets accepted	Pets accepted
Charges per week (98): From Ffr: *(low season)* to Ffr: *(high season)*	Low season (2 persons) Ffr 1,450; high season (4 persons) 2,900; extra person 210; pet 20; weekend rates available outside 5 May - 30 August	Low season (2 persons) Ffr 1,450; high season (4 persons) 2,900; extra person 210; pet 20; weekend rates available outside 5 May - 30 August	Low season (4 persons) Ffr 1,750; high season (6 persons) 3,500; extra person 210; pet 20; weekend rates available outside 5 May - 30 August
Amount/% of deposit	30% (plus Ffr 100 fee in July/August)	30% (plus Ffr 100 fee in July/August)	30% (plus Ffr 100 fee in July/August)

8316 Parc Camping-Caravaning Les Cigales, Le Muy

Family run site in a quiet location, convenient for the attractions of this popular area.

In a natural setting, this medium sized site is well tucked in, 1 km. from the busy N7. Whilst it offers the opportunity for a peaceful stay, it also makes an excellent base for exploring the coast or the hinterland and the Gorges du Verdon. The terrain is typical of the area with rough, sloped and stony, dry ground, but pitches are mostly level and benefit from the shade given by trees which include cork, oak and pine, plus the sweet smelling mimosa. A feature is the swimming pool and sunbathing area, and also the patio at the restaurant/bar. Entertainment is organised in season, with a disco twice weekly and daytime activities for children and senior citizens. Salads, fresh food, etc., are available at the restaurant (July/August) and there is a shop (June – Sept). It is 2 km. to Le Muy where a Sunday market is held. For sports enthusiasts, canoeing, riding and hang-gliding are organised. A `Sites et Paysages' member.

Directions: Site is signed off approach to autoroute péage on A8 at Le Muy exit and is 2 km. west of Le Muy on N7.

Open: 28 March – 31 October.

Address: 83490 Le Muy. Tel: (0)4.94.45.12.08. Fax: (0)4.94.45.92.80.

RENTED ACCOMMODATION	CHALETS Type A	CHALETS Type B	CHALETS Type C
Number of persons	2/4 persons	4 persons	5/6 persons
Bedrooms	One bedroom: 1 x double bed	Two bedrooms: 1 x double bed, 1 x twin beds	Two bedrooms: 1 x double bed, 1 x 3 single beds
Living/Dining area	Table and seating; convertible double bed	Table and seating	Table and seating; sofa bed
Kitchen area	2 hot-plates, refrigerator, sink, crockery, cutlery and utensils	2 hot-plates, refrigerator, sink, crockery, cutlery and utensils	2 hot-plates, refrigerator, sink, crockery, cutlery and utensils
Bathroom/shower	Washbasin, shower, WC	Washbasin, shower, WC	Washbasin, shower, WC
Additional facilities	Paved terrace, private garden, table and chairs	Paved terrace, private garden, table and chairs	Paved terrace, private garden, table and chairs
Bedding	Duvets and pillows provided	Duvets and pillows provided	Duvets and pillows provided
Pets	Pets accepted	Pets accepted	Pets accepted
Charges per week (98): From Ffr: (low season) to Ffr: (high season)	Ffr 1,100 - 3,300	Ffr 1,400 - 3,600	Ffr 1,600 - 3,800
Amount/% of deposit	Ffr 180 fee	Ffr 180 fee	Ffr 180 fee

Campings
SITES & PAYSAGES

The 50 'Sites et Paysages' campsites are located in all regions of France. They are a group of family run sites designed to provide an essentially 'green' environment coupled with a family atmosphere and a genuine sense of hospitality.

In general, sites in this chain offer a high standard of service and a wide variety of leisure facilities including swimming pools, children's clubs and in the main season, some entertainment for both adults and children. Many of the sites in the Sites et Paysages chain have been selected for the Alan Rogers' Good Camps Guide for France.

Provence

8317 Camping Domaine de la Bergerie, Roquebrune-sur-Argens

Large, well organised site with a holiday environment to suit all ages and tastes.

This is an excellent site which takes you away from all the bustle of the Mediterranean to total relaxation amongst the natural perfumes of Provence. Here, where cork oak, pine and mimosa flourish, is a 70 ha. campsite which varies from landscaped areas for mobile homes to flat, grassy terrain with avenues of pitches for caravans and tents. A well stocked supermarket is uphill behind the touring pitches. The restaurant/bar, a converted farm building, is surrounded by shady patios, whilst inside it oozes character with high beams and archways leading to intimate corners. Alongside is an extravagantly designed complex with three swimming pools (15 May – 30 Sept) and a keep fit centre. There are tennis courts, volleyball, mini football and more. Tournaments are organised and evening shows, cabarets, discos and dancing at the amphitheatre. Fishing on site, riding, water skiing and rock climbing nearby. St Aygulf or Ste Maxime are 7 km.

Directions: Leave A8 at Le Muy exit on N7 towards Fréjus. Proceed for 9 km., then right onto D7 signed St Aygulf. Continue for 8 km. and then right at roundabout onto D8; site is on the right.
Open: 15 February - 15 November.
Address: Vallée du Fournel, 83520 Roquebrune-sur-Argens. Tel: (0)4.94.82.90.11. Fax: (0)4.94.82.93.42.

RENTED ACCOMMODATION	MOBILE HOMES *Classical Luxury*	MOBILE HOMES *Classical Super Luxury*	MOBILE HOMES *Residential*
Number of persons	4 or 6 persons (<30 sq.m)	4, 6 or 8 persons (>30 sq.m)	4, 6 or 8 persons
Bedrooms	One or two bedrooms: 1 x double bed, 1 x twin beds	Two or three bedrooms: 1 x double bed, 1 or 2 x twin beds	Two or three bedrooms: 1 x double bed, 1 or 2 x twin beds
Living/Dining area	Electric heating, table and seating; convertible double bed	Electric heating, table and seating; convertible double bed	Electric heating, table and seating; convertible double bed
Kitchen area	Gas hob, traditional or microwave oven, refrigerator, sink, crockery, cutlery and utensils	Gas hob, traditional or microwave oven, refrigerator, sink, crockery, cutlery and utensils	Gas hob, traditional or microwave oven, refrigerator, sink, crockery, cutlery and utensils
Bathroom/shower	Washbasin, shower, WC	Washbasin, shower, WC	Washbasin, shower; separate WC
Additional facilities	Paved patio with rigid canopy, private garden and parking, table and chairs	Paved patio with rigid canopy, private garden and parking, table and chairs	Paved patio with rigid canopy, private garden and parking, table and chairs
Bedding	Blankets or duvets and pillows provided	Blankets or duvets and pillows provided	Blankets or duvets and pillows provided
Pets	Pets accepted	Pets accepted	Pets accepted
Charges per week (98): From Ffr: *(low season)* to Ffr: *(high season)*	4 berth Ffr 1,700 - 3,400; 6 berth 1,850 - 3,700	4 berth Ffr 1,850 - 3,700; 6 berth 2,000 - 4,000, 8 berth 2,150 - 4,350	4 berth Ffr 1,900 - 3,850; 6 berth 2,000 - 4,150, 8 berth 2,250 - 4,500
Amount/% of deposit	30%	30%	30%

N8402 Domaine Naturiste de Bélézy, Bédoin, nr Carpentras

Excellent naturist site with many amenities and activities, at the foot of Mt Ventoux.

Excellent medium sized site thoughtfully managed allowing one to enjoy the relaxed French approach to naturism. So far as naturism is concerned the emphasis is on personal choice (and weather conditions!), the only requirement being complete nudity in the pool and pool area. The leisure area in natural parkland includes numerous sports facilities, including tennis courts and three swimming pools (one open and heated April–Sept). The old Mas (Provencal farmhouse) houses a virtually sound-proof disco and nearby are the restaurant/bar and terrace. The variety of activities includes painting and pottery courses, language lessons, archery, music (bring own instrument), a sauna and guided walks. A hydrotherapy centre (1 April–15 Sept) offers courses of massages, steam baths, acupuncture and a variety of treatments including osteopathy and Chinese medicine (on payment). Shop on site. It is possible to walk into Bédoin – the market is fascinating. Bélézy operates in four seasons and a comprehensive booklet details exactly what is available and when.

Directions: From A7 autoroute or RN7 at Orange, take D950 southeast to Carpentras, then northeast via the D974 to Bédoin. Site in Bédoin, 2 km. northeast of the village.

Open: 14 March - 8 November.

RENTED ACCOMMODATION	MAISONNETTE
Number of persons	5 persons
Bedrooms	One bedroom 3 x single beds, 1 double bed on mezzanine
Living/Dining area	Table and chairs, electric heating
Kitchen area	2 hot-plates, refrigerator, microwave, coffee machine, sink, utensils, crockery and cutlery
Bathroom/shower	Shower, washbasin; separate WC
Additional facilities	Terrace with pergola and small garden, sun-loungers
Bedding	Pillows and blankets provided
Pets	Pets not accepted
Charges per week (98): From Ffr: (low season) to Ffr: (high season)	Ffr 2,670 - 4,215; recreation fee 3.50 - 5.50 per day (child 2.50 - 4.00); low season weekend rates available
Amount/% of deposit	Ffr 1,000 per week plus Ffr 180 fee/cancellation insurance

Provence

8404 Camping Le Jantou, Le Thor, nr Avignon

Family run, attractive site beside River Sorgue.

The nicest feature of this attractive site is the 18th century 'mas' (Provencal farmhouse) and outbuildings which, together with a huge plane tree, form a centre piece courtyard for the site facilities. The fairly small site was originally designed and constructed in the late 70s (it has only been owned by the Tricart family for the last few years). In July/August, the site has a snack bar and a little restaurant serving stews, plat du jour, etc. Whilst there is a shop for essentials on site, a small supermarket is within a short walk. Some live entertainment is organised in season. There is a swimming pool, bicycle hire and a new children's playground. A quite fast flowing river runs past the site which is suitable for fishing (short term licences available from the site), but not really for swimming due to the current. It is approached through a gate (unlocked) in a fence.

Directions: Leave A7 autoroute at Avignon Nord exit onto D942 towards Carpentras. Turn immediately south on D6 for 8½ km. to join N100. Turn east for 3½ km. to Le Thor. Site signed before entering village.
Open: all year.
Address: 84250 Le Thor. Tel: (0)4.90.33.90.07. Fax: (0)4.90.33.79.84.
E-mail: lejantou@avignon.pacwan.net. Internet: http://www.elansud.fr/lejantou/

RENTED ACCOMMODATION	MOBILE HOMES *Lock 17*	MOBILE HOMES *Lock 22*	MOBILE HOMES *Lock 28*
Number of persons	4 persons	4-6 persons	4-6 persons
Bedrooms	Two bedrooms: 1 x double bed, 1 x twin beds	Two bedrooms: 1 x double bed, 1 x twin beds	Two bedrooms: 1 x double bed, 1 x twin beds
Living/Dining area	Electric heating, table and seating	Sofa bed (2 persons), electric heating, gas fire, table and seating	Sofa bed (2 persons), electric heating, gas fire, table and seating
Kitchen area	3 ring gas hob, refrigerator, sink, crockery, cutlery and utensils	3 ring gas hob, oven (some), refrigerator, sink, crockery, cutlery and utensils	3 ring gas hob, oven (some), refrigerator, sink, crockery, cutlery and utensils
Bathroom/shower	Washbasin, shower, WC	Washbasin, shower, WC	Washbasin, shower, WC
Additional facilities	Garden table, chairs and sunshade	Garden table, chairs and sunshade	Garden table, chairs and sunshade
Bedding	Blankets and pillows provided (sheets for hire)	Blankets and pillows provided (sheets for hire)	Blankets and pillows provided (sheets for hire)
Pets	Pets accepted	Pets accepted	Pets accepted
Charges per week (98): From Ffr: *(low season)* to Ffr: *(high season)*	Ffr 1,450 - 2,460; nightly rates available outside high season	Ffr 1,560 - 2,680; nightly rates available outside high season	Ffr 1,680 - 2,890; nightly rates available outside high season
Amount/% of deposit	20% plus Ffr 80 fee	20% plus Ffr 80 fee	20% plus Ffr 80 fee

Rhône Valley

Major city: Lyon
Départements: 01 Ain, 07 Ardèche, 26 Drôme
42 Loire, 69 Rhône

The Rhône Valley is one of Europe's main arteries – this traditional route carries millions of travellers and millions of tons of freight by rail (TGV), by autoroute and by water to the Mediterranean. However, either side of this busy corridor are areas of great interest and natural beauty. From the sun-baked Drôme, with its ever-changing landscapes, culminating in the isolated mountains of the Vercors; the deep gorges and high plateaux of the Ardèche, studded with prehistoric caves to lush valleys filled with orchards and the vineyards of the Beaujolais and the Rhône Valley. The region's 2,000 year history as a cultural crossroads has blessed the area with a rich blend of customs, architecture and sights of interest. The city of Lyon was developed by the Romans as a trading centre and is now the second largest city of France. Although heavily industrialised, it has a charming old quarter and is renowned for its gastronomy. Not far from Lyon lies the Dombes, the `land of a thousand lakes', the medieval village of Pérouges and the Roman ruins of Vienne with its yearly jazz festival.

Cuisine of the region
From Lyon to Bresse and Bugey by way of the Dombes, food is an art and a science. The poultry, cheese, freshwater fish, mushrooms and wines are superb
Bresse (Poulet, Poularde, Volaille de) – the best French poultry, fed on corn and when killed bathed in milk; flesh is white and delicate
Gras-double – ox tripe, served with onions
Poulet demi-deuil (half-mourning) – called this because of thin slices of truffle placed under the chicken breast
Poulet au vinaigre – chicken, shallots, tomatoes, white wine, wine vinegar and a cream sauce
Rosette – a large pork sausage
Sabodet – Lyonnais sausage of pig's head, pork and beef, served hot

Wine
Beaujolais, Côte Rotie, St Julien, Condrieu, Tain-Hermitage, Chiroubles and Julienas are some of the wines produced in this region

Places of interest
Beaujolais – vineyards and golden-stone villages
Bourg-en-Bresse – 16th/17th century church of Notre-Dame, craft shops, museum of Ain
Dombes – land of a thousand lakes, ornithological park
Lyon – Gallo-Roman artifacts, Renaissance quarter, historical Fabric Museum, silk museum.
Montélimar – nougat capital of France
Pérouges – lovely medieval village, Galette de Pérouges
St Etienne – museum of Modern Art
Vallon-Pont d'Arc – base from which to visit Gorges de l'Ardèche; canoe and rafting centre
Vienne – Roman remains, Gothic style cathedral, 6th century church St Pierre

Rhone Valley

0702 Camping-Caravaning L'Ardèchois, St Sauveur-de-Montagut

Well equipped site in spectacular setting.

This small site is quite a way off the beaten track and the approach road is winding and narrow in places. It is worth the effort, however, to find such an attractive hillside site offering good amenities. Some pitches are alongside the small fast-flowing river, while the rest are on higher, sloping ground nearer the restaurant/bar. The main access roads are tarmac but are quite steep. The bar/restaurant, shop and new soundproof 'salle de jeux' have been created by the careful conversion of old buildings and provide modern amenities in an attractive style (the shop opens from 15 May, the restaurant from 1 May). There is a TV room and table tennis, with bicycle hire and fishing available on site. The swimming pool (heated from 1 May) has a bar, snack bar and terrace. The site owners have developed an extensive and unusual excursion programme for exploring this attractive area on foot or by car. Used by tour operators and popular with the Dutch.

Directions: From Valence take the N86 south for 12 km, turn right onto D120 to St Sauveur de Montagut, then take the D102 towards Mézilhac for 8 km. to site.
Open: Easter – 30 September.
Address: 07190 St Sauveur-de-Montagut. Tel: (0)4.75.66.61.87. Fax: (0)4.75.66.63.67.

RENTED ACCOMMODATION	MOBILE HOMES *Type A*	MOBILE HOMES *Type B*	CHALETS
Number of persons	5 persons	6 persons	5 persons
Bedrooms	Two bedrooms: 1 x double bed, 1 x twin beds	Two bedrooms: 1 x double bed, 1 x twin beds	Two bedrooms: 1 x double bed, 1 x twin beds
Living/Dining area	Convertible single bed, table and seating	Convertible double bed, electric heating, table and seating	Convertible single bed, electric heating, table and seating
Kitchen area	4 gas hot-plates, refrigerator, sink, utensils, crockery and cutlery	4 gas hot-plates, refrigerator, sink, utensils, crockery and cutlery	2 gas hot-plates, refrigerator, sink, utensils, crockery and cutlery
Bathroom/shower	Shower, washbasin, WC (50% units heated)	Shower, washbasin, WC, electric heating	Shower, washbasin, WC, electric heating
Additional facilities	Table and chairs on pitch	Table and chairs on pitch	Large terrace with table and chairs
Bedding	Pillows and blankets provided; sheets for hire	Pillows and blankets provided; sheets for hire	Pillows and blankets provided; sheets for hire
Pets	Pets accepted	Pets accepted	Pets accepted
Charges per week (98): From Ffr: *(low season)* to Ffr: *(high season)*	Ffr 1,500 - 3,200; dog 70; min. 2 weeks 4 July - 22 August	Ffr 1,640 - 3,340; dog 70; min. booking 2 weeks 4 July - 22 August	Ffr 1,800 - 3,200; animal 70; min. booking 2 weeks 4 July - 22 August
Amount/% of deposit	25% plus Ffr 150 fee	25% plus Ffr 150 fee	25% plus Ffr 150 fee

0704 Camping La Rouveyrolle, Casteljau, nr Les Vans

Attractive, family run site in peaceful surroundings beside the Chassezac river gorge.

Family run and aimed at families, this is a very tranquil small site by the river in attractive countryside with vineyards and orchards. An attractively shaped swimming pool, positioned to catch the sun all day, was built after the water level in the river dropped following the building of a dam upstream. The site offers a pleasant bar/restaurant (13 June – 15 Sept) serving a 'dish of the day' and takeaway, with animation in July/August. A shop also opens in high season – the village is 500 m. There are tennis courts and a children's playground. Swimming and canoeing are possible at the river beach (100 m). Riding, pot-holing and rock climbing (with guides) are available. The Cévennes and the Ardèche Gorges (20 km) are near; excursions can be arranged. The site is used by tour operators.

Directions: From A7 at Montélimar, take D102 west to Aubenas, then D104, south through Joyeuse and Chandolas. Turn right just after the bridge over the Chassezac onto the D252. Turn right after 1.75 km. (site signed) then right at next crossroads. Site is 1 km. signed to right (don't turn into village La Rouveyrolle).
Open: 1 April - 20 September.
Address: Casteljau, 07460 Berrias et Casteljau. Tel: (0)4.75.39.00.67. Fax: (0)4.75.39.07.28.

RENTED ACCOMMODATION	MOBILE HOMES *Type A*	MOBILE HOMES *Type B*
Number of persons	4/5 persons	6 persons
Bedrooms	Two bedrooms: 1 x double bed, 1 x twin beds	Two bedrooms: 1 x double bed, 1 x twin beds
Living/Dining area	Electric heating, table and seating, plus convertible double bed	Electric heating, table and seating, plus convertible double bed
Kitchen area	3 gas hot-plates, refrigerator, sink, crockery, cutlery and utensils	3 gas hot-plates, refrigerator, sink, crockery, cutlery and utensils
Bathroom/shower	Washbasin, shower, WC	Washbasin, shower, WC
Additional facilities	Garden table and chairs	Garden table and chairs
Bedding	Blankets and pillows provided; sheets for hire	Blankets and pillows provided; sheets for hire
Pets	Pets accepted	Pets accepted
Charges per week (98): From Ffr: *(low season)* to Ffr: *(high season)*	Ffr 1,300 - 2,550	Ffr 1,300 - 2,800
Amount/% of deposit	30% plus Ffr 60 fee	30% plus Ffr 60 fee

Rhone Valley

0705 Camping-Caravaning Le Ranc Davaine, St Alban Auriolles, Ruoms

'Lively but tasteful' – family oriented site in southern Ardèche.

This is a quite large site with an extensive programme of entertainment, especially for families with small children and an attractive partly open air restaurant beside the pool where listening to Bach, Handel and Vivaldi makes a change from Johnny Halliday. There is an attractive, large, irregularly shaped swimming pool overlooked by terraces and the bar/restaurant which serves a good range of meals in very pleasant surroundings, made more attractive in the evenings by the lighting and floodlighting. The entertainment programme (July/August) is extensive and varied with a particular emphasis on the participation by younger children in a quite imaginative way. The amenities include a restaurant, pizzeria and takeaway, large shop, children's play area, tennis, table tennis, archery, minigolf and an extensive programme of watersports and excursions on and to the river Ardèche. The site is popular with tour operators. A 'Sites et Paysages' member.

Directions: Continue south on D111 after Ruoms. Turn right just before Grospierres on D246, across bridge and then left on D208 towards Chandolas and site.
Open: 1 April – 15 September.
Address: St Alban Auriolles, 07120 Ruoms. Tel: (0)4.75.39.60.55. Fax: (0)4.75.39.38.50.

RENTED ACCOMMODATION	MOBILE HOMES Type A	MOBILE HOMES Type B	CHALETS Type B
Number of persons	4 persons (21 or 18 sq.m)	6 persons (25 sq.m)	6 persons
Bedrooms	Two bedrooms: 1 x double bed, 1 x twin beds	Two bedrooms: 1 x double bed, 1 x twin beds	Three bedrooms: 1 x double bed, 1 x twin beds, 1 x bunk beds
Living/Dining area	Table and seating	Table and seating, convertible double sofa bed	Table and seating
Kitchen area	4 gas hot-plates, mini oven, refrigerator, sink, crockery, cutlery and utensils	4 gas hot-plates, mini oven, refrigerator, sink, crockery, cutlery and utensils	4 gas hot-plates, mini oven, refrigerator, sink, crockery, cutlery and utensils
Bathroom/shower	Washbasin, shower, WC	Washbasin, shower, WC	Washbasin, shower; separate WC
Additional facilities	Garden table and chairs, 2 sunbeds, sunshade	Garden table and chairs, 2 sunbeds, sunshade	Garden table and chairs, 2 sunbeds, sunshade
Bedding	Blankets and pillows provided	Blankets and pillows provided	Blankets and pillows provided
Pets	Pets accepted	Pets accepted	Pets accepted
Charges per week (98): From Ffr: *(low season)* to Ffr: *(high season)*	Ffr 1,500 - 3,280	Ffr 1,700 - 3,680	Ffr 1,900 - 3,980
Amount/% of deposit	20% plus Ffr 220 fee	20% plus Ffr 220 fee	20% plus Ffr 220 fee

Campings
SITES & PAYSAGES

The 50 'Sites et Paysages' campsites are located in all regions of France. They are a group of family run sites designed to provide an essentially 'green' environment coupled with a family atmosphere and a genuine sense of hospitality.

In general, sites in this chain offer a high standard of service and a wide variety of leisure facilities including swimming pools, children's clubs and in the main season, some entertainment for both adults and children. Many of the sites in the Sites et Paysages chain have been selected for the Alan Rogers' Good Camps Guide for France.

0707 Camping Les Ranchisses, Chassiers, Largentière

Family site on the Route de Valgorge.

The Chevalier family combine farming and wine-making with running a campsite and an Auberge. In a somewhat lesser known area of the Ardèche at Chassiers, on the route de Valgorge, Les Ranchisses has developed into a medium sized family site with a fairly extensive range of facilities. These include a medium sized, heated pool (from 15 April) with sunbathing areas and, somewhat apart from the pitches, the Auberge developed from the original 1824 building used to house silk-worms. Also open to the public, traditional dishes are served both indoors and outside in very attractive surroundings. A shop opens in high season. There is frontage onto a small lake which is connected to the river, providing opportunities for fishing or simple canoeing and, judged by appearances, at least one part of this is pretty safe for youngsters. Bicycle hire. The medieval village of Largentière (1 km.) is well worth a visit, with a Tuesday market and a medieval festival in July.

Directions: From Largentière take the Route de Valgorge (D24) and Les Ranchisses is the first site on the left hand side.

Open: 1 April – 4 October.

Address: Route de Valgorge, Chassiers, 07110 Largentière. Tel: (0)4.75.88.31.97. Fax: (0)4.75.88.32.73.

RENTED ACCOMMODATION	MOBILE HOMES *22 or 27 ft*
Number of persons	4-6 persons
Bedrooms	Two bedrooms: 1 x double bed, 1 x twin beds
Living/Dining area	Table and seating, plus convertible double bed
Kitchen area	Gas hot-plates, refrigerator, sink, crockery, cutlery and utensils
Bathroom/shower	Washbasin, shower, WC
Additional facilities	Terrace with garden table and chairs, sunshade
Bedding	Duvets and pillows provided; sheets for hire
Pets	Small pets accepted
Charges per week (98): From Ffr: *(low season)* to Ffr: *(high season)*	22 ft: Ffr 950 - 2,750, 27 ft: 1,100 - 2,950; weekend rates available
Amount/% of deposit	30% plus Ffr 150 fee

Rhone Valley

0709 Castel Camping Domaine des Plantas, Les Ollières-sur-Eyrieux

Good quality site in a spectacular setting on the banks of the Eyrieux river.

This small site offers an attractive alternative to those in the more popular, and often crowded, southern parts of the Ardèche. The Eyrieux valley is less well known, but arguably just as attractive as those further south. Perhaps the only drawback to this site is the narrow twisting 3 km. approach road. There is a beach beside the quite fast-flowing, but fairly shallow river which is used for bathing (a swimming pool is planned). The bar, restaurant and disco are in an original building which is quite impressive with a Protestant history and visible from the road long before you reach it. Many activities are possible – mountain biking, canoeing, canyoning, riding and 'randonnées pedestres'. A small shop opens in July/August, otherwise you can order bread and milk. No barbecues are allowed in July/August. An adventure play area is beside the river – near the goats!

Directions: South of Valence exit N86 at La Voulte and follow the D120 west for Les Ollières sur Eyrieux (20 km). After bridge in the village, take left turn and follow site signs – the road is single track.
Open: 4 April – 26 September (all services from 1 June).
Address: 07360 Les Ollières-sur-Eyrieux. Tel: (0)4.75.66.21.53. Fax: (0)4.75.66.23.65.

RENTED ACCOMMODATION	MOBILE HOMES	CHALETS *Type A*	CHALETS *Type B*
Number of persons	4-6 persons	4 persons	6 persons
Bedrooms	Two bedrooms: 1 x double bed, 1 x twin beds	Two bedrooms: 1 x double bed, 1 x twin beds	Two bedrooms: 1 x double bed, 1 x double bed plus bunk beds
Living/Dining area	Table and seating, plus convertible double bed	Table and seating	Table and seating
Kitchen area	2 gas hot-plates, refrigerator, sink, crockery, cutlery and utensils	2 gas hot-plates, refrigerator, sink, crockery, cutlery and utensils	2 gas hot-plates, refrigerator, sink, crockery, cutlery and utensils
Bathroom/shower	Washbasin, shower, WC	Washbasin, shower, WC	Washbasin, shower, WC
Additional facilities	Garden table and chairs, sunshade	Garden table and chairs, sunshade	Terrace with garden furniture
Bedding	Duvets and pillows provided	Duvets and pillows provided	Duvets and pillows provided
Pets	Pets accepted	Pets accepted	Pets accepted
Charges per week (98): From Ffr: *(low season)* to Ffr: *(high season)*	Ffr 1,400 - 2,800; weekend rates available in low season	Ffr 1,600 - 3,000; weekend rates available in low season	Ffr 1,750 - 3,600; weekend rates available in low season
Amount/% of deposit	25% plus Ffr 120 fee	25% plus Ffr 120 fee	25% plus Ffr 120 fee

2603 Camping Le Grand Lierne, Chabeuil, nr Valence

Conveniently and attractively situated family site.

This medium sized site provides a pleasant base to explore this little known area between the Ardèche and the Vercors mountains and the Côte du Rhône wine area. There is a feeling of spaciousness and good views to the mountains on either side of the valley. An entertainment programme has an emphasis on activities for children, with various excursions, and a disco for teenagers is well managed to avoid noise. There are two small heated swimming pools, one covered in low season, a children's pool and a 50 m. water slide. A bar/snack bar with terrace provides both 'eating in' and takeaway (all season). Other amenities include a shop, tennis, children's playgrounds and trampoline, minigolf, table tennis, volleyball, a football field, small climbing wall and bicycle hire. Library. Golf, archery, riding and hang gliding are near. A 'Sites et Paysages' member.

Directions: Site signed in Chabeuil about 11 km. east of Valence (18 km. from autoroute). It is best to approach Chabeuil from the south side of Valence via the Valence ring road, thence onto the D68 to Chabeuil itself.

Open: 1 April – 30 September.

Address: BP.8, 26120 Chabeuil. Tel: (0)4.75.59.83.14. Fax: (0)4.75.59.87.95.

RENTED ACCOMMODATION	MOBILE HOMES *Types A and B*	CHALETS *Types A and B*
Number of persons	4 persons (A) - 6 persons (B)	5 persons (A) - 7 persons (B)
Bedrooms	Two bedrooms: 1 x double bed, 1 x twin beds	Two bedrooms: 1 x two beds, 1 x three beds
Living/Dining area	Electric heating, table and seating, plus double bed in type B	Electric heating, table and seating, plus double bed in type B
Kitchen area	3 ring gas hob, oven (type B only), refrigerator, sink, crockery, cutlery and utensils	3 ring gas hob, oven (type B only), refrigerator, sink, crockery, cutlery and utensils
Bathroom/shower	Washbasin, shower, WC	Washbasin, shower, WC (separate WC in type B)
Additional facilities	Garden table, chairs and 2 sunbeds	Terrace with 2 sunbeds
Bedding	Blankets and pillows provided	Blankets and pillows provided
Pets	Pets not accepted	Pets not accepted
Charges per week (98): From Ffr: *(low season)* to Ffr: *(high season)*	Type A: Ffr 1,400 - 2,990, type B: 1,500 - 3,490	Type A: Ffr 1,500 - 3,290, type B: 1,700 - 3,790
Amount/% of deposit	25% plus Ffr 220 fee	25% plus Ffr 220 fee

Campings
SITES & PAYSAGES

The 50 'Sites et Paysages' campsites are located in all regions of France. They are a group of family run sites designed to provide an essentially 'green' environment coupled with a family atmosphere and a genuine sense of hospitality.

In general, sites in this chain offer a high standard of service and a wide variety of leisure facilities including swimming pools, children's clubs and in the main season, some entertainment for both adults and children. Many of the sites in the Sites et Paysages chain have been selected for the Alan Rogers' Good Camps Guide for France.

Rhone Valley

2608 Camping Le Gallo-Romain, Barbières, nr Valence

Small site with pool, cradled in the foothills of the Vercors.

Le Gallo-Romain is enviably situated in one of the prettiest approaches to the spectacular Vercors plateau, providing visitors with a marvellous range of walks and drives. The site is located in natural woodland, with the ground sloping down to a pretty stream. This bounds the southeastern edge of the site, joining the river Barberolle, which then runs round the southwest perimeter. There is a fair sized swimming pool and a small shallow pool for young children. Sports facilities include table tennis, volleyball, and a small, shaded children's play area. An bar and restaurant is supplemented by a terrace overlooking the pool, where some entertainment is organised in high season. Takeaway food is provided. There are shops and restaurants nearby in the delightful town of Barbières, and the hypermarkets of Valence are not far.

Directions: Leave A49/E713 autoroute at exit 7 (Romans-sur-Isère) and turn south on D149, following signs to Col de Tourniol. Barbières is approx. 12 km. along this road. Drive carefully through narrow streets in the village; the site is a little way past it on the right.
Open: 2 May – 26 September.
Address: Quartier des Pommarets, 26300 Barbières. Tel: (0)4.75.47.44.07. Fax: as phone.

RENTED ACCOMMODATION	MOBILE HOMES
Number of persons	4-6 persons
Bedrooms	Two bedrooms: 1 x double bed, 1 x twin beds
Living/Dining area	Table and seating, double sofa bed
Kitchen area	Cooking range, fridge/freezer, sink, utensils, crockery and cutlery
Bathroom/shower	Shower, bath, washbasin, WC
Bedding	Blankets and pillows provided
Pets	Pets accepted
Charges per week (98): From Ffr: *(low season)* to Ffr: *(high season)*	Ffr 1,400 - 2,500
Amount/% of deposit	Ffr 600

Savoy/Dauphiny Alps

Major city: Grenoble
Départements: 38 Isère, 73 Savoie, 74 Haute-Savoie

Lying between the Rhône Valley and the Alpine borders with Switzerland and Italy are the old provinces of Savoie and Dauphine. This is an area of enormous granite outcrops, deeply riven by spectacular glacier hewn and river etched valleys. It has become one of the world's leading wintersport playgrounds and in the summer provides a range of outdoor activities. From Chambéry, north to the shores of Lac Léman (Lake Geneva) are many towns and villages that, since Roman times, attracted visitors to take the waters. Aix-les-Bains, Evian and Annecy were three major lakeside spa resorts of the Victorians; while Chamonix, under Mont Blanc, and Grenoble, capital of Dauphine, attracted the more active (often British) 19th century travellers who pioneered modern ski-ing and 'alpinism'. Today's modern ski resorts are Tignes, Val d'Isère, Megeve and Courchevel, whilst Grenoble is a bustling town with academic eminence in high technology and industry. To the north is the region of Chartreuse famous for its monastery, and liqueur! Italy and Switzerland are within easy reach for day excursions.

Cuisine of the region
'Plat gratine' applies to a wide varity of dishes; in the Alps this means cooked in breadcrumbs; gratins of all sorts show how well milk, cream and cheese combine together.
Farcement (Farçon Savoyard) – potatoes baked with cream, eggs, bacon, dried pears and prunes; a hearty stomach filler
Féra – a freshwater lake fish
Fondue – hot melted cheese and white wine; a classic of the region
Gratin Dauphinois – a classic potato dish with cream, cheese and garlic
Gratin Savoyard – another classic potato dish with cheese and butter
Lavaret – a freshwater lake fish, like salmon
Longeole – a country sausage
Lotte – a burbot, not unlike an eel
Omble chevalier – a char, it looks like a large salmon trout
Tartiflette – potato, bacon, onions and Reblochon cheese

Places of interest
Aix-les-Bains – spa resort on the Lac du Bourget, boat excursions to the Royal Abbey of Hautecombe
Albertville – 1992 Winter Olympics, museum
Annecy – canal-filled lakeside town, 12th century château, old quarter.
Chambéry – old quarter, Dukes of Savoie château, Savoie museum.
Chamonix – site of first Winter Olympics in 1924; world capital of mountain climbing; Mont Blanc tunnel, 11.6 km. long (for many years the longest tunnel in the world)
Evian-les-Bains – spa and casino on Lake Geneva, home of Evian water
Grenoble – University city; a cable car takes visitors across the River Isère and up to the Fort de la Bastille, from where there are panoramic views of the city and mountains beyond.

Savoy/Dauphiny Alps

3806 Camping Les Trois Lacs, Trept, nr Sablonnieres

Medium sized country site on edge of three lakes.

In flat, open country in the north of Dauphine, Trois Lacs is a pleasant relaxing base to enjoy either the countryside, the historic places of the region or the programme of leisure activities provided. The land around the lakes has been well landscaped and the camping area is on one side of the largest lake with tall trees on one side and views of distant mountains. The attractive bar/restaurant near reception serves drinks and snacks and there are other snack bars around the lakes. A mobile shop calls in high season and there are other shops at Trept (2 km). Well away from the camping area is a large building, open on one side, for roller skating and entertainment which is provided in July/August. There are two small children's playgrounds and a games area. The smallest lake is kept for fishing and the others for boating and watersports with one section for swimming with a water slide. Other activities include walking, riding, mountain biking, tennis and minigolf.

Directions: Leave the N75 Grenoble – Bourg-en-Bresse road at Morestel and travel west on D517 when site will be found between Sablonnieres and Trept.

Open: Campsite 15 April – 15 September, chalets all year except 10 September – 10 October.

Address: 38460 Trept. Tel: (0)4.74.92.92.06. Fax: (0)4.74.92.93.35.

RENTED ACCOMMODATION	CHALETS
Number of persons	4-5 persons
Bedrooms	One bedroom: 1 x single bed, 2 x bunk beds
Living/Dining area	Table and seating, double sofa bed
Kitchen area	2 ring gas hob, refrigerator, sink, utensils, crockery and cutlery
Bathroom/shower	Shower, washbasin, WC
Additional facilities	Terrace
Bedding	Pillows and blankets provided; sheets for hire
Pets	Pets accepted
Charges per week (98): From Ffr: (low season) to Ffr: (high season)	Ffr 1,840 - 2,300, additional week 1,600 - 2,000
Amount/% of deposit	50%

7404 Camp de la Ravoire, Doussard, nr Annecy

Small, quality site with pool, overlooking Lake Annecy.

De la Ravoire, some 800 m. from the lake, has gained the coveted 4 star rating by the quality of its sanitary block, its neat tidy appearance and the quietness of its location in this popular tourist region. The pitches, on well mown grass and separated by small shrubs, have little shade, although there are trees on the lake side of the site. The outdoor pool is overlooked by the terrace of the snack bar where limited food items may be stocked. Near this building is a children's play area. A good restaurant is on the lake-side where the camp road leaves the main road, with others near, plus shops in Doussard village. Those looking for a quiet, quality site in this most attractive region without the 'animation' programmes which so many French camps feel are necessary will find this a peaceful base, although disco noise from a camp by the lake may drift across under some weather conditions. The site is used by a tour operator.

Directions: Site is signed from the Annecy-Albertville road, just north of Bout-du-Lac. (Watch carefully, signs are small!)
Open: Christmas – 31 October.
Address: Bout du Lac, Route de la Ravoire, 74210 Doussard. Tel: (0)4.50.44.37.80. Fax: (0)4.50.32.90.60.

RENTED ACCOMMODATION	CHALETS
Number of persons	2-6 persons
Bedrooms	Two bedrooms: 1 x double bed, 1 x twin beds
Living/Dining area	Table and seating, TV on request, double sofa bed
Kitchen area	2 ring gas hob and oven, fridge/freezer, dishwasher, sink, utensils, crockery and cutlery
Bathroom/shower	Shower, washbasin; separate WC
Additional facilities	Covered terrace with garden table and chairs
Bedding	Pillows and blankets provided
Pets	Pets not accepted
Charges per week (98): From Ffr: *(low season)* to Ffr: *(high season)*	Low season (Christmas – 30 May and from 12 September) Ffr 2,000 for 1st week, then 1,700 for following week; mid season 2,600, then 2,300; high season 3,900 then 3,600
Amount/% of deposit	Ffr 800 per week booked

Western Loire

Major cities; Angers, Nantes

Départements: 44 Loire-Atlantique, 49 Maine-et-Loire, 53 Mayenne, 72 Sarthe, 85 Vendée

The Western Loire region's five départements to the south of Brittany have become popular for British visitors involving no more than a day's drive from the channel ports. The region includes 300 km. of Atlantic coastline, long sandy beaches and little islands like the Ile de Noirmoutier and the Ile d'Yeu contrasting with the lush, green countryside through which flows the Loire River. Only the western stretch is included in this region and most of the great Loire châteaux lie in the Loire Valley region, but the Western Loire is not without its history with many monuments and medieval towns. At its heart lies Angers, capital of the historic province of Anjou, home of feudal warlords and the Plantagenet kings of England. To the southeast, the Vendée, centre of the counter-revolutionary royalist movement between 1793 and 1799, is a peaceful, windswept area popular with the holidaymaker in the summer.

Cuisine of the region
Such specialties as rillettes, andouillettes, tripes, mushrooms and the regional cheeses of Trappiste d' Entrammes and Cremet d' Angers, Petit Sable and Ardoises d'Angers cookies. Challans, in the Vendée, is known for its quality ducks.

Wine
The white wines of Anjou and Saumur may be dry or sweet. There are also fruity rosés, both dry and sweet, produced mainly from the Cabernet grape which has given its name to Cabernet d' Anjou and Cabernet de Saumur. Among the whites, Côteaux de Saumur are lighter and drier and preserve their quality well, Côteaux du Layon and Côteaux de l' Aubance, very fine and sweet, are richer and age very well. A large proportion of the production from the Saumur region is made by the Champagne method.

Places of interest.
Angers – art town, medieval castle and tapestries, cathedral
Brissac – 15th century castle
Le Croisic – little fishing port, Naval Museum
Fontevraud – 11th century Royal Abbey
Goulaine – 15th-16th century castle with beautiful furnished apartments
Laval – castle, `Douanier Rousseau' art gallery, boat trips on the Mayenne
La Baule – resort with lovely sandy bay and beach
Le Lude – medieval fortress, sound and light show
Le Mans – the annual 24-hour car race attracts visitors from all over the world; car museum, old town, cathedral
Le Puy du Fou – 15th-16th century castle, sound and light show involving over 700 participants
Les Sables d'Olonne – fishing port and seaside resort
Noirmoutier – linked to the mainland by a 3 mile bridge
Saumur – 13th century castle, Cadre Noir National School of Horse Riding, wine cellars, and Mushroom Museum

4409 Castel Camping Château de Deffay, Pontchâteau

Relaxed, family managed site, near the Côte Armor and Brière Regional National Park.

Château de Deffay has a rural setting and has been developed to blend into the natural environment of the estate. The old courtyard of the smaller château (which dates from before 1400) houses the bar and small restaurant with takeaway, well stocked shop and is where the solar heated swimming pool and paddling pool are located (all 15 May – 15 Sept). The larger château (built in 1880) and another lake stand away from this area providing pleasant walking. There is a play area for children on grass, a TV room below the bar and a separate room for table tennis. Entertainment is organised in season. Tennis and swimming, pedaloes and fishing in the lake, are free. Riding. Bicycle hire. The Guérande Peninsula, La Baule bay and the natural wilderness of the 'Grande Brière' are all near. Golf 5 km. This is a small, fairly 'laid-back' site, not over organised or supervised.

Directions: Site signed from D33 Pontchâteau-Herbignac road near Ste-Reine. Also from D773 and N165.
Open: 4 April – 24 October.
Address: BP 18, Ste-Reine, 44160 Pontchâteau. Tel: (0)2.40.88.00.57 (winter: (0)2.40.01.63.84).
Fax: (0)2.40.01.66.55.

RENTED ACCOMMODATION	CHALETS Type A	CHALETS Type B	CHALETS Types C and D
Number of persons	2 persons	4 persons	4-6 persons
Bedrooms	None	Two bedrooms: 1 x double bed, 1 x twin beds	Two bedrooms: 1 x double bed, 1 x bunk beds
Living/Dining area	Sofa bed (2 persons), table and seating	Table and seating	Table and seating, buffet in type D, sofa bed (C: 1 person, D: 2 persons)
Kitchen area	Electric hot-plates, refrigerator, coffee machine, sink, utensils, crockery and cutlery	Electric hot-plates, refrigerator, coffee machine, sink, utensils, crockery and cutlery	Electric hot-plates, oven and grill in type D, refrigerator, coffee machine, sink, utensils, crockery and cutlery
Bathroom/shower	Shower, washbasin, WC	Shower, washbasin, WC	Shower, washbasin, WC
Additional facilities	Covered terrace with garden table and chairs	Covered terrace with garden table and chairs	Covered terrace with garden table and chairs
Bedding	Blankets and pillows provided	Blankets and pillows provided	Blankets and pillows provided
Pets	Pets accepted	Pets accepted	Pets accepted
Charges per week (98): From Ffr: *(low season)* to Ffr: *(high season)*	Ffr 800 - 1,600; weekend and nightly rates available outside 27 June - 29 August.	Ffr 1,300 - 2,700; weekend and nightly rates available outside 27 June - 29 August.	Type C: Ffr 1,500 - 3,000, type D: 1,700 - 3,400; weekend and nightly rates available outside 27 June - 29 August.
Amount/% of deposit	Ffr 500 plus fee 100	Ffr 500 plus fee 100	Ffr 500 plus fee 100

Western Loire

4410 Camping Caravaning International Le Patisseau, Pornic

Friendly quiet site near fishing port of Pornic with its own pool.

Le Patisseau is a nice friendly site, rurally situated 2½ km. from the sea, with a good welcome. The site has a small restaurant and bar (both 27 June - 29 August) on a terrace near the medium sized pool (all season). Two water slides have been added with their own pool. There is a games area with volleyball and table tennis, children's play areas, one large on sand, and bicycle hire. With a new reception area and two new sanitary blocks, the site continues to improve its facilities. The toilet blocks are modern, tiled and well cleaned, with free hot showers, cabins with washbasins and fully equipped laundry rooms. Shop (all season). A railway line runs through the bottom half of the site but with trains only two or three times a day. Pornic is a delightful fishing village and the coastline is interesting with secluded sandy coves and inlets.

Directions: Site is signed at the roundabout junction of the D751 (Pornic – Nantes) road, and from the town centre.

Open: 1 May – 12 September, chalets all year (limited facilities outside July/August).

Address: Le Patisseau, 44210 Pornic. Tel: (0)2.40.82.10.39. Fax: (0)2.40.82.22.81.

RENTED ACCOMMODATION	MOBILE HOMES *Types M4 and M6*	CHALETS	TENTS
Number of persons	M4 (24 sq.m) 4 persons, M6 (28 sq.m) 6 persons	6 persons	4/5 persons
Bedrooms	Two bedrooms: 1 x double bed, 1 x twin beds	Two bedrooms: 1 x double bed, 1 x twin beds	Two bedrooms: 1 x double bed, 1 x 3 single beds
Living/Dining area	Table and seating, M6 with sofa bed (2 persons)	Heating (extra), table and seating, sofa bed (2 persons)	Table and seating
Kitchen area	Gas or electric hot-plates, refrigerator, sink, utensils, crockery and cutlery	Gas or electric hot-plates, refrigerator, sink, utensils, crockery and cutlery	2 gas hot-plates, refrigerator, utensils, crockery and cutlery
Bathroom/shower	Shower, washbasin, WC; (M6 with separate WC)	Shower, washbasin, WC	None
Additional facilities	Terrace with barbecue	Terrace with barbecue	Barbecue
Bedding	Pillows provided; sheets and blankets for hire	Pillows provided; sheets and blankets for hire	Pillows provided; sheets and blankets for hire
Pets	Pets not accepted	Pets not accepted	Pets not accepted
Charges per week (98): From Ffr: *(low season)* to Ffr: *(high season)*	M4: Ffr 800 - 3,290, M6: 900 - 3,490; weekend rates available May, June and Sept.	Ffr 1,000 - 3,490; weekend rates available outside July/August; heating extra	Ffr 600 - 2,590
Amount/% of deposit	25%	25%	25%

8508 Camping La Puerta del Sol, St Hilaire de Riez, nr St Gilles-Croix

Well designed, good quality site with swimming pool and other amenities.

La Puerta del Sol is a modern site developed on ambitious lines resulting in a very good, environmentally pleasing site with excellent amenities. The ambience achieved is friendly, welcoming and lively, without being intrusive to those who seek a peaceful and relaxing holiday in an area where so often quite frenzied activity is the order of the day. The Spanish camp name is reflected in the architectural style of the buildings which contain reception, bar, takeaway and restaurant. An attractive heated swimming pool is by the bar with a terrace. There is a mini-market (20 June - 31 August) and a general room also used for `animation' events; sports competitions and games, evening entertainment and dancing. Excursions are organised in July/August. Barbecue area, children's adventure play areas (on sand), tennis and a games room. The nearest sandy beach is 5 km. and St Jean-de-Monts 7.

Directions: Site is 1 km. north of Le Pissot (which is 7 km. north of St Gilles Croix-de-Vie on D38) on the D59 road towards Le Perrier. Watch carefully for camp sign, you come on it quite suddenly.
Open: Easter holidays, then 15 May - 20 September.
Address: Les Borderies, 85270 St Hilaire de Riez. Tel: (0)2.51.49.10.10. Fax: (0)2.51.49.84.84.

RENTED ACCOMMODATION	CHALETS *Wooden*	CHALETS *Metal*	MOBILE HOMES
Number of persons	4/6 persons	4/5 persons	4 persons
Bedrooms	Two bedrooms: 1 x twin beds, 1 x bunk beds	Two bedrooms: 1 x double bed, 1 x twin beds	Two bedrooms: 1 x double bed, 1 x twin beds
Living/Dining area	Table and seating, sofa bed (2 persons)	Table and seating, sofa bed (2 persons)	Table and seating
Kitchen area	2 gas hot-plates, refrigerator, sink, utensils, crockery and cutlery	2 gas hot-plates, refrigerator, sink, utensils, crockery and cutlery	2 gas hot-plates, refrigerator, sink, utensils, crockery and cutlery
Bathroom/shower	Shower, washbasin; separate WC	Shower, washbasin; separate WC	Shower, washbasin, WC
Additional facilities	Covered terrace (10 sq.m) with garden table and chairs	Covered terrace (8 sq.m) with garden table and chairs	Awning with garden table and chairs, sunshade
Bedding	Blankets and pillows provided	Blankets and pillows provided	Blankets and pillows provided
Pets	Pets accepted	Pets accepted	Pets accepted
Charges per week (98): From Ffr: *(low season)* to Ffr: *(high season)*	Ffr 1,500 - 3,900; weekend and nightly rates available outside 4 July - 22 August	Ffr 1,500 - 3,800	Ffr 1,300 - 3,200
Amount/% of deposit	Ffr 1,000 per week booked plus 200 fee	Ffr 1,000 per week booked plus 200 fee	Ffr 1,000 per week booked plus 200 fee

Western Loire

8509 Camping L'Abri des Pins, St Jean-de-Monts, nr Challans

Family run, well equipped site with pool on outskirts of popular resort.

L'Abri des Pins is on the outskirts of the pleasant, modern resort of St Jean-de-Monts, separated from the sea and long sandy beach by a strip of pinewood. One can walk about 600 m. through the wood to the beach from the back of the medium sized site or drive slightly further and park. Bathing is said to be safer here than on most of the beaches on this coast, but is nevertheless supervised. There are two heated swimming pools and a water slide, plus a small pool for children, with a paved sunbathing area (open mid May – mid Sept). Facilities include a shop and bar/restaurant with takeaway (all 15 June – 1 Sept), tennis, table tennis, pétanque, TV room and games room, a children's playground and a fitness suite. Entertainment is organised for children in July/August. Riding, sailing and windsurfing hire facilities are near. Accommodation is also available at the sister site (not inspected).

Directions: Site is 4 km. from the town centre on the St Jean-de-Monts to Notre Dame-de-Monts/Noirmoutiers road (D38).
Open: 30 May – 12 September.
Address: 85160 St Jean-de-Monts. Tel: (0)2.51.58.83.86 (winter: (0)2.40.73.09.70).
Fax: (0)2.51.59.30.47 (winter (0)2.40.71.98.04).

RENTED ACCOMMODATION	MOBILE HOMES	CHALETS Type A	CHALETS Type B
Number of persons	6 persons	6 persons	4 persons
Bedrooms	Two bedrooms: 1 x double bed, 1 x two single beds	Two bedrooms: 1 x double bed, 1 x two single beds	One bedroom: 1 x double bed
Living/Dining area	Gas fire, table and seating, sofa bed (2 persons)	Gas fire, table and seating, sofa bed (2 persons)	Gas fire, table, seating and chairs; 2 single sofa beds
Kitchen area	2 ring gas hob (no oven or grill), refrigerator, sink, utensils, crockery and cutlery	2 ring gas hob (no oven or grill), refrigerator, sink, utensils, crockery and cutlery	2 ring gas hob (no oven or grill), refrigerator, sink, utensils, crockery and cutlery
Bathroom/shower	Shower, washbasin, WC	Shower, washbasin; separate WC	Shower, washbasin, WC
Additional facilities		Terrace	
Bedding	Blankets and pillows provided	Blankets and pillows provided	Blankets and pillows provided
Pets	Pets not accepted	Pets not accepted	Pets not accepted
Charges per week (98): From Ffr: (low season) to Ffr: (high season)	Ffr 1,300 - 3,600	Ffr 1,690 - 3,800	Ffr 1,300 - 3,450
Amount/% of deposit	Ffr 1,500 plus fee 100	Ffr 1,500 plus fee 100	Ffr 1,500 plus fee 100

8513 Camping Pong, Landevieille

Pleasant, well kept site, 4 km. from the coast at Brétignolles.

In a rural situation, 12 km. south of St Gilles-Croix-de-Vie, this is a comfortable, family run site. The original part of the medium sized site around the small, fenced fishing lake has a mixture of mature trees, whereas, in the newer, terraced area, the trees and bushes edging the pitches are less developed. A new, heated semi-oval pool with jacuzzi, combined with the original pool, toboggan and paddling pools (with many water games), make a very attractive leisure area complete with palm trees and sun loungers (all from 15 May). There is a small shop with bread, milk and takeaway meals (from June) and a new bar with terrace overlooking the pool. Other facilities include a small gym, TV lounge, games room, fenced, sand based children's play area complete with Wendy house. Tennis 200 m. Golf, markets, vineyards all nearby. The site is 2½ km. from the large Lac du Jaunay (canoeing and pedaloes), 14 km. from Lac d'Apremont and its XVI century château and the nearest beach is 4 km. There are no tour operators.

Directions: Site is on the D32 St Gilles-Croix-de-Vie to La Mothe road just south of Landevieille and is signed.
Open: 1 May – 19 September.
Address: Rue du Stade, 85220 Landevieille. Tel: (0)2.51.22.92.63. Fax: (0)2.51.22.99.25.

RENTED ACCOMMODATION	MOBILE HOMES Type A and B	CHALETS Campéco
Number of persons	Type A: 8.6 x 3 m, type B: 8 x 3 m. Both 4/6 persons	5 persons
Bedrooms	Two bedrooms: 1 x double bed, 1 x two single beds	One bedroom: 1 x double bed, 1 x twin beds
Living/Dining area	Table and seating; sofa bed (2 persons)	Table and seating; sofa bed
Kitchen area	Hot-plates, refrigerator, sink, utensils, crockery and cutlery	Hot-plates, refrigerator, sink, utensils, crockery and cutlery
Bathroom/shower	Shower, washbasin, WC	Shower, washbasin, WC
Additional facilities	Terrace with garden table and chairs	Terrace with garden table
Bedding	Blankets and pillows provided	Blankets and pillows provided
Pets	Pets accepted	Pets accepted
Charges per week (98): From Ffr: *(low season)* to Ffr: *(high season)*	Type A: Ffr 1,000 - 2,850, type B 1,050 - 3,050	Ffr 1,000 - 2,700
Amount/% of deposit	25%	25%

The other titles in the ALAN ROGERS' series for independent campers and caravanners are:

- ● **Good Camps Guide – Britain & Ireland**

- ● **Good Camps Guide – France**

- ● **Good Camps Guide – Europe**

- ● **Camping & Caravanning All Year Round**

OUR FRANCE & SPAIN *Direct*

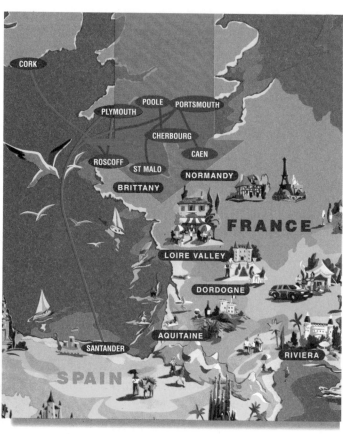

Travelling to Holiday France or Spain?
Why drive the long way round when you can sail direct?
We land you closer to where you'd like to be.

Brittany Ferries
The Holiday Fleet

BROCHURES 0990 143 554 (24HRS) RESERVATIONS 0990 360 360
OR SEE YOUR TRAVEL AGENT

Alan Rogers' CARTE D'OR 1998/99
SAVE MONEY

Purchase of the Carte d'Or provides the following benefits:

Campsite Discounts – 5% (high season) to 15% (low season) on rental of accommodation

Essential Travel Pack – from the Caravan & Camping Service as described overleaf

---

Carte d'Or Application

I would like to take advantage of the benefits described in this Guide for holders of the Alan Rogers Carte d'Or and hereby enclose payment * of £10 for a 1998/99 Carte d'Or.

Name:

Address:

Telephone:

I enclose a cheque for £10 in favour of Alan Rogers' Guides

I wish to pay Visa or Mastercard

Details of card:

Number: Expiry Date:

Request for Brochures and Booking Forms, etc.

I am interested in a holiday at the following campsites featured in this guide:
Please send me further information (max. 3 sites)
(brochure, full tariff, booking conditions and booking form)

	Site No.	Site Name
1		
2		
3		

Name:

Address:

Please send these forms to: Deneway Guides & Travel, Chesil Lodge, West Bexington, Dorchester DT2 9DG.

Please note that we cannot deal with enquiries/requests by telephone.

If, at the same time as requesting the above information, you are applying for an Alan Rogers Carte d'Or, the cost of postage will be covered by your Carte d'Or fee.

If you are not applying for a Carte d'Or please enclose a self-addressed stamped A4 envelope (150 grams, 1st class 49p, 2nd class 38p, as at March '98).

When you send to us for additional campsite information, booking conditions, etc. we would stress that these are produced by, and the responsibility of, the individual campsites themselves. We have no control over this information and the editors and the publishers cannot be held in any way responsible for these or for any consequences of them. If you make a booking, your contract will be between yourself and the individual campsite (we are not a tour operator).

Alan Rogers' CARTE D'OR

EXCLUSIVE OFFER

The Essential Travel Pack
from Caravan & Camping Service

Save money on your holiday this year with discounted Channel Crossings and the Essential Travel Pack from Caravan & Camping Service – exclusive to holders of the Alan Rogers Carte d'Or.

Caravan & Camping Service specialises in camping and caravanning holidays abroad and has prepared an Essential Travel Pack of insurance, holiday guide and maps to help you get more out of your holiday and save money.

As a Carte d'Or holder you benefit from a minimum 5% discount on Channel Crossings booked through Caravan & Camping Service and when you purchase your personal and vehicle breakdown & emergency insurance from Caravan & Camping Service you will receive all these valauable extras.*

- Michelin Tourist Guide for France
- Large scale Michelin Touring Map of France
- Detailed Michelin regional map – essential for sightseeing
- GB Sticker

Premiums	9 Days		17 Days	
	Standard	Plus Cover	Standard	Plus Cover
Personal per person	£10.50	£15.00	£13.50	£19.00
Child (0-3)	FREE	FREE	FREE	FREE
Car	£24.50	£29.00	£30.50	£35.00
Trailer	£11.00	£11.00	£14.00	£14.00
Motor Caravan	£35.00	£42.00	£40.00	£49.00
Camping Equipment	£7.00 per party for up to 31 days			

Please note that these premiums apply to 1998 only, and may be subject to change for 1999.

We will be pleased to send you full details of insurance cover and limits – just call 0171 792 1944

* Please note the minimum purchase requirement is personal insurance for two persons and car – which must be under 12 years old. If you take insurance only there will be charge of £2.50 for post and packing. If you also book your ferry with Caravan & Camping Service there will be no post and packaging charge.

Start saving money now call 0171 792 1944 today for a low price quotation on your Channel crossing or post the form opposite

CARAVAN & CAMPING SERVICE FORM

CARAVAN
& CAMPING
SERVICE

DETAILS OF YOUR PARTY

Name of party leader:	
Address:	
	Post Code:
Tel. Work:	Home:

Names of all party members including the leader and ages at the time of travel if under 18

Mr/Mrs/Miss	Initials	Surname	Age	Mr/Mrs/Miss	Initials	Surname	Age

FERRY REQUIREMENTS

Outward	1st choice		Outward	1st choice
Date			Date	
From (Port)			From (Port)	
To (Port)			To (Port)	
Departure Time			Departure Time	
Accomm. on board			Accomm. on board	

SITE DETAILS

Site	Arrival date	Departure date	Site name	Site address (for map)
1				
2				

HOLIDAY INSURANCE

Insurance: (please tick)   **Emergency Breakdown Insurance**

Personal Plan:	☐	Car	Standard ☐	Plus ☐
Camping Equipment:	☐	Motor Home	Standard ☐	Plus ☐
Bicycle insurance	☐	Trailer/Caravan	Standard ☐	Plus ☐

for vehicles up to 12 years old

Outward travel date: . . . .   Inward travel date: . . . .

SEND TO: Caravan & Camping Service, 69 Westbourne Grove, London W2 4UJ. Please do not send any payment.

Naturist Sites

During the past several years we have had very favourable feedback from readers concerning our choice of naturist sites, which we first introduced in the 1992 edition of our Good Camps Guide – France. Over the last five years we have gradually added a few more to that guide and are pleased to feature two of them in this guide to rented accommodation (nos. 3405N and 8402N).

Apart from the need to have a 'Naturist Licence' (see below), there is no need to be a practising naturist before visiting these sites. In fact, at least as far as British visitors are concerned, many are what might be described as `holiday naturists' as distinct from the practice of naturism at other times. The emphasis in all the sites featured in this guide at least, is on naturism as `life in harmony with nature', and respect for oneself and others and for the environment, rather than simply on nudity. In fact nudity is really only obligatory in the area of the swimming pools.

There are a number of 'rules', which amount to sensible and considerate guidelines designed to ensure that no-one invades someone else's privacy, creates any nuisance, or damages the environment. Whether as a result of these 'rules', the naturist philosophy generally, or the attitude of site owners and campers alike, we have been very impressed by all the naturist sites we have selected. Without exception they had a friendly and welcoming ambience, were all extremely clean and tidy and, in most cases, provided much larger than average pitches, with a wide range of activities both sporting and cultural.

The purpose of our including a number of naturist sites in our guides is to provide an 'introduction to naturist camping in France' for British holidaymakers; we were actually surprised by the number of British campers we met on naturist sites, many of whom had `stumbled across naturism almost by accident' but had found, like us, that these sites were amongst the nicest they had encountered. We mentioned the Naturist Licence – French Law requires all campers over 16 years of age on naturist sites to have a 'licence'. These can be obtained in advance from either the British or French national naturist associations, but are also available on arrival at any recognised naturist site (a passport type photograph is required).

ELECTROLUX –
FOR THE LIFE OF LEISURE

With the life we lead today leisure is of increasing importance, so is the need to have cool fresh food and drinks to hand wherever you are.

Electrolux have the most comprehensive range of portable refrigerators and coolers in the industry. They have a product for every conceivable use and application.

The mobilLife range of portable refrigerators is ideal for use either at home or away. There are models suitable for use on outings with the kids, or just in the garden for barbecues.

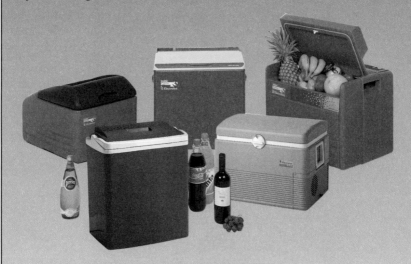

HOLIDAY

Stocking up for the holiday? Taking the children or grandchildren with you? Where to store the left-over Christmas turkey?

Electrolux has the answer. Their top of the range mobilLifes are portable top-opening absorption refrigerators. There is a choice of models and they are all three-way just like the model fitted in a caravan. You can run from gas or 230v while stationary, or plug into the cigar lighter 12v socket whilst on the move. They are ideal when you are camping, or useful as an additional refrigerator at home. Whatever the occasion Electrolux can help solve the problem.

Sitting in your car in long summer traffic jams in the sweltering heat, wouldn't it be great to just reach into the back of your car and take out a long cool drink?

Electrolux mobilLife thermoelectric coolers work on the Peltier system from a 12v supply, so you can plug them directly into the cigarette lighter of the car, and have cool drinks to hand at any time. No more do you need to search for a roadside café, or queue in busy motorway service stations. Refreshment is to hand at any time of day or night. With the aid of an adaptor, you can run your mobilLife cooler on the 24v system on a truck or boat. A 230v adaptor means you can use it at home as well. Some of the products even allow you to reverse the plug and use your mobilLife as a food warmer, ideal for an outing on colder days, or for keeping the takeaway warm.

Reasonably priced, these coolers are also ideal for day trips and excursions. Whatever the application Electrolux has a portable product to suit.

The Wine Regions of France

The Bluffer's Guide to Wine

by Mike Cazelet

For thy health drink wine, for thy wealth drink water.
But is it better to meet thy Maker young and rich or old and poor?

Old Burgundian proverb

We British have a problem with wine. We love it, in fact we drink more wine per head than almost any other non-mainstream wine producing nation. And our consumption is rising at a staggering ten per cent per year. But we also know we know nothing about wine. "I don't know much about wine, but I know what I like" is a favourite saying. For that I blame the television pundits, always rabbiting on about tasting a hint of "honeysuckle at dawn" or "sun-kissed wild blackberries."

Tackle the experts and ask them what on earth they are talking about, and you'll get fobbed off with a long explanation which basically comes down to "If you don't know what I'm talking about it merely proves I am a superior human being with an educated palate, whilst you ....."

Understandably the mystique surrounding wine has frightened off many of those who would like to know more. We can't promise to turn you into a wine expert, but in the next few pages perhaps we can break the spell which surrounds the subject of wine.

I'm still no wine expert, but years ago I had to spend a few days in Burgundy. During that time I met a man who opened my mind and eyes to the pleasure of wine. Since then I've met French wine experts by the score, tramped through châteaux, both large and small, and sampled wines both grand and humble.

The new wine producing nations are good, but some would say they've taken commercialisation too far. Each label may be produced from hundreds of acres, and it is chemists who control production to maintain consistent quality – and taste. The result is a product which is good, but usually horribly predictable. France has adopted modern production methods, but their

vineyards are often small, and the taste and perfume of their product will reflect the inherited skill of the producers. Consequently French wines vary enormously. Even from one small vineyard, ten years of production will have produced ten different wines. Each subtly different from each other and reflecting the imponderables like winter rain and summer sun and temperature.

At first glance wine seems like such a simple commodity to produce. Take a ripe grape and crush it. The sugars in the juice mix with the yeast on the skin and fermentation starts. Nourished by the sugar the yeast multiplies and turns the sugar into alcohol. When all the sugar is consumed, or the alcohol level has built up to a certain point, the yeast dies. What is left is wine, but not necessarily as we might recognise it.

The skill of wine making is choosing exactly the right time to pick the grapes and then controlling the fermentation so there is the right mix of acidity, sweetness and alcoholic content. Sometimes the skill also involves blending wines from different producers to make something which is greater than the sum of its constituent parts. And remember that frequently the producers are working with a product which will mature and change before it is consumed.

Wine is produced in most of France. There is even a small vineyard near Sacre Cœur in the centre of Paris. However it takes a combination of well drained soil and fairly predictable weather to produce wine of a consistent quality and quantity. In this feature we are only dealing with France's principal wine production areas. If you should be fortunate enough to stumble across a vineyard well away from one of these areas, don't be frightened away. You might just have discovered an unknown gem.

I once found a tiny vineyard high in France's Haute Provence mountains. The white wine we tasted was unusual, and certainly good enough to be worth buying a small case. Later the locals told us that we had bought some of the only produce from this vineyard which was really fit to drink.

Despite the fact that wines can vary between adjoining fields and even from the top to the bottom of a single field, there are consistencies of taste which make the produce of a single area clearly different. If you are about to set off for France read this guide. If your holiday area just happens to be in a wine producing area, this is what you're going to have a chance to savour.

Alsace

Perhaps more than any other part of Europe, Alsace has had a troubled past. The area has passed back and forth between German and French ownership, and armies have trampled its vineyards into the ground. Despite all that Alsace has risen to be an area of vital importance to France's wine industry. It wasn't always so. From the Franco-Prussian Wars until the end of the First World War Alsace's white wines were so nondescript they were just sold as vin ordinaire. When they attempted to copy the German wines with their extra sweetness, the result was disappointing. But now the area produces wines which are dry, full flavoured and stronger bodied than the equivalent product from across the border.

Places to visit in Alsace
Without doubt the one place every visitor to Alsace must visit is the village of Riquewihr. Whilst virtually every other village in the area was decimated by war, Riquewihr is untouched since the 18th century. Although Colmar isn't strictly in the wine production area, it is where most of the wine merchants reside and the old quarter seems to be set in the Middle Ages.

Where to buy in Alsace
Virtually anywhere, but in particular from the small wine merchants in Colmar. Look in particular for wines made with the Sylvaner and Pinot Gris grape variety. Both are for everyday drinking, and can be ridiculously cheap. If lucky enough to spot of bottle of Alsace produced Pinot Gris rosé, grab it. They don't produce much, and it is virtually unknown outside Alsace.

Beaujolais

Poor Beaujolais. The area got a reputation for producing young wines frequently of no great character. What made it worse was that a few unscrupulous operators were dumping wines from other areas on to the market with labels claiming they were from Beaujolais. At one time Britain, alone, drank more Beaujolais Nouveau than the total production of Beaujolais.

But all that has fortunately changed. Nevertheless the Beaujolais area is still a massive producer of wine. About 80 million litres a year which is about a quarter more than is produced in the Bordeaux region.

The nouveau wines should be drunk soon after they are bottled, and by March at the latest. This way they are soft and fruity. However if you want a similar wine with a bit more maturity, the grand cru wines from Moulin à Vent and Chénas will improve from a few years after production.

Where to visit in Beaujolais

Co-incidentally both Moulin à Vent and Chénas are worth a visit. Also on every visitor's itinerary is the town of Bresse which is famous for its yellow, corn fed chickens. Virtually every restaurant in the town serves dishes using the local chickens, and I've never been disappointed in any of them.

Where to buy in Beaujolais

For a couple of weeks after November 15th when the Beaujolais Nouveau is released, virtually every wine producing village is jammed with foreign registered cars and vans buying up the new wine and rushing it back home for sale.

Being a young wine there aren't any significant differences between the production of one vineyard over another. Nor do prices vary significantly. It's more a case of finding somewhere to park and buying the wine within carrying distance.

Surprisingly the cheapest place to buy wine during the summer months is from the hypermarkets around Bresse where prices can be up to half what you would pay in Calais.

Bordeaux

If Beaujolais is the largest production area by volume, then Bordeaux is the largest production area of fine wines. The extraordinary thing is that part of the credit for Bordeaux's success is due to us – the Brits. In 1152 Henry II married Queen Eleanor of Aquitaine whose lands included the wine producing area of Bordeaux. She introduced the British to the thin, red wines of Bordeaux which were know by the British as claret.

Over 300 years the British developed a taste for claret, and it was considered a cheap essential drink at every man's table. Such was the demand that new areas were planted out with vines. The entire Médoc wine producing area was developed to satisfy British demand. But then we lost Bordeaux and went on to develop Portugal's wine production area, and particularly the development of the fortified wine we know as Port.

Bordeaux is unusual in that it produces both white and red wines in almost equal quantities, and the labelling system seems designed to create confusion. Take Graves which we know as a

reasonably dry white wine. That name is also given to the area which includes the city of Bordeaux itself. And within that area there are red wine production units which don't use the Graves name on their label, but rather use the name of the Parish in which they were produced. To add to the confusion the word château doesn't mean a castle or grand country house, and can be given to a wine producing unit with a mere farm house at its centre.

Where to visit in Bordeaux
Most of Bordeaux's wine production area consists of nothing but rolling hills of vines centred around a nondescript farm house. The exception is the hillside village of St Emilion. From the castle ramparts you can see over the sun bleached roofs of the village, and at most pavement cafés buy a glass of premier cru St Emilion as if it was a glass of mineral water.
Wander up the side streets and seemingly every other shop sells wines and offers tastings. In particular stop outside the printer who produces the labels for the principal local producers.
For tourists the city of Bordeaux is a better bet. From Napoléon's Pont de Pierre bridge you can get a good view of the 6 mile long quay from which wine is still shipped. At one time the wine was shipped to England in giant 250 gallon oak casks called Tuns, and all ships were rated at a certain tonnage which was the measure of how many of these casks they could carry. In Bordeaux make a point of seeing the 14,000 piece Bohemian glass chandelier in the foyer of the Grand Theatre, and the 29 acre Esplanade des Quinconces.

Where to buy in Bordeaux
The answer is everywhere. Everyone who has anything to do with the production of wine, will sell direct to the consumer. The problem with buying direct from the châteaux is that all they will offer is what they produce. For a wider selection, and still at silly prices, try one of the wine co-operatives who will have the products of a number of small producers for sale.
I particularly like the wine co-operative at Rauzan, 8 miles south east of Bordeaux and just off the D670. Their stocks include a good range of reds and whites, and occasionally they sell the rare Bordeaux rosé which they say is as close as we will ever get to the original claret which captivated England over 800 years ago.

Burgundy

In Burgundy they will tell you that whilst Bordeaux produces fine wines, Burgundy produces great wines. Certainly their products tend to be fuller bodied wines, both white and red, which often need time in the bottle to reach full maturity.
Burgundy's wine production area is in a narrow band which runs between the A6 motorway and

the low range of hills to the west – the Côte d'Or. If you take the N14 out of Dijon through to just south of Beaune every village name is a reminder of just important this is as a wine producing area.

The signposts look like a trip down a wine merchant's shelves; Gevrey-Chambertin, Musigny, Vosne-Romanée – allegedly the most expensive wines in Burgundy – Nuits St George, Aloxe-Corton. And it goes on mile after mile.

Virtually every wine producer seems to be offering tastings, and will be equally willing to sell their products. This can be a risky business, because once you've tasted you will probably feel some obligation to buy. The real experts say that wines in Burgundy can vary enormously over a very short distance. They go further and claim that a 500 metre wide band down the centre of the Côte d'Or produces wines enormously superior to wines produced just a few yards higher or lower on the slopes.

Unlike Bordeaux, the Burgundians don't tend to overuse the word Château. Many of the châteaux in the wine production areas tend to be small and a bit disappointing. For the grander houses you'll need to go the other side of the A6 motorway, towards the river Saône.

Where to visit in Burgundy
Nobody can visit Burgundy without going to the 15th century Hôtel Dieu, also known as the Hospice d'Beaune. It is both an active home for the elderly and where the annual Burgundy wine auctions are held. Unfortunately to get there you'll have to brave the Beaune by-pass, and probably queue up to get a parking space. But once inside take the conducted tour and you'll see the wonderful patterned tiled roofs and even the old hospital wards where patients were laid two to a bed.

Dijon is another city well worth a visit. Unfortunately development has ruined much of the original medieval city centre, but there are still sufficient grand buildings to make it easy to understand how Dijon used to be a centre of power in medieval Europe.

Where to buy in Burgundy
I would suggest that buying directly from the producer can be slightly risky unless you really know your wine. It's far safer to buy from someone who has a range of wines on offer. The owner of Château Pierreclos, like many others, runs conducted tours round the house, followed by wine tasting in the caves – cellars. The range of stock is good, their prices equally so. Alternatively the Marché Aux Vins opposite the Hôtel Dieu in Beaune has tasting sessions, and a great range of wines at surprisingly cheap prices.

Failing that try the wine shops in the various villages – particularly Santaney – which will only sell locally produced wines, but that still gives the visitor an opportunity to find something they like.

Champagne
A few years ago when British politicians were looking for the green shoots of recovery which would herald the end of recession, they suggested that increased use of electricity would be the first sign that things were on the turn.

They got it wrong. France's champagne producers can tell precisely how we view our future by looking at the forward orders from the British wine trade. Britain is one of the world's greatest champagne drinking nations. Like the French we don't restrict champagne consumption just to meal times. We drink it to celebrate when things are going well, and frequently we drink it because it makes us feel better.

Scientifically there is justification for doing so, because drinking champagne has been proven to make us feel better. Well that's my excuse, and I'm sticking to it.

It was a monk – Dom Pérignon – who discovered that the late harvest in Champagne meant that wine bottled that winter hadn't stopped fermenting, but merely shut down during the cold months. If the wine is bottled then the secondary fermentation the next year gave the wine a light sparkle.

The growth of the Champagne industry is due to another famous name – Veuve Clicquot – the widow Clicquot. The Russian army was quartered in Reims in the days leading up to the Battle of Waterloo. They acquired a taste for champagne, and when they returned home she chartered ships so they could continue to enjoy their favourite drink. From that humble beginning the entire world-wide export market for champagne grew.

All champagne is a blend, and the only difference between dry (brut) and sweet (sec) champagnes, is that the latter has sugar syrup added. Demi-sec (semi-sweet) has smaller amounts of sugar added. Champagne is made with a mix of white grapes from the area around Eperney and black grapes from the valley of the Marne and the Mountains of Reims. In recent years some champagnes have been made from all white grapes, and are usually labelled blanc de blanc. Although supposedly lighter in taste, blanc de blanc champagnes aren't, although they are more expensive.

Places to visit in Champagne
In Cramant, near Eperney, they produce a unique champagne which has less fizz than conventional champagne areas. They maintain that their product is closer to how champagne used to taste.
Both Eperney and Reims are worth a visit, and in particular the cathedral at Reims is a must. Under the city of Reims lie miles of caves in which the champagne is stored whilst it slowly ages to maturity. Most of the great champagne houses run education tours and tastings.

Where to buy in Champagne
You can buy direct from the producers, but the best bargains are usually to be found in the small shops just off the Cathedral square in Reims.

Jura
The Jura wine production area is the gentle slopes which lead from Burgundy towards Switzerland. At the moment this is an area which produces a few good wines, rather than anything of great importance.
The Jura principally produces white wines, but unlike anything else produced in France. At their best they are so strong they appear to be almost yellow. Whilst intended for drinking with a meal, they perform best if enjoyed as an aperitif to sharpen the appetite before eating.
For a white Jura wine which you can enjoy with your meal look for Côtes du Jura ordinaire.
The Jura's best product is rosé. Some experts say that the rosé production now outstrips that of any other of France's wine producing areas. To taste a Jura rosé is more like a light red than a white with a touch of red in.
The Jura region produces an enormous range of red wines. Some, like Marnebour, are extraordinary sweet and taste more like a mock Madeira than real red wine. On the other hand Barberousse is a full bodied red not dissimilar to the produce of Burgundy.

Where to visit in the Jura
The only town or city worth visiting in the area is Besançon, although in fairness it would never feature very highly on any list of tourist attractions. There is a citadel with good views over the city, and the cathedral is a glorious mixture of influences ranging from a Roman altar to a 19th century astronomic clock.

Where to buy in the Jura
Much of the Jura's wine production is processed by a single factory outside the old town of Arbois. Buy direct from this factory and you'll be paying prices similar to that paid by the wine merchants.

Languedoc-Roussillon
The majority of British wine enthusiasts would probably think of the wines from Languedoc-Roussillon as being newcomers to our market. But Fitou comes from this area, and has long been a favourite in the British market. The reason wines from this area have been comparatively unknown is that for generations the producers concentrated on quantity rather than quality.
When, a decade or so ago, the European Community was grappling with the problem of the European Wine Lake, it was partly the produce of this area which was causing the problems. The few wines from this area which did have any character were frequently blended with the produce of Algiers.
The producers have learnt their lessons. Rather than quantity they are now concentrating on quality. Inevitably this is going to eventually force up prices, but at the moment you can buy a good middle class wine at a junk wine price.
The Languedoc-Roussillon area is the gently rolling hills which lead up from Narbonne and Perpignan to the Pyrénées.
Their product is principally full bodied reds not dissimilar to those produced in the Rhône. But unlike the Rhône wines, these are ready for drinking whilst still comparatively young. And also unlike Rhône wines, those from Languedoc-Roussillon will often stay at their optimum drinking level for some years.

Where to visit in Languedoc-Roussillon
Like much of this area Narbonne has yet to adjust to its potential as a tourist town. Much of the town is industrialised and it is also a major centre for warehousing in southern France. The unfinished Gothic cathedral dominates the town, and there is a superb archaeological museum near the cathedral which shows how Rome and North Africa have influenced the area.
Perpignan is far more interesting. Although this is France the principal influence is Catalan Spanish. The old fortress dominates the centre of the city, and many of the side streets are more Spanish than French.

Where to buy in Languedoc-Roussillon
Almost every wine producer will be more than happy to sell you some of his products. However it seems that modern ideas are radiating out from Narbonne, so the closer you get to the city the better chance you will have of buying wines of quality. In 1997 it was possible to buy a good 1996 red from a producer on the outskirts of Narbonne for the equivalent of sixty pence a bottle. If you want to buy without risk look to the wine wholesalers on the industrial estate to the north of the city.

Loire
Experts often talk about the wines of the Loire creating the impression that it is one tightly defined geographical area. But the Loire river is more than 500 meandering miles long and inevitably the wines reflect the changing climate and terrain.
Wine is produced down most of the river's length, but only in a few areas is the produce worthy of note.
Around Saumur they produce a sparkling white wine not dissimilar to a demi sec (semi-sweet) champagne but at anything up to half the price.
From around the port of Nantes comes Sancerre and Pouilly-Fumé. Don't confuse Pouilly-Fumé with Pouilly-Fuissé which is in Burgundy. Both wines have a slight hint of sweetness without actually being sweet. Being originally produced for consumption in a fishing area, both wines are at their best when drunk with fish.
The Loire seaside wines are known as Muscadets, but that is the name of the predominant grape rather than a town or village. Like Beaujolais they are best drunk within a year of production. If you do bring some home you will almost certainly find that the wine has gone slightly cloudy as sediment is shaken up. It can take up to six months with the bottle laying on its side before all the sediment has settled out.
Perhaps the best wines from the Loire are the rosés from Anjou. Anjou rosé is the cheaper, and Anjou rosé de cabernet is slightly more expensive and a little less sweet.
The Loire isn't a great producer of red wines. Those which are produced are often like a Beaujolais with a hint of tannin, and perhaps just a shade dryer. Margeaux is a name which is just starting to appear in British supermarkets as a cheap everyday drinking wine.

Where to visit in the Loire
Almost the entire Loire valley is famous for châteaux. If you love these grand country houses then it is well worth investing in a specialised guide book. If you only visit one château make it the Château de Beauregard just down the road from Chambord. It is particularly famous for its Delft tiled floors and timbered ceilings, but perhaps more importantly it isn't on most people's châteaux routes.

If your interests are more general visit Orléans which Joan of Arc (the Maid of Orléans) rescued from the British after a siege of 8 months. Although the city appears in most guide books the reality is that wars and commercial development have destroyed much of its charm.

Where to buy in the Loire
Perhaps more than in any other part of France there is very little to be gained trying to buy wine direct from the producers. It is as if the distributors have a standing order to buy the best, leaving the mundane for the tourists.

Surprisingly some of the best bargains are to be found in the hypermarkets, and usually under a banner saying l'occasion. I think what happens is that the hypermarkets buy up any good wine which hasn't yet been grabbed up by the local distributors, and sell it on at good prices for local consumption.

Provence
The name Provence is given to a massive area which reaches from Marseille to the Italian border, and from the Mediterranean coast right up into the high Alpes. But wine production is principally concentrated in a small area around Marseille.

Inevitably wine production reflects the climate. During the summer temperatures often soar above 100° F, and when the Mistral winds blow only stumpy vines can stay firmly rooted into the ground.

For white wines there are two villages worth noting. Bandol just to the east of Marseille produces a good everyday drinking white, whilst the product of Cassis is perhaps slightly better and worth bringing back from your holiday.

Bandol also produces a full bodied red with an unfortunate reputation for not travelling well. For the best of the reds look for Château Simone from Palette which is just to the east of Aix-en-Provence.

Where to visit in Provence
In the main wine production area Marseille has to be the main attraction. The city has such a turbulent past that it will take a fat guide book to introduce you to all the sights, sounds and smells which make up this most cosmopolitan of cities.

Eastward of Marseille lies the fishing port of Cassis which is generally accepted as being the least spoilt on France's Mediterranean coast. It also happens to be the centre for one of Provence's best white wines which shouldn't be confused with the crème de cassis – blackcurrent liqueur which forms the basis for Kir.

Aix-en-Provence is another tourist attraction, although also rather over-crowded in peak season. Cyclists should make a visit to Mont Ventoux near Carpentras which is one of the classic Tour de France stages. The fit can try cycling from the bottom to the top. The wise get a family member to take them to the top so they can coast down.

Where to buy in Provence
The best bargains are to be had from anywhere in Bandol or Palette. The Cassis you can buy in the port of the same name is only really suitable for consuming while you are in Provence.

Rhône
The Rhône is one of France's longest rivers, but the wine producing area which tends to use the Rhône name is the 150 mile stretch from Lyon to Avignon. Strictly speaking Châteauneuf-de-Pape doesn't come in that area, but its products are rich and dark and more like a Rhône than Provence wine.

The white Rhône wines are often described as being an acquired taste. Unlike whites from the north they are powerful beverages and often have an alcoholic content as high as 15%.

The Rhône valley is better know for its production of red wines. Unfortunately for years the name was disgraced as the name was affixed to some cheap and nasty, rough reds which flooded onto the British market.

Most Rhône reds are made purely from the Syrah grape, which almost guarantees a heavy, full bodied wine. Add the almost guaranteed summer sun and high temperatures and you've got a wine which is consistent in character. To enjoy them at their best all these wines need a good six years maturing in the bottle before drinking.

The title Côte du Rhône Village can only be applied to wines produced in a dozen or so communities north of Avignon. In the Rhône valley these wines cost only a little more than a straight wine, but the quality suggests they should cost a lot more.

Places to visit in the Rhône Valley.
All of us attempted to learn French at school by learning the rhyme "Sur le pont, d'Avignon" so when in Avignon you have to visit that spectacular bridge. The town is very pretty, if a little touristy.

The city of Lyon is a totally different kettle of fish. Once the Capital of France, Lyon manages to mix the best of the old with the best of the new. The Place de la Terreur in the centre of the city is where the guillotine was placed during the French revolution – until it wore out through overuse. Also in Lyon are reminders of the city's position during the Second World War as a Resistance centre.

Where to buy in the Rhône valley.
As with much of France's wine producing areas there are good bargains to be had almost everywhere. But the best place seems to be the Grower's Co-operative in the village of Chusclan. Their reds and rosés are good drinking wines, and their subtle whites and light reds are so good you'll often not find them on sale anywhere else.

Savoie

The Savoie Alpes are those mountains which line Switzerland's southern border with France. In this sparse mountainous country little grows, but there are small pockets of wine producing land. Crépy produces a light white wine which is fine for everyday drinking, but not noble enough to lay down. In Savoie the locals use it in fondue Savoieard with a mixture of Gruyère and Abondance cheese. Unlike the more traditional fondue only slightly dried out French stick bread is dipped into the boiling cheese / wine mixture.

The best of Savoie's wines comes from Seyssel where they produce a delicate, dry sparkling white wine which is almost indistinguishable from good champagne – but much cheaper.

Where to visit in Savoie

The Savoie Alpes are not yet well developed as a summer tourist area, and many of the ski towns look drab and asleep without a coating of snow. However Albertville has an active night-life and Bourg St Maurice is the centre of Savoie café society.

Whilst in Savoie you have to drive up to Mont Blanc. You can see the mountain from 99 miles away in Lyon, but up close its sheer size explains why it still challenges climbers generations after it was first conquered.

Where to buy in Savoie

The best bargains in Savoie wines are usually to be found in small village shops. However there is a wine shop in the centre of Seyssel which sells the local sparking white at a price which could put you off champagne for life.

South West Coast (Aquitaine and parts of the Midi Pyrénées)

The final one of our wine production areas comes under the catch-all title of South West France. It includes vineyards right on the border with Bordeaux and extends down to the border with Spain.

In fairness this area is still new to both the tourist trade and the wine trade. Twenty years ago what was a sparsely populated region where the only wines were for local consumption is suddenly springing into life.

Some of the local wines are already creeping into the wine merchants list, and for the adventurous traveller there are hundreds more to be sampled and bought before the wine trade wakes up, or more likely before the producers decide to cheapen their product in the search for quantity rather than quality.

I've picked just three places to mention. The unfortunately named La Clape at the mouth of the River Aube produces one of the most full bodied whites I have ever tried. The vines usually grow in the shade of pine trees which might have some effect on the taste and body. It makes no difference where you buy, the price will always be low and the quality high. But in five years time? Who knows.

For red wines I've chosen the better known Bergerac and Cahors. Bergerac is a full bodied red which at its best competes with the best from the Bordeaux area.

The wines from Cahors are unfortunately changing. For generations of locals the wine from this area was always known as a black wine – so dark you couldn't see through the bottle. But all that is changing as the producers are being urged to produce lighter wines which apparently everyone wants. But don't be fooled. The original black wines are still available and still set an example for what a full bodied wine should taste like.

Few wine guides will mention the small wine producers around the cities of Pau and Lourdes. The wines which are produced in these areas vary from disgusting to very good, and only tasting will tell you which is which. These are not wines for buying from supermarkets. Rather as you drive along keep your eyes open. If you see a field of vines and a sign say dégustation (tasting) stop and try it.

Where to visit in South West France

The coastal region south of Bordeaux is a great tourist area, but without much in the way of grand tourist attractions. However moving into the foothills of the Pyrénées and you'll stumble across some amazing sights. The cities of Pau and Lourdes are both well worth a visit.

Lourdes is best know for the miracles said to have been performed there and Pau is perhaps equally well known for the annual F3000 motor race which is held round the streets. But look at little closer and Pau in particular has some charms which aren't immediately obvious.

Stand at one end of the boulevard des Pyrénées and the street makes a perfect framework for the mountain backdrop. Turning away from the mountains and you'll see the château given over to the memory of the French monarch Henry IV which is well worth a visit.

Where to buy wine in South West France

I've already mentioned the best of the wine production areas, and these are also the best places to look for bargains. It really is a question of being prepared to stop if you see anywhere that looks interesting. In Cahors, in particular, it is worth asking if the producer has any vin noir.

But equally there are now some producers who are more interested in quantity than quality, so practise saying non if you aren't impressed with what they have to offer.

Exploring French Canals
by Dennis Needham

France by the back door. This may well describe the inland waterway system of France, creeping, for the most part unobserved, through the very heart of the country. From the smallest village to the mightiest city, canals and rivers provided the heartbeat for industry and trade. For years they were the silver highway on which France prospered.

From the wine-growing regions of the south to the heavily industrialised north, the ability to move product from maker to consumer was crucial. Roads were poor, the iron horse still a dream for the future.

Unlike the English canals, France, with an abundant supply of water, could afford to build on a grand scale. We in England are (rightly) proud of our canal heritage, but the French were there long before us.

The Canal du Midi from Toulouse to the Mediterranean was opened in 1681 – almost a century before the English canal age got under way. The work was almost entirely down to the efforts of one man, Pierre-Paul Ricquet, Baron of Bonrepos. He was born in Béziers in 1604 and had no apparent engineering connections.

Appreciating the benefits that transport would bring to the Languedoc, his vision was quite remarkable. A canal from Toulouse would need to climb uphill to Col de Naurouze west of Castelnaudary before plunging downhill to meet the Med.

Water supply to a canal in this arid region would have been a great problem had not Ricquet appreciated it from the start. He built an enormous reservoir in the Montagnes Noir to the north and created a channel to deliver a regular supply to the summit level.

His planning was so wonderful that, despite the long hot French summers, it was not until the end of summer 1986 that this supply finally failed: a remarkable achievement. Indeed, the canal is considered so historically significant that it is now designated a World Heritage Site.

Not that there was any ground-breaking as far as the Midi was concerned. The Canal de Briare, linking the Loire with the Seine above Paris was probably the first summit level (linking two places by climbing a hill and descending again) canal in the world.

To explore these forgotten highways is to peer into the very heart of France itself. Forget the sometimes off-handed way the French treat their visitors; along these charming by-ways, the true spirit of the country is revealed.

Villages, still delightfully remote from central authority, existing with very little change in lifestyle.

The River Rance at Dinan

The boulangérie still produces 'proper' bread where his opposite number in town now frequently works with pre-prepared frozen dough. Inexpensive menus are available in the local café, a carafe of refulgent red wine on the table and extremely drinkable. The whole pace of life so starkly different to the cities: much more noticeably so than in England.

All this navigable water has one thing in common: fascination. It is also easily explored: by foot, on two wheels or four. Towpaths are to be found alongside the canals and many of the rivers. They vary from small tracks to good quality roads. With only a rudimentary knowledge of the countryside it is possible to organise one-way walks or cycle rides or more extended visits to some of the wonders by car.

Walking is probably the best option – if only because you can always work out a way to progress. Some areas are difficult for bikes, others impossible for cars. The French public transport system is good to variable but can usually be utilised with confidence.

To illustrate. One walk, easily accomplished, is along the Canal du Midi, close to the Pyrénées. The wonderful city of Carcassonne with its walled Cité has a bus depot quite close to the canal. By walking east for some 10 km, the canal arrives in Trèbes. From here, a bus will return you to the city.

Along the way, you will see French style locks (écluse), ancient bridges and a fair chunk of peaceful French countryside. The locals have yet to discover the pleasures of towpath trekking. Carcassonne is a city of two very distinct parts. The modern thriving commercial area; and the cité. The former has lots of fascinating interest and modern shopping. The latter is the most complete medieval walled city in Europe. It's also the one place in the region that is commercialised.

Several other points on the Midi are worth checking out. Béziers is a quite marvellous city connected – as are so many in this area – with the Cathars. This was a Christian-based religion popular several hundred years ago that was ruthlessly put down by the Catholic church.

At Fonserannes, close to Béziers, a 'water slope' supplements the locks. This has a huge machine that moves boats between the two levels and is quite a sight to see.

Also on the Midi, a meal at La Cascade near Port Robine is well recommended. 'The Two Malcolm's', English ex-Thespians produce an adventurous menu scoring heavily on quality, less so on quantity. The ancient building is only partially modernised, but the atmosphere is delightful indoors, refreshing if outside, overlooking a small river.

Much of the French canal system is to be found to the northeast of a line drawn by the river Seine – itself an important waterway artery. The river is navigable from Marcilly-sur-Seine – north of the N19 Troyes to Paris road – right through the capital and to the sea at Le Havre, 535 km. away.

One attractive area is to be found north of Dijon. This is the source of the Seine, a pretty little grotto, surrounded by trees. This developed and acknowledged area is in direct contrast to the source of the Thames in England whose location is very much an ad-hoc event.

In the Nord/Pas de Calais regions, Arques positively demands a visit. Its beautiful glassware famed throughout the world. Less well known, but equally impressive is the massive boat lift at Les Fontinettes, a vertical boat lift, now replaced by a deep lock. This was built by Edwin Clarke who gained his experience on the Anderton boat lift in Cheshire.

More than a century ago, the original locks here were so busy that delays of up to five days were encountered. The lift – with a 13.1 m. level change – was opened in 1888 and performed satisfactorily until the increasing size of French barges saw it become obsolete in 1967. A new lock was built a little further along the canal. This can handle boats up to 3,000 tonnes. An English narrow canal boat carries 30 tonnes!

Today, the lift is open to visitors as it stands, a péniche (French barge) in the tank, a memory to a bygone age.

The Canal de St Quentin runs from Cambrai, due south for 92 km. to Chauny. Here, the first use of tanks was recorded in the First World War in the huge battle that ranged around this area during that conflict.

30 km. south of Cambrai is Bony Tunnel, at 5670 m, the longest in Europe. It was completed in 1810 under the direction of Napoleon and drained during both World Wars. At one stage, the Germans used it as a Command Centre and hospital. It is easy to access by road to the east of Le Catelet.

Many consider this corner of France to be flat and uninteresting. The rolling hills and delightful canal cuttings along the 25 km. long summit level will easily give the lie to this perception.

Moving further east towards the Alsace, a magnificent inclined plane is located at St Louis-Arzviller on the Canal de la Marne ar Rhin. The is rural France at its best. The steep sided Zorn valley was a challenge to the canal builders and many locks were needed to lift the canal to the watershed.

This concrete inclined plane was built in 1969 and replaced seventeen locks. It's a wonderful sight to see and the whole experience has been developed with visitors in mind. You can take a boat trip, walk (or cycle) around the old locks, still intact although de-watered or join one of the

Ancient bridge on the Canal du Midi

excursions around the site.

It's easy to find too. Leave Strasbourg on the N4 towards Nancy. At 39 km. is Saverne. There is a left turn beyond here along the D98 which leads to the lift.

Still in this corner of France, Flavigny-sur-Moselle – close to Nancy – is the location of a wonderful aqueduct over the Moselle river. Stone built and over 125 m. long, it carries the canal southwards towards the river Saône.

Having whetted your appetite on this hors d'œuvre, the main course will be found at Briare on the Canal Latéral à la Loire. This is right at the northern end of the canal, just beyond the basin area opposite where the Canal de Briare arrives. As mentioned earlier, this was the first summit level canal in Europe, being built in 1642.

At nearly 663 m. long, this is probably the longest aqueduct in the world. It was built sixty years after the main canal by Société des Établissements Eiffel (who had a hand in building a tower somewhere) and crosses the river on fifteen massive columns. Originally, the barges crossed at river level but frequent floods caused such delay that this magnificent structure was proposed. There are lights illuminating the dual towing paths which make it look particularly beautiful after dark.

Away from the natural beauty of these canals and rivers, there are some pretty weird spectacles as well. In Sète, on the Mediterranean coast north of Narbonne. Here, jousting boats are to be found. Flamboyantly decorated rowing boats have a large raised platform on the prow. Oarsman row furiously towards each other whilst musicians work everyone to a fever pitch with trumpets and drums. The boats rush headlong towards each other with a man on each platform and the winner is the one who does not meet a watery fate.

High on the list of beautiful canals in France must be the Canal du Nivernais. 174 km. long, it was built to link the rivers Loire and Yonne, providing connections between Paris and the Saône.

In many ways, it has direct parallels with English waterways in that, because of a non-standard middle section, there was so little traffic that closure was threatened in the 1960s. A hire boat company, the first to be established in France, started operations on the river Marne in the Champagne district in 1957 and moved to Baye at the southern end of the Nivernais' summit level a decade later.

This ensured that closure plans then being mooted, were not put into operation. Actually, the beauty of this line was soon being reported around the world and today, it vies with the Canal du Midi for popularity.

Incidentally, some of the towing paths along this 10 km. summit are variously difficult to use/non-

A French barge (péniche) converted to live aboard.

existent. A shame: there are some dramatic lengths of water hereabouts.

Heading south from Auxerre, the navigation makes its way up the Yonne valley – indeed, the river is used for much of the route as far as Clamecy. Over the heavily wooded summit, the canal then drops down to Decize and the Loire, 30 km. southeast of Nevers on the N7.

Elsewhere, Brittany, long a favourite with English visitors is well blessed with navigations both natural and artificial. The Erdre is a quite beautiful river, the Canal du Nantes à Brest – although derelict for some of its length – has delightful reaches, passing through Redon – noted for its historic buildings – and La Gacilly with its pottery.

One huge plus to the waterway system of France is that they travel for miles through the major wine-growing areas. Until comparatively recent times, the canals were the main method of moving wine around the country. Many canals have Caves alongside, acres of vines growing right to the water's edge.

This gives you a unique opportunity to discover the real wines of France, especially using the guide contained within these covers.

Although this trade is virtually no more, the waterways of France do allow you the opportunity to relax in the sun and watch commercial traffic – a rarity in England – alongside holiday boats. To watch their skippers steering these deeply-laden behemoths of the waterways into locks and bridges scarcely wider than the craft itself is to marvel at their skill.

Opportunities for the landlubber to get afloat for an hour or two are many and varied. Trip boats operate from Dinard up the river Rance to that wonderful city-on-a-hill, Dinan, one of the finest preserved medieval towns anywhere.

On the Canal de Nantes à Brest you can cruise north from Nantes, several day tripping boats operate along the Canal du Midi. Burgundy Cruisers at Vermenton – just off the Canal du Nivernais – are one of several yards around the country with English managers and offer their luxury hire cruisers by the day when available.

Use the French waterways then to reach into the very heart of this wonderfully individualistic – if occasionally bloody-minded – nation. Seek them out, enjoy them. But don't share your new-found Utopia with anyone. After all, you don't want everyone to know do you?

© **Dennis Needham**

The Waterways of France

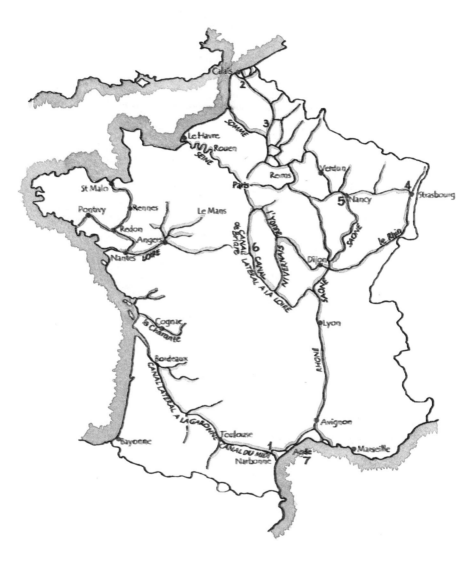

This map shows the major waterways of France. The numbers 1-7 show the location of features referred to in Dennis Needham's article.

1. Fonserannes Water Slope
2. Les Fontineetes Boat Lift
3. Bony Tunnel
4. St. Louis-Arzviller Inclined Plane
5. Flavigny-sur-Moselle Aqueduct
6. Briare Aqueduct
7. Sète Boat Jousting

Campsite Map
– showing the location of the sites featured in this guide

Indexes

This guide is organised geographically using the official French regional structure – these regions are listed alphabetically in the guide and a sketch map on page 6 shows their geographical location within France. Each of these regions contains a number of départements' (see pages 6 and 7), each of which has an official number. We have used these numbers to prefix our site numbers (the four figure number which preceeds the site name). The map above shows the approximate location of each of the featured campsites using these numbers. We include two indexes on the following pages. Index 1 is by region (as the campsites appear in the guide) and Index 2 lists the campsites using the départment in which each one is situated (i.e. numerically by départment and campsite number).

Index 2 – by départment number

Allier	0305	La Petite Valette
Alpes-H-Provence	0401	Hippocampe
	0402	Le Camp du Verdon
	0403	Moulin de Ventre
Alpes-Maritimes	0605	La Vieille Ferme
Ardèche	0702	L'Ardèchois
	0704	La Rouveyrolle
	0705	Ranc Davaine
	0707	Les Ranchisses
	0709	Domaine de Plantas
Ariège	0906	Le Pré Lombard
Aude	1106	Au Pin d'Arnauteille
Aveyron	1202	Les Rivages
	1207	Grange de Monteillac
Cantal	1504	De Coursavy
Charente-Maritime	1708	Les Chirats
	1713	Ile Blanche
Côte d'Or	2100	Lac de Panthier
Côtes d'Armor	2201	Les Capucines
	2204	Le Châtelet
	2212	Le Cap Horn
Creuse	2301	Château de Poinsouze
Dordogne	2400	La Tuilière
	2403	Les Périères
	2404	Le Moulin du Roch
	2405	Hauts de Ratebout
	2409	Soleil Plage
	2410	Le Moulinal
	2411	Aqua Viva
	2416	Le Grand Dague
	2420	De la Plage
Doubs	2503	Bois de Reveuge
Drôme	2603	Le Grand Lierne
	2608	Le Gallo-Romain
Finistère	2901	Le Ty-Nadan
	2905	Orangerie Lanniron
	2906	Le Pil Koad
	2908	Le Panoramic
	2910	Pen-ar-Steir
	2912	Manoir de Kerlut
Gard	3000	Domaine de Gaujac
	3009	Château de Boisson
	3012	TCS L'Ile des Papes
	3014	Soubeyranne
Gers	3201	Camp de Florence
	3207	Angeles
Gironde	3301	La Dune
	3304	Les Viviers
	3306	Camping Palace
Hérault	3403	Le Napoleon
	3404	Lou Village
	3405N	Le Mas de Lignières
	3406	L'Oliveraie
	3407	Le Sérignan Plage

Ile-et-Vilaine	3500	Le Vieux Chêne
	3502	Château des Ormes
Indre et Loir	3701	La Mignardière
Isère	3806	Les Trois Lacs
Landes	4003	Les Pins du Soleil
	4004	La Paillotte
	4010	La Rive
	4013	La Côte
	4014	Lou P'tit Poun
Loir et Cher	4101	Parc du Val de Loire
	4103	Parc des Alicourts
Haut-Loire	4303	De Vaubarlet
Loire-Atlantique	4409	Château de Deffay
	4410	Int. Le Patisseau
Loiret	4501	Les Bois du Bardelet
Lot	4603	Les Pins
	4605	Le Rêve
Lot-et-Garonne	4701	Moulin de Périé
	4703	Château de Fonrives
Manche	5000	L'Etang des Haizes
	5003	Lez-Eaux
	5005	Le Cormoran
Morbihan	5602	La Plage
	5604	De Penboch
Nièvre	5801	Des Bains
	5804	Le Village Européen
Puy-de-Dôme	6302	Etang de Flêchat
	6303	L'Europe
Pyrénées-Atlantique	6407	Le Ruisseau
	6409	La Chêneraie
	6411	Col d'Ibardin
Pyrénées-Orientales	6601	California
	6602	Ma Prairie
	6607	Le Brasilia
Saône-et-Loire	7105	Moulin de Cologne
	7107	Château l'Epervière
Haute-Savoie	7404	La Ravoire
Seine-et-Marne	7704	Le Parc de la Colline
Deux-Sèvres	7902	Courte Vallée
Somme	8004	Du Royon
	8007	La Ferme des Aulnes
Tarn	8101	Entre Deux Lacs
Var	8316	Les Cigales
	8317	La Bergerie
Vaucluse	8402N	De Bélézy
	8404	Le Jantou
Vendée	8508	La Puerta del Sol
	8509	L'Abri des Pins
	8513	Camping Pong
Vienne	8604	Le Futuriste

Index 1 – by region

Aquitaine
2400 Camping La Tuilière
2403 Camping Les Périères
2404 Castel Camping Le Moulin du Roch
2405 Castel Camping Les Hauts de Ratebout
2409 Camping Soleil Plage
2410 Camping-Caravaning Le Moulinal
2411 Camping-Caravaning Aqua Viva
2416 Camping Le Grand Dague
2420 Camping de la Plage
3301 Camping de la Dune
3304 Camping-Caravaning Airotel Les Viviers
3306 Camping Palace
4003 Les Pins du Soleil
4004 Camping La Paillotte
4010 Camping La Rive
4013 Camping-Caravaning de la Côte
4014 Camping-Caravaning Lou P'tit Poun
4701 Camping-Caravaning Moulin de Périé
4703 Castel Camping Le Château de Fonrives
6407 Castel Camping Le Ruisseau
6409 Camping La Chêneraie
6411 Camping du Col d'Ibardin

Auvergne
0305 Camping-Caravaning La Petite Valette
1504 Camping de Coursavy
4303 Camping de Vaubarlet
6302 Camping L'Etang de Flêchat
6303 Hôtel de Plein Air L'Europe

Brittany
2201 Camping Les Capucines
2204 Camping Le Châtelet
2212 Camping Le Cap Horn
2901 Castel Camping Le Ty-Nadan
2905 Castel Camping L'Orangerie de Lanniron
2906 Camping-Caravaning Le Pil Koad
2908 Camping Le Panoramic
2910 Camping du Manoir de Pen-ar-Steir
2912 Camping Manoir de Kerlut
3500 Ferme-Camping Le Vieux Chêne
3502 Castel Camping Le Château des Ormes
5602 Camping de la Plage
5604 Camping de Penboch

Burgundy
2100 Campings Les Voiliers & Lac de Panthier
5801 Camping Des Bains
5804 Le Village Européen
7105 Camping Moulin de Cologne
7107 Castel Camping Château de l'Epervière

Côte d'Azur
0605 Camping La Vieille Ferme

Franche-Comté
2503 Camping du Bois de Reveuge

Languedoc-Roussillon
1106 Camping Au Pin d'Arnauteille
3000 Domaine de Gaujac
3009 Castel Camping Le Château de Boisson
3012 Camping TCS L'Ile des Papes
3014 Camping-Caravaning Soubeyranne
3403 Camping International Le Napoleon
3404 Camping Lou Village
3405N Camping Naturiste Le Mas de Lignières
3406 Hôtel de Plein Air L'Oliveraie
3407 Camping Village Le Sérignan Plage

6601 Camping-Caravaning California
6602 Camping-Caravaning Ma Prairie
6607 Camping Le Brasilia

Limousin
2301 Castel Camping Château de Poinsouze

Loire Valley
3701 Camping de la Mignardière
4101 Le Parc du Val de Loire
4103 Camping Sologne Parc des Alicourts
4501 Camping Les Bois du Bardelet

Midi-Pyrénées
0906 Camping Le Pré Lombard
1202 Les Rivages
1207 Camping La Grange de Monteillac
3201 Le Camp de Florence
3207 Camping-Caravaning Angeles
4603 Camping Les Pins
4605 Camping Le Rêve
8101 Camping Relais d'Entre Deux Lacs

Normandy
5000 Camping L'Etang des Haizes
5003 Castel Camping Lez-Eaux
5005 Camping Le Cormoran

Paris/Ile de France
7704 Le Parc de la Colline

Picardy
8004 Caravaning du Royon
8007 Caravaning La Ferme des Aulnes

Poitou-Charentes
1708 Camping Les Chirats
1713 Camping-Caravaning L'Ile Blanche
7902 Camping de Courte Vallée
8604 Camping Le Futuriste

Provence
0402 Hôtel de Plein Air L'Hippocampe
0402 Castel Le Camp du Verdon
0403 Camping Lac de Moulin de Ventre
8316 Parc Caravaning Les Cigales
8317 Camping Domaine de la Bergerie
8402N Domaine Naturiste de Bélézy
8404 Camping Le Jantou

Rhône Valley
0702 Camping-Caravaning L'Ardèchois
0704 Camping La Rouveyrolle
0705 Camping-Caravaning Ranc Davaine
0707 Camping Les Ranchisses
0709 Camping Domaine de Plantas
2603 Camping Le Grand Lierne
2608 Camping Le Gallo-Romain

Savoy/Dauphiny Alps
3806 Camping Les Trois Lacs
7404 Camp de la Ravoire

Western Loire
4409 Castel Camping Le Château de Deffay
4410 Camping-Caravaning Int. Le Patisseau
8508 Camping La Puerta del Sol
8509 Camping L'Abri des Pins
8513 Camping Pong